Drawing in Real Perspective

Published by
Mandrake of Oxford
PO Box 250
OXFORD
OX1 1AP (UK)

Printed on acid free paper certification from three leading environmental organizations: the Forest Stewardship Council™ (FSC®), the Sustainable Forestry Initiative® (SFI®) and the Programme for the Endorsement of Forestry Certification (PEFC™)

The Art of the Living

Drawing in Real Perspective

A new approach to space

With natural and immediate application

Translation Rebekah Start

Supervisor Robert Shupp.

Xavier Bolot

"The sum of his work easily pulls the reader in his wake"

Xavier Bolot delivers to us the fruit of his reflections on the subject of visual perception of surfaces with passion and sincerity. He has read with eagerness everything concerning these codes or "perspectives." And in discovering the rifts in each of them, he wishes to experiment with their limits and launch himself in a grand adventure by proposing a body of work that asks, "Can one realize a more instinctive perspective?"

He imposes this challenge with ardor and tenacity.

The sum of his work easily pulls the reader in his wake and can convince us with enthusiasm his faith in the perspective and of its future.

Jean Mary, Honorary Professor of Perspective of Art Schools

"I find it remarkable all your drawings in the Third Section"

I share perfectly the sentiments of Michèle Arnold and Jean Mary with regard to your work.

I find it remarkable all your drawings in the Third Section. Can I keep a little of your work? Without perspective no element of surface is more important than another.

In architecture I have studied the optic corrections of the Parthenon and painted a number of contraperspectives.

Thank you for showing me the energy of drawing.

Paul Roche-Ponthus, Artist and Researcher

"With him all the way to the jubilant finale"

I am disconcerted by the construction of a book and the progression of thought. The construction seems to be that of a scientific work with an educational value : each chapter can be read for itself while we can return to the others at anytime as they are interrelated. The reader is solicited as an architect, artist and conscious observer. But as one progresses through the reading, the work is revealed, to the reader that I am, to be in direct relation with the very particular and personal spirit of the author. In the beginning I had the impression to be in a space, a large room, one could say "where I see nothing but markers placed in a repetitive fashion : Rectilinear Perspective, Curvilinear Perspective. With these references to the history of "seeing" and a documentation examined closely from an artistic and scientific point of view, a feeling of repetition settles in, with at each turn a progression in the marking out of lines.

It is a step-by-step advancement. I am in the room and am allowed to drive, a little astonished, curious without too much reticence . . . just enough to establish confidence. I observe, discover little by little and hold my breath.

Advancing step by step in observation which, after having an outline, places me, places us the readers, in the interior of a space to look at, as in the center of "the cylinder of perception." We turn on the axe of a cylinder (the observer is the axe, his eye the center). Little by little, very progressively this position forces us to look at, to really see and "believe what we see."

The author seems to put in place this mechanism, which we wind up making our own, so as he wants to make us understand, to convince us, to put us in a state of seeing "for real."

He has arrived, and he knows it, because in the end we share with him a sort of jubilant explosion.

It's like child's play: he himself is liberated of his demonstration, he accompanies us patiently, we have followed his path, he has come to his conclusions or more simply stated, he has arrived at the end: so that the reader makes his own experience, and makes his mark. He also lets go of narrow and stifling, constraints illusory of academicism, to finally live in his free space.

What he tells us is very instructive, interesting beyond conviction, having a condition of a release of principles, which is not immediate, guides us to the center of a cylinder, dares us to turn around with him all the way to the jubilant finale which opens us to the living world.

I am happy with the journey, which has taken me towards regions to explore and raised multiple questions about our presence in this world.

In brief I thank Xavier Bolot to have allowed me to read his work.

Michèle Arnold, psychoanalyst.

Contents

Acknowledgements

I warmly thank all those who helped me in this research while reading my work and giving me their remarks and comments. These amicable readers intervened in two phases.

The first phase of reading involved confiding in high-level experts, concerning the approached domains in this work, having in common their taste for Fine Art and the multiple aspects of perception. They are listed in alphabetic order:

Michèle Arnold, Psychoanalyst

Dominique Bolot, Architect DESA and DPLG,

Jean Mary, former Professor at the National Superior School of Art of Bourges, France

Jean Renault, PhD in Mathematics, University of Berkley, California; Professor University of Orleans

The second phase tested the clarity and readability of the book, with thanks to:

Jean-Chrysostome Bolot, PhD in Computers, University of Maryland, Maine; Engineer with Sprint, Mountain View California

Aurelie Constant, Director of Communications for the International Wine Academy of Rome.

Archimedes Garcia, Electrical Engineer, GIAT;

Douglas Kinsinger, Translator Expert, SAP, Frankfurt Germany

Bernard Lancereau, section engineer,

Eric Mengual, Lawyer, Photographer; Director of the Faculty of Law, Bourges;

Christine Perrin, Consul to the Court of Appeals of Versailles;

Marie Emeriau, Speech Therapist.

My recognition especially goes to those who have brought me assistance throughout the duration. I thank my brother Dominique, architect, caricaturist and painter, who when we were adolescents, taught me everything about drawing and painting by his example of sensibility, precision and imagination, and who has helped and encouraged me ever since.

I thank for her benevolent attention, Isabelle Renault, potter and lecturer.

I thank Jean Mary, professor at the National Superior School of Fine Arts of Bourges, France, who has shown great interest in my work and has given me her reactions at several stages of this book.

I keep the memory of Jean Claro, former professor at the School of Fine Arts of Poitiers, France, who encouraged me with enthusiasm when we drew together in Bourges.

I thank for their intelligence : Rebekah Start, artist, Michigan, who translated my work into English, and Robert Shupp, former Chairman of the French Department U.H. Houston, Texas, who revised and discussed my texts in French and English.

I thank Mr. Paul Devautour, Director of the National Superior School of Fine Arts of Bourges, France, for the welcome he gave me and the logistics he arranged for my disposition in the forms of a library, location and materials for The Free Workshop.

This list is certainly not exhaustive and I ask those that I may forget to excuse me.

Foreword

A new approach to space

I Origin of the book

I was in Pisa, in Italy, on that particular day. I came from Carrara where I had the opportunity to work with some friends from the School of Fine Arts. We had explored Santa Pietra at the foot of the grandiose quarry, and we passed by Pisa before going on to San Giminiano. We visited the museum, which is found at the end of the immense esplanade. There I discovered a loggia, which permitted a point of view in the opposite direction typically used for photograph taking.

The view is striking; one does not find it at ground level, far from the monuments, as is the case when one arrives by the principal entry of Campo.

One finds it in the foreground, across the frame drawn by the columns of the loggia, in the middle of the gigantic space outlined by the impressive mass of the Leaning Tower, the Dome, which gives the impression of

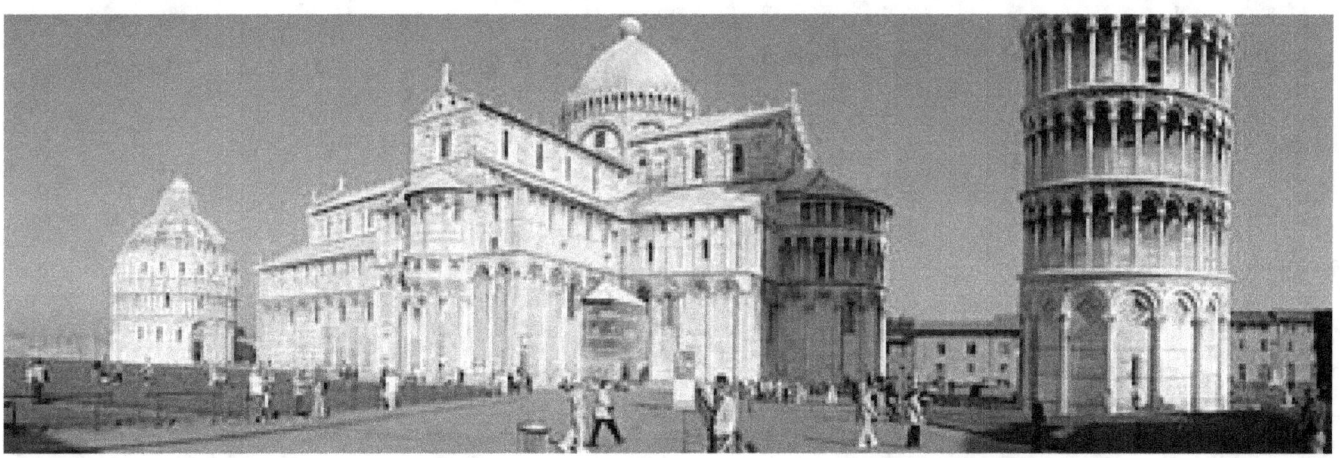

being at the foot of an aircraft carrier, and Baptistere, which seems to have the height of the cupola of Saint Peter of Rome.

On the left you see a row of buildings, corresponding to an aisle of a museum, which seems to be small in size compared with the enormous masses, which come from the right. It was difficult to imagine that these have been immobile on this spot for such a long time; the impression of invasion that they provoked was strong.

Here one loses one's landmarks, the distances between the naves are difficult to evaluate. I took my drawing paper in the format of 50 x 60cm, and attempted to grasp this impression. It was a miserable attempt and my drawing was completely flat.

A friend, who joined me, suggested that perhaps the wall of the loggia prevented me from seeing the sides of the central alley that came towards us from the principal entrance of the Campo.

I started drawing again, standing, leaning against a low wall, in a way that I could see the sides of the alley which I represented by two straight lines coming from a vanishing point on the principle door. In vain, the construction of the drawing was ridiculous.

A friend, who joined us in her turn, concluded that one does not need lines and promised, upon returning to Carrara, to rifle through her book on M.C. Escher who made his drawings curvilinear. This mystery had to be solved and thus the adventure commenced.

This experience at Pisa was exemplary: it is impossible in classic Rectilinear Perspective to translate certain situations. This troubled me all the more since I have had for a long time a fixed idea: the art of the living. I had already encountered difficulties in this domain. These masses at Pisa were living: how to transmit this impression onto a sheet of paper?

Already at Carrara, as in France, when in a drawing session with a live model, a friend said to me "your shortcut is perfect" I responded to him "No, this is not what I see." And we remained in frustration. What do I see? What have I not seen? Which senses must I activate to see the living, to translate what I sense with the certitude of its presence?

Some philosophers have tried to contribute to this approach. Descartes brought us very little with his *Dioptrique*. Indeed Man is not a simple mechanic implementing technology.

Husserl took the opposite side of the master in his contradiction. Man, who is aware of the living is not the only conscience that exists. And more, I have indeed an intention when I laboured to translate the living, my perception would have then to be organized around this objective.

A triangle, whichever point of view I have on it in space, always has three sides, which make up a part of its "essence". But which figure should I retain to draw it? When I draw a portrait, I see well that there are several viewpoints to give it all its facets. How to catch the invariants of volume of a face and under which angle do I present it if I must leave only one picture?

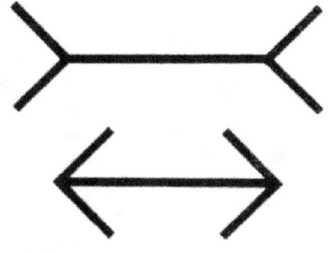

Merleau-Ponty developed his ideas with subtlety. But he tells of his surprise, in his chapter *"The Sensation"* of his book *The Phenomenology of perception,* about our errors reading the illustration of Müller-Lyer, two parallel segments equal in length, limited by inversed arrowheads, *having a* semblance of unequal lengths.

Writing of that, he notes, in fact, the natural function of the eye which is no longer today, for the neurosciences, a camera, but a *directional sensor* piloted by a *predictive monitor* preparing actions for the survival of the species.

The formulation of philosophic intuitions narrowly depends on scientific-knowledge of the time, those which are the work of courageous men who do not hesitate to transgress their culture, unless a philosopher has already done it.

All shake the Pandora's box of linked questions and strive to interpret the contents in an order in which things occur, with a sole tool: simple mechanistic images.

"You will see that our reason has short wings," said Virgil to Dante, as they advanced towards the circles of Hell in *The Divine Comedy*. But the idea grows that what I see depends on me.

How to apply this problem of representation of perception to drawing? One thing is certain since Plato: the physical world is not the perceived world. On the other hand, the Renaissance created a sensation by proposing in a convincing manner the diverse ways of representing perceived space, even if they only did so by rediscovered skills mastered two thousand years ago by the Greeks.

Therefore, there are three worlds when I draw:

The physical world, which I seek to understand as a physicist, this is a hard job, for we, for example, do not know, even today, very clearly what is gravity.

The perceived world, which I seek to understand, because neurophysicists have discovered the brain as Christopher Columbus discovered India. However neurophysicists confirm already, at this first stage of their discovery, each being's autonomy of perception.

The represented world, in which artists of all sorts evolve, and seem, starting from their earlier works, to bounce on rubber walls. In taking the simplest case, if a line in space can be defined objectively, what is my natural perception? For it is the latter that allows me to reveal the living. When I perceive living things, which route do I follow to develop this perception on the map of my paper?

While returning to Carrara I consulted the book evoked at Pisa on M.C. Escher., treating of natural cylindrical perception. Bruno Ernst is the author. He has the intuition of the trigonometric projection of which

Escher was not aware, "but this demonstration drives us too far", he said.

David Hockney had the same visual intuition of naturally cylindrical space when he reconstructed the landscape of the Grand Canyon of Arizona with two hundred photos. Struck by these coincidences, my engineer's blood churned, as I am familiar with this undulating world.

I went to work and I realized, in seeing again the same paintings, spanning the centuries, that these questions were not articulated for the first time, as is testified by the works of Fouquet, before the Renaissance and, as we shall see, numerous artists leading up to David Hockney during the 20th century. It appears that one cannot represent space in Rectilinear Perspective, but in Curvilinear Perspective. But with which curves?

From Vitruve to Bruno Ernst we do not have any scientific publications on this theme, with the exception of the work on spherical perspective of Barre and Flocon who described however a non-realistic world.

We need then to uncover a natural perspective bringing a practical tool to the artist.

I have sought, for a long time, with Jean Mary, the most accurate term, or the least false, for this concept pushing us on the road to the perception of the living. I finally chose the term *real* because, joined to *perspective*, it seems *iconoclastic* and calls for a questioning mind.

2 Words of Warning

1. The goal of this book is not to study the history of curvilinear perspective. Curvilinear Perspective has been particularly trampled upon since the Renaissance, without supplanting Roman Rectilinear Perspective rediscovered at this period, for lack of comparable scientific support of that of its rival.

We therefore look to pass on this stage and fix a clear objective: representing the living. This latter goal has driven us to present a practical tool, simple to use, intuitive, which explains scientifically the structure of representation as seen by our natural perception.

2. Real perspective is not the only technique that permits successful representation of the living, for once accurate lines are placed, it remains to be known which types of lines and which colors are needed to translate the living. But that is not our discussion today.

3. I have done myself the schemas, drawings, and transferring on transparencies of what we see of space through a transparent plane. The tracings carried out on a transparent plate, are only the reflections of perceived nature, in our natural space, cylindrical and trigonometric.

The Schemas serve a pedagogic aim and represent a volume under different angles, with trigonometric receding lines and elliptical contour lines. But this network that structures space is intuitive because it corresponds to our natural perception. The drawings are *free,* they are therefore carried out and realized in an instant, in symbiosis with the living, their execution does not take, for a student, more than three to five minutes on a format of 50cm x 60cm or 80cm x 100cm.

To represent the living, a realistic drawing does not need to be over loaded and thickened (with details) during long sessions, nor does it need to be covered with shading. An *accurate* living drawing brings the essential, it is therefore *finished,* but neither is it a photograph nor an anatomical relief.

3 Presentation of the position

It could seem surprising to see an analysis of drawing proposed that relies on a perspective other than traditional Rectilinear Perspective. We propose a curved universe, but not just any universe, one that corresponds to the fashion in which our eyes and brain function. We bring a scientific, geometric, and algebraic demonstration, the consequences of the almost-cylindrical nature of our perceived universe.

In fact, our current culture of perspective is still fundamentally one from the 17th century, when an edict by Colbert gave a monopoly of artistic teaching to Le Brun, the director of the Royal Academy. Therefore the perspective taught is that when two rectilinear receding lines converge to a point.

The most famous promoter of this technique was Alberti, an Italian from the Renaissance who wrote a treatise on this subject. This technique fathered the academic style rejected by artists as early as the end of the 19th century.

Nevertheless, as early as Antiquity, the Greeks considered that their visual environment was curvilinear. They constructed temples with columns converging in a manner that gave the spectator the impression of contemplating a building with perfectly straight angles. We had to wait till 1920 the architect Geoges Gromort to check this facts.

The Greek heritage was not totally forgotten, even during grand moments of glory for Rectilinear Perspective. Indeed, numerous famous painters tried to work in Curvilinear Perspective, even if they subsequently abandoned it for lack of understanding the exact form of the curves used.

In contemporary art, drawing is the most often misunderstood. Perspective, the integral motor of drawing, undergoes the same.

What is our perception of the world?

How do we see our environment and its volumes? In other words, how do we perceive things when we disregard our culture? How to represent this perception? We attempt to respond to this approaching Real Perspective. We utilize numerous examples that permit us to reply to these questions.

We propose a new culture of depth to

- Relearn to see and allow us to be guided by our natural perception.

- Open the doors to the living by an intuitive approach.

- Permit the artist a simple implementation of his drawings, rapidly and securely.

4 Contents of a treaty on perspective

In their book, Barre and Flocon developed in 1968 their technique of *spherical perspective*. To put things into perspective we must take several factors into account:

1. All spatial reality lives (directly apprehended by the senses of vision, touch, hearing, or by conscious memories or unconscious sentiments).

2. An observer and organizer (painter, designer, photographer).

3. On a flat surface (image, work).

4. A style of transformation (system of placing things in order).

Contrary to accepted opinions, no one style of transformation is self-evident. As we will see, it depends on what one wants to transform, because no process of transformation can correspond to total and confused spontaneous perception. On the other hand, each one corresponds to a certain image type, therefore to a sorting of things out in chaos perceptive.

We must understand that, following the example of the scientific approach, there is no question of representing the world as it actually exists, but rather such as one can observe it in certain conditions.

André Barre and Albert Flocon, *Curvilinear Perspective, from visual space to the constructed image.*

In order to follow an innovating scientific approach, I propose, with what we call *Real Perspective*, the following points:

1. We distinguish three worlds of reality, which we explain as: the physical, the perceived and the represented.

2. We opt in the choice of these realities for that of the living world.

3. Our *objective* shall be: to search for the living being. These two last

points forbid us to opt for the technique of spherical perspective, which can represents objects situated behind the observer, and thus a virtual world.

4. We shall start from the physiological perception of man to understand his visual universe (the cylinder), *and then* we will search for an *analytical tool* adapted for this universe.

So we will avoid presenting false tools which could conduct one to a world of representation in contradiction with the perceived reality: skimpy volumes of the Rectilinear Perspective, or onirical world of the spherical perspective.

Lobatchevski, Gauss or Reimann each conceived other mathematical spaces, but these quadric structured spaces do not correspond to our objective.

The *objective* must precede the *tool* and not the inverse. Our objective is the search for the living being ; the tool will be a result of that search. We have therefore, for the first time in our knowledge, published the calculations of the lines structuring the representation of visual cylindrical space, which corresponds to our physiology.

For that we must forget our classic culture, without disavowing its historical contributions. We shall deduct from it a simple, instinctive, and practical method of representation of natural space.

5. What do we mean by real or natural?

When we present a new concept or when we explore virgin territory, we lack the vocabulary to describe these newly discovered territories. The explorer must therefore create a neologism, which will be necessary for him to explain, or better yet use ancient words in a new context that will be necessary for him to describe. I have chosen to keep a vocabulary the least daunting as possible and thus opt to use ancient words. Thus it remains to place the terms "real" and "natural" in their new context.

We sought to join to the word perspective with the most appropriate adjectives such as "panoramic" and "optical." But all these terms have introduced is a false direction and a restriction at the same time.

The approach to Real Perspective, here presented, surpasses the idea of a simple recipe mechanically applied.

Innovation claims a new concept, and a title to name it. This title accompanies the researcher throughout his course of discovery of its new facets. This is what we will do with Real Perspective. If these two terms, *perspective* and *real* are old, their juxtaposition is iconoclastic, this is fortunate, because this birth brandish a new questioning.

What do we call real? Where is Nature?

We shall try to understand nature. This is not easy, for our ways of apprehending its phenomena are limited. We make discoveries daily in astronomy, microphysics, or neurosciences, which prove our given tools insufficient and we cannot imagine what would enable us to go further. We are as a child upon the breast of his mother attempting to understand the exterior world.

What do we call real when there are several realities, in particular that of the *physical* world, that of the *perceived* world and that of the *represented* world?

Let us take the example of the adventure of physicist Fresnel (1788, 1827) who was interested in light.

At the time, the theory of Descartes (1596, 1650) allowed the following: light is propagated in a straight line, consequently if I make a small hole in a sheet of cardboard and if I placed on one side of the sheet a light source and the other side a screen, I must therefore see an illuminated point on the screen.

Admittedly, but Fresnel saw rings.

Fresnel was dismayed for the following points were no longer coherent:

1. The physical world (light conveyed by the radiation of the sun)

2. A new perception (one sees rings on a screen)

3. And the former representation which appeared, as always, to make an image mechanically simple (rays of light are lines which cross the shutters of my room)

What does this mean?

Fresnel did not have any other resources than that of proposing an innovative concept:

1. The physical world (the consistency of light poses a problem for me) would consist of periodically emitted rays.

2. A gap in the date of arrival of the waves on the screen (called a phase difference) makes it so that their impacts would add up or cancel each other out positively or negatively to create the perceived world.

3. This phenomenon can be represented with the aid of small arrows, which turn like needles of a watch for adding or opposing.

Notice two basic things:

1. The poetic imagination of a physicist has nothing to envy compared to that of an artist. A physicist looks serious while fusing his inspiration with some equations, of which a winning combination will perhaps permit him to understand a new observation.

2. Fresnel's concept was unable to replace that of Descartes, which remains essential for optic instrumentation. In the same way when Planck said light is made up of small grains of energy, his new concept did not erase those of his predecessors. (This concept of Planck's makes it possible to explain, for example, why a ray of light is able to turn small windmills which one sees in store

windows of trinket and gadget shops, in the manner that a stream turns a wheel of a water mill.)

Therefore to define the physical world of light we need at least three concepts (that of Descartes, Fresnel and Planck) and we know that we cannot stay there. That was the job of de Broglie, Schrödinger, Einstein and Heisenberg.

Meanwhile physicists say that concrete reality is that of the physical world. This is reassuring for them.

The conscious artist is also confronted by these three realities: the physical, concrete one; the perceived one; and the potentially represented one.

In this study we shall be interested in the reality of the perceived world, which is the one that touches me profoundly.

Where is nature? As far as we are concerned, biologists and physiologists have as many difficulties describing this as the physicists have.

We shall limit our investigation to visual perception, although it is nourished with multiple sources. Let us attempt the adventure, man has always progressed thus!

6. The world of visual perception

In this work we will remain centered on optical vision. The other means of vision are the multi-sensory perceptions of the artist, which are essential and very effective.

We will consider those means in another work.

The artist is therefore confronted by three worlds:

- The physical world,

- The perceived world,

- The world of representation.

To pass from one world to another, a transformation must take place each time, that is to say an explanation accompanied by a tool.

Take a *line* for example.

In the physical world, let us point out that a line is a concept invented by man, who traced streets in straight lines for villages along the banks of the Indus. These are villages that have been abandoned nearly five thousand years ago.

In the perceived world, Greeks noted that two parallel lines converge at the horizon. This did not prevent their schools of mathematics from using the concept of parallel straight lines, which by definition, never meet.

When it was a question of representing two straight lines, for example two vertical columns, the Greeks built them convergent to give the impression that they would have been vertical.

In other words, the materialization of a representation depends on the objective of the architect who wanted, in this case, to give an impression of solidity to his temples.

This would suggest that the Greeks gave an angle to their columns to correct the *physiological perception* of the eye, which diverges the columns towards the sky.

The architect surely considered this correctional angle as one of his functional objective.

Notice then that there are two perceptions:

• Our physiological perception

• And our cultural perception, which is the intervention of our brain, which *interprets and predicts* according to its memorized experiences.

We will remain attached in this work to physiological perception, that we will qualify simply as "natural", if we would like to leave the beaten path of Rectilinear Perspective, which has been imposed upon us in France since Louis XIV. The artist has the right to update today, once again, his ideas on perspective, taking into account the discoveries of our century in physiology, psychology, computer sciences, neurosciences and physics.

7. Objective of the book

Rectilinear Perspective, which is the most commonly used since the Renaissance, is no longer obligatory in the eyes of today's artist. What tool, giving the impression of space on a sheet of paper, corresponds to our culture today?

Notice that the most diverse group of artists were interested episodically in Curvilinear Perspective, without however dealing at length with it, because of their lack of control over its nature. Matisse, Degas, Robert Delaunay, Félicien Rops, Villon, Rembrandt, Isaac van Swanenburg, Seurat, Lucien Levy-Dhurmer, felt intuitively the force of life that this type of perspective is capable of bringing, provided they knew the appropriate curves. There remains, in effect, a sizeable obstacle to overcome in mastering this tool: what is the nature of curves in Curvilinear Perspective that corresponds to our natural perception, what do we call "real" here?

The objective of this book is to respond to this question and to open new fields of possibilities, while taking care not to imprison the artist with dicta.

We have the intention of seeing the living side of a space, of a building or a still life. We would like to facilitate perception of a living model, and also learn to see proportions that we perceive naturally and how that will help us capture its presence.

Without being conscious of such goals and without study, we do not believe what we see. It is much easier to believe in what we do not see.

The aim of this book is to understand space as it is captured by our natural perception, that is to say physiological, forgetting our cultural prejudices imposed on us by Rectilinear Perspective.

8. Method

1. The understanding of perspective is the basis for the comprehension of a drawing. It is illusory to attempt perspective understood while copying a drawing. Drawing is first of all an active reflection.

We will show by examples the intuitive feeling of Real Perspective. We will then study, only for the scientists and architects among us, the exact nature of these curves. But we will come back immediately for the artists to the practical, natural use of "Real Perspective," which proves to be intuitive and simple, stripped of calculations and anguish. The "force" of the living therefore emerges naturally.

2. To understand space we shall explain that there are three realities:

• the physical world, which physicist takes as concrete truth,

• the perceived world that psychologists take for real,

• the world of representation in which artists evolve,

These three worlds are conductive to structure discourse and to advance in number of explanations of observed phenomenon's.

By consequence, throughout this work, we will not hesitate to remind the reader in which world he is situated, without fear of repetition; because, each time, the reader will therefore feel comfortable in his progressive perception of space.

3. It is not possible in a book to present objects in three dimensions, since a page has only two dimensions. It would mislead the reader to ask him to reproduce a drawing of a hand. It is necessary for him to learn how to draw the hand in three dimensions that is in front of him. For the reader to *see* in the proposed new culture of Real Perspective, must therefore *understand* the space that is around him. To See is to Understand. So, we will not present recipes for copying images from a flat sheet.

3.1. On the contrary, we shall endeavor to develop an understanding of real space while encouraging the reader to create, by himself, drawings perceived through a transparent plate and to observe his environment as he attempts to draw it.

3.2. We shall explain that space transferred onto a sheet of paper registers in arcs, like those of fireworks. The reader will then be able to transfer onto the drawing, obtained on a transparent plate, the vanishing point, trigonometric receding lines and the contour lines. The reader will be able to practice observation, in this new understanding of space, having forgotten cultural prejudices, and will see immediately the volumes before his eyes.

3.3. With experience, an artist will be able to store away his transparent plate and construct his drawing directly on the sheet of paper by adopting the reverse steps: by having his model under his eyes, he will begin by drawing the structure of space. He will choose his vanishing point to center his picture, and will trace the receding and contour lines in function of distance which he would like to have vis-à-vis the model in his drawing. By thus creating his arcs of fireworks, he will choose the intensity of his magnifying-glass effect. The artist will therefore be able, with a few references points, to draw his model by following the angles of its volume. The whole operation takes only a few minutes.

3.4. At the end of a few weeks of experience, the artist no longer has any need to trace his network of receding and contour lines for his drawing. When a child learns how to ride a bicycle and has a fear of speed and does not want to look ahead, nothing will serve him, if he does not understand that he must go fast and that it is fun.

An artist must work quickly, looking in front of himself (at his subject) to seize the volumes before his eyes, in only a few seconds and in symbiosis with the living moment. He must look as little as possible at his drawing, anguished by a waterfall of corrections that are the result of a bad setup.

The tool of Real Perspective permits him this accurate setup. Again he must accept that a vertical wall must not forcibly be straight on his sheet of paper.

By drawing *actively* not only can one attain an accurate line, but a completed portrait. But we shall show numerous examples.

Look now at the last illustration on page 188

9. Readers

The concept of Real Perspective is not only a practical tool for artists but also a new sensible and scientific approach to perception and of the representation of space that will interest many professions..

My experience with teaching showed me that scientific work, as elaborate as it is, is comprehended by everyone when it is clearly explained, and without jargon. This is why at no time shall we use scholarly terms, and we have made an annex to explain trigonometry in simple terms a child could understand.

Science was not born to be reserved for a privileged and jealous inner circle of readers. In 1930, only one circle of initiates knew the ideas of Einstein. Thirty years later $E=MC2$ was shown in amphitheatres of the faculties of science, and fifty years later the idea of the exhaustion of matter in the form of radiation is popular.

In 1980, Marr and his contemporaries presented a theory of perception of forms. Twenty years after, the treatment by software makes it possible to transform a photograph into a line drawing. Today the neurosciences are a typical example of the fruit of opening up the ivory towers.

It is no longer necessary, in order to understand the advantages of Real Perspective, to have read entire libraries which tell, all of them, the history of Rectilinear Perspective or that show paintings in Curvilinear Perspective without recognizing, without understanding and without explaining them. In effect, if we want to advance in our understanding of space, we must simply reflect calmly on our traditional notions, without fear of taking a new look at them.

This book therefore is addressed to all the amateurs of art no matter their level, beginners, students, professors and professionals. It will also interest philosophers of the phenomenology of perception because "we do not believe what we see" since a line in space is perceived as a curve, which must in its turn be transformed as it is projected onto paper. It will also interest architects since one of their peers constructed the column of Trajan in Rome by using real Curvilinear Perspective. It will interest mathematicians such as Wilhem Schickhard or Bruno Ernst; also physiologists, computer scientists, psychologists, neurophysiologists, sociologists, neurobiologists, psychiatrists and anthropologists who will see a new application of the knowledge they accumulate and transmit. This book would not have been written without the illumination of all these professions. Therefore neuroscience finds itself at the crossroads of multiple origins.

> "Must we give up participation in the vast movement of knowledge, which moreover runs such an extraordinary adventure?" Albert Flocon.

10. What is perspective?

A little memory aid

10.1 Definition 10.2 Examples of representations 10.3 Diversity of techniques used 10.4 Technique of Rectilinear Perspective 10.5 Inconveniences of Rectilinear Perspective

10.1 Definition

The word "perspective" comes from the Latin word "perpiscere" which means to *perceive*. Perspective is the art of representing, on a flat surface, objects spread out in space in a manner so that their representation corresponds to visual *perception* that we are able to have in our three-dimensional environment.

But we know today that our perception is not limited to our eyes, which remain very poor cameras. The fovea only captures under an angle of three degrees, the macula occult just a part of the visual field and the number of pixels perceived decreases very quickly under the periphery of the retina. What's more, the eye is constantly moving and vibrating.

Thanks to physiologists and neurophysiologists we know today that our visual perception is the result of work done by our brain, which makes decisions from a sampling of information received by the eye. The decisions made by the brain are made within a framework of a scenario of actions making it possible to anticipate an event; anticipation being necessary for our survival.

Now, we construct our scenarios by experience, from our memories and with our culture. This is true in particular each time that man wants to reproduce his impression of space in a drawing. According to the personality of the artist and of the culture of the period that it transports, acquired results differ, every culture having its references that are at times completely different from those of other cultures.

The modern, western, cosmopolitan man is confronted by an accumulation of information, which has evolved rapidly. Which culture shall prevail? Which techniques of depth expression will see the light of day?

10.2 Examples of Representation

Let us see first two examples without depth.

Without perspective

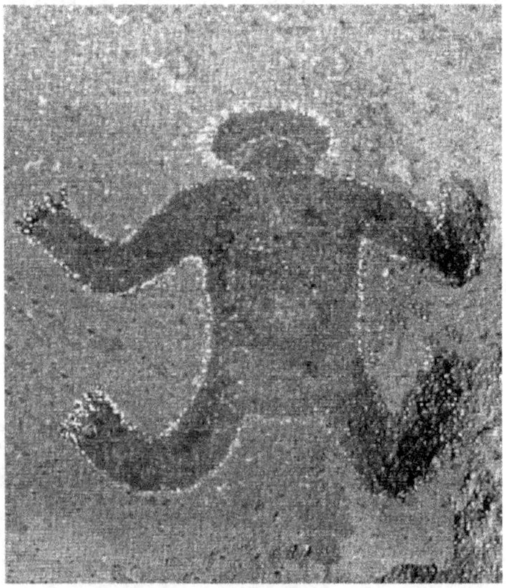

Without perspective

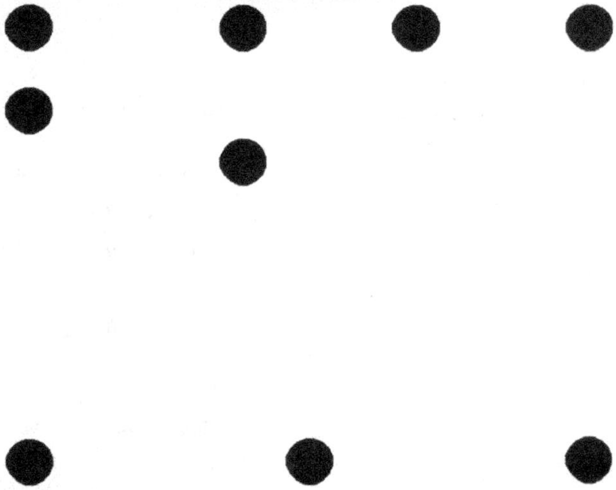

On the left evocation of flat figures on a flat background, California, Mutua Flat. Photo by Jean Clottes. On the right «6.4.62», composition by Paul Roche-Ponthus, 1962.

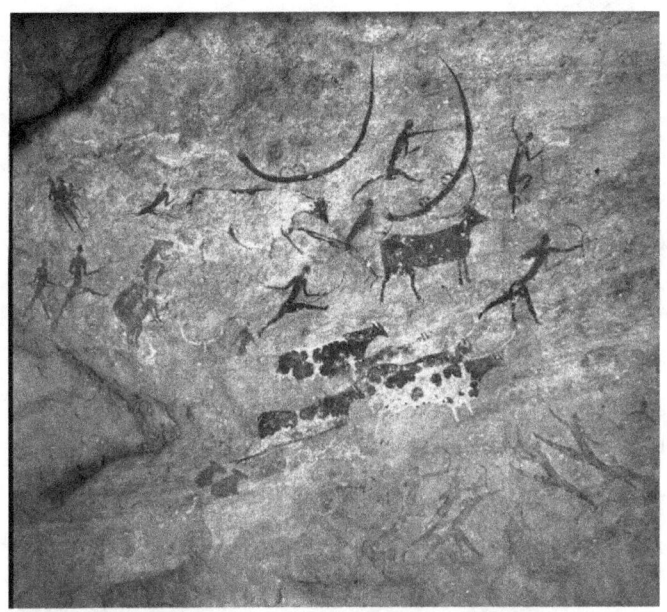

In parallel perspective

Space appears in this kind of perspective. The observer is situated above a herd of cattle. Perhaps he is seeing it from a promontory. This high-angle view allows him to divide the animals in space.

Let me add that certain animals, masking partially others, are accentuating by this effect of *covering* the impression of being spread out in space. This perspective is called parallel because one does not see the foreshortening of distant space. The sides of the path would stay parallel whether they are close or far away.

The first parallel perspectives appeared in Europe during the Magdalenian era (-13000) as in Ekain, in Spain or Eyzies in Dordogne. One can, moreover the techniques of parallel perspective and of covering between figures, admire the suppleness and workmanship of the lines.

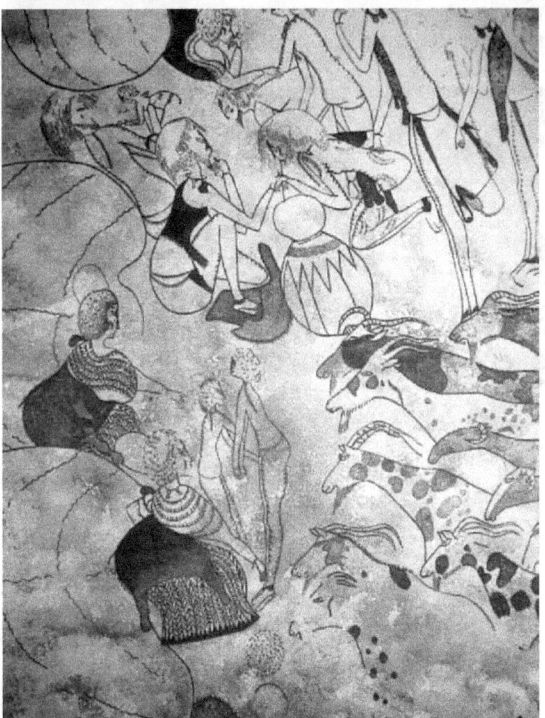

Sahara, Tassili n'Ajjer. Jabarun. *Photo by Jean Dominique Lajoux.* Shepherds, cattle herd, the hunt.

Sahara , between -3000 and -300. Tahilahi, civilization of shepherds. *Photo by Gabriel Camps.*

Without perspective

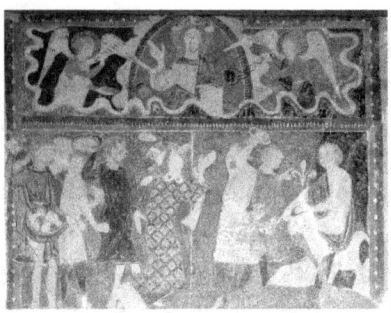

In Parallel Perspective

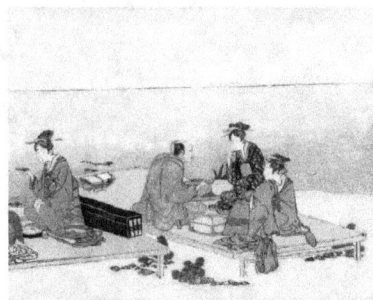

On the left fresco, 1200, in the little church of Longpré, Loir valley, France, shows a scene on a flat background. The only impression of depth is given by the treatment of the figures.

On the right a Chokosai Eiri painting, Japan between 1790-1800, shows the use of parallel perspective. The edges of the tables stay parallel. We have the impression that the side of the table the furthest away is larger than the side the nearest.

A sketch in Rectilinear Perspective

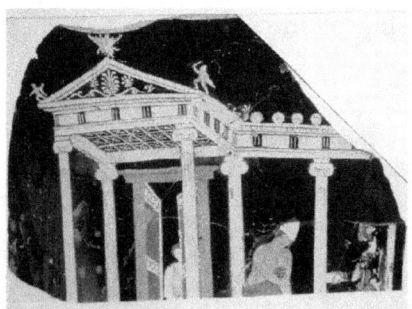

In Rectilinear Perspective

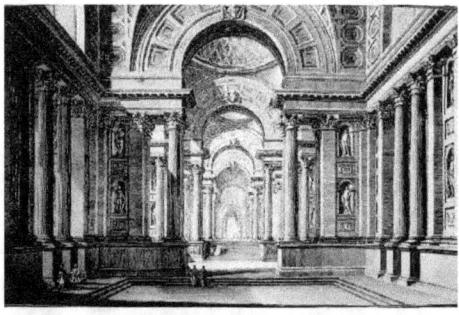

On the left pottery found in Tarente, 400AD. In the background the upper edges of the double doors seem to converge, therefore giving the impression of depth.

On the right the Italian optical illusion made a reputation of excellence for the system of Rectilinear Perspective adopted by certain Masters in the Renaissance, which served as a model for several centuries. Here over a theatrical perspective of Piranese about 1740. As we shall see, the rectilinear structure of such décor gives all its effects only in a narrow window (a street is perceived in proportion to a portico) and applied to forms made of straight lines.

In Spherical Perspective   **In Real Perspective**

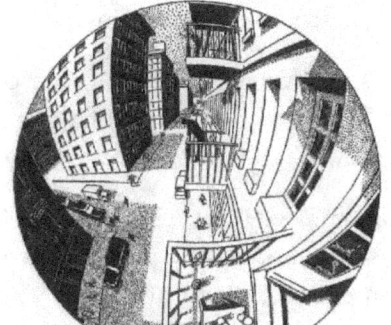   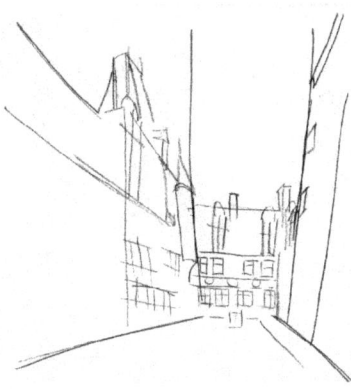

On the left, a drawing by Barre and Flocon (1930) connects all of a street in a cramped space.

On the right, a tracing on a transparent plate, in the style of Leonard de Vinci, gives to a medieval courtyard a handsome volume.

In Spherical Perspective   **In Real Perspective**

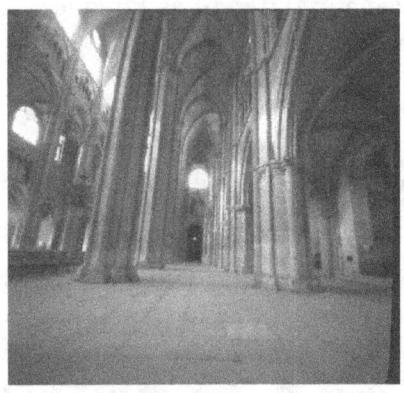   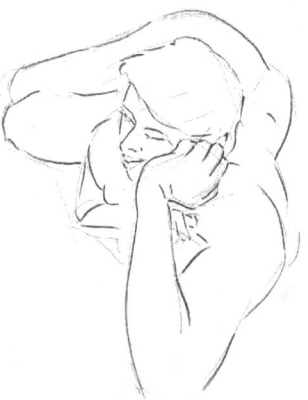

On the left, Erick Mengual, restored, with his pin-hole (a camera without optic lenses) give on the photo plan of the cube box a spherical construction of the lateral naves in the gothic cathedral (Bourges, France).

On the right, notice the presence and force of a drawing executed in five minutes, naturally and in complete security with Real Perspective.

10.3. Diversity of techniques used

Each way of presenting figures in a drawing brings an impression more or less marked by the depth that an artist searches to make felt.

1. In certain cave paintings; as in Eyzies (15,000BCE) the observer is situated above the subject (the herd of animals) having by consequence a high-angle view in this one.

2. The Chinese have traditionally used the perspective called parallel. In this technique the edges of a house stay parallel, giving the impression, for our western culture, that a house gets larger towards its most distant side. Therefore the surrounding space remains open and seems to be able to be indefinitely extensible. So one obtains the same type of spreading out of space seen in cave paintings.

3. The Greeks (circa 500BCE) used Real Perspective, which served for constructing their temples, to give them an aspect of endless solidity, by creating the impression of a building with right angles.

4. Thereafter this perspective did not cease to be used across the centuries by artists as innovative and different as Fouquet, Van Eyck, Vinci, Delacroix, Villon, Escher, or Matisse.

5. The Italians from the Renaissance starting with Giotto (1266-1337) are renowned for their Rectilinear Perspective, which was developed to the point of optical illusion such as the one employed to decorate the Olympic Theatre of Vicense.

6. Starting from the 13th century, the Flemish used aerial perspective, which consisted of rendering the horizon bluer to accentuate its distance.

7. Various Masters used spherical perspective in an empirical way by drawing what was seen in a convex mirror (van Eyck, Parmigianino). In 1930 Barre and Flocon described their perspective by using arcs of a circle and lines.

8. In 1950 Bruno Ernst and MC Escher were interested in the perspective of a cylindrical universe, however, without publishing a complete theory applicable to drawing.

9. Today we introduce the concept of "Real Perspective" by defining the nature of the curves used.

The question posed is: which perspective best translates our natural process of perception, in coherence with neurosciences.

10.4 The Technique of Rectilinear Perspective

We present this technique because it is, rightly or wrongly, the most widely known in our western culture. The issue is to be able to space out, for example, trees alongside a road giving us a sense of depth. It is necessary then to give the trees an adequate dimension so that they recede progressively.

This technique was discovered by Alberti (1404-1472) taking the example of a tiling. The idea is that the observer sees the picture plane through a window. So, on the right part of the drawing one could draw a grid facing us and on the left we see the profile of the observer looking at the grid

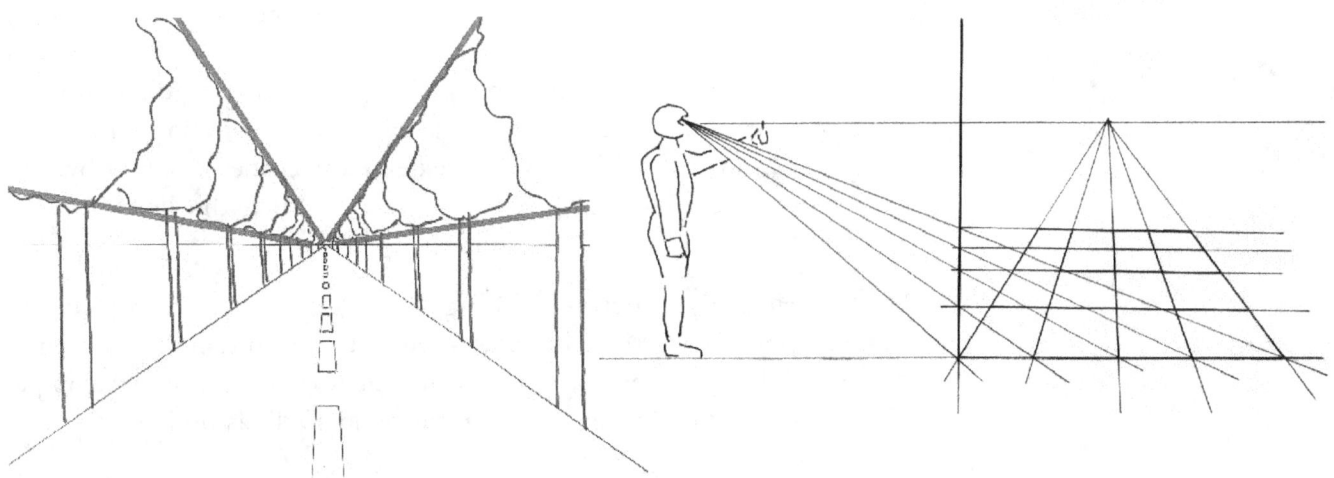

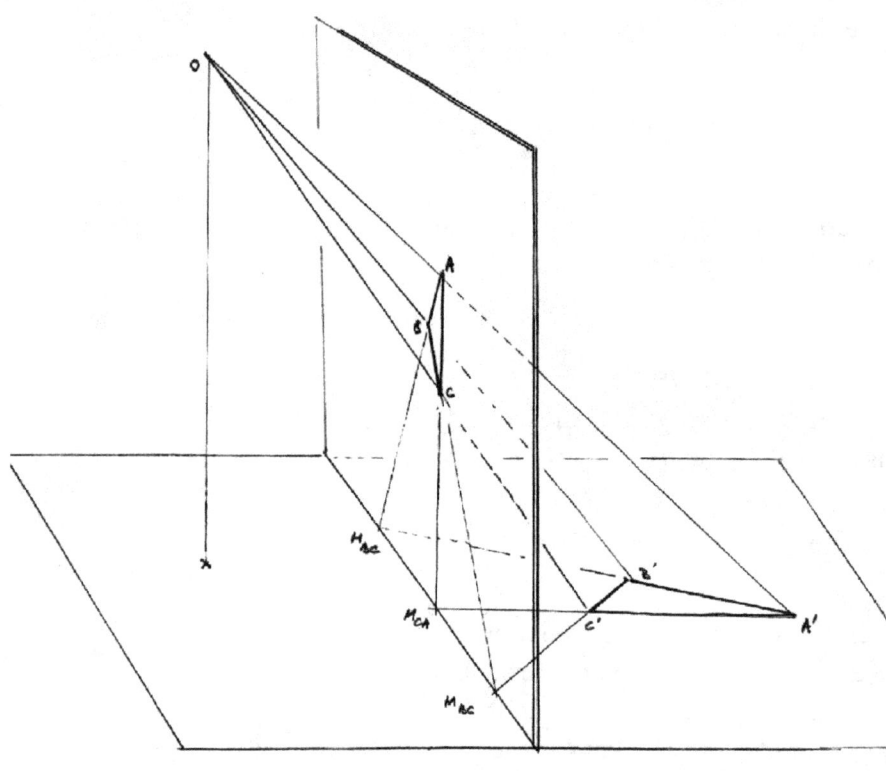

through a window. The window plays the role of a piece of drawing paper of the painter.

Now then, the sides of the grid are equal. This allows us to take into account, at the same time, the size of a square in length and depth. The lines joining the eye of the observer to the foot of the grid, allow, going across the pane, to see that tiles in the picture are systematically foreshortened as they recede into the distance. However, this simple diagram disheartens often the artists.

This technique was the object of brilliant developments. The theorem of mathematician Desargues (1593-1662) makes it possible to define the contour lines of shadows casted by a luminous source placed at point O. More valid at the time in the surface and in space this theorem makes it possible to bring to two dimensions a space of three dimensions: "if two triangles have their summits aligned starting at point O, the lines which extend their sides cut two by two according to three aligned points." In solar lighting the lines become parallel.

The descriptive geometry of Monge brings with the method called "running point" the projection of simple volumes: cubes, spheres, cones, and torus. This grand occupation of candidates to the Paris Polytechnique School was eliminated from programs around 1970, as useless.

10.5 Inconveniences of Rectilinear Perspective

- Space and volume are correctly expressed only in field widths of 30 degrees and for distant objects.

- Shortcuts and the magnifying-glass effect are not correctly expressed; Guillaume Apollinaire said, *"It's a miserable system for making things look smaller."*

- If architectural optical illusion is spectacular, they are less than in Real Perspective. (*I have change the word curvilinear*)

- The personages in a scene do not render the reality of life.

- Art students are very often paralyzed by the techniques of geometry, which panics them as the mysterious lowest common denominator, lowest common multiple, square root, and other mathematic "nastiness" of "horrible" childhood memories.

11
What is "Real Perspective"?

11.1 Objective

"Real Perspective" is the technique that allows us to translate the living, by putting down correctly the volumes that we have before our eyes.

Let us be reminded on this occasion that Real Perspective is not the only technique which allows successful representation of the living; for once accurate lines are placed it remains to be seen which type of line and what colors should be used to translate the living. That is not our discussion today.

11.2 Steps to constructing the tool

The objective must be defined *before the tool* and not the opposite.

The steps consist of identifying the nature of our natural perception, that is to say taking into account the physiology between the eye and the brain. The eye scans space starting from its position. The brain is in charge of imagining a stable environment to be able to take actions. According to neurosciences the eye is a directional sensor, directed by a predictive center. Our visual universe is cylindrical and we will mathematically calculate receding and contour lines.

We will determine that this natural network in the shape of grid-like cluster of fireworks is familiar to us. We shall note therefore that our classic culture has taught us, rightly or wrongly, how to see according to classic norms in the Rectilinear Perspective and not according to the instinct of our physiological apparatus.

11.3 Definition

At the level of the tool, one could say that Real Perspective finds itself to be a particular Curvilinear Perspective, with trigonometric receding lines and with ellipsoidal contour lines. It is successfully the tool of Real Perspective, constructed from our physiological perception, correspondiing to our natural perception.

11.4 Sources

Real Perspective takes its theoretical source from M.C.Escher and David Hockney. In 1947, M.C. Escher represented in his lithograph "Up and Down" a patio, constructed on the hypothesis we are in a space of cylindrical perception. It uses in effect sinusoidal arcs, but without being conscious of it, according to his mathematician friend Bruno Ernst, who was the first to explain the articulation of the transformations linking the three physical, perceived and represented spaces.

In 1992, David Hockney, who photographed the Grand Canion in Arizona with 200 viewpoints, also supports that we are surrounded by a cylindrical space of visual perception, because of the position of our two eyes which allow us to see more in width than in height.

Beforehand, Leonard de Vinci, when he drew through a glass pane, worked in Real Perspective. While returning from Bologna, Dürer also worked on tracings on a glass pane and made "perspectographs" which allowed him to report onto a sheet of paper what he saw through his apparatus. However, from the point of view of the method of construction, the apparatuses of the era permitted only a production of drawing point-by-point, comparable with Monge's "running point method."

Lanci made an apparatus, which allowed an artist to mark on a cylindrical screen a point in space that he observed. Barre and Flocon brought an invaluable testimony by showing that it was possible to theorize a type of Curvilinear Perspective. But all of this seemed well known since the ancient Greeks, who left us the convexity of the grounds of their temples, the table of arcs of circles of Ptolemy and the column of Trajan in Rome built by Apollodore from Damas (113). Unfortunately, Roman rectilinear reference erased their work.

11.5 Nature

Real Perspective confirms the preceding affirmations looking for how to go instinctively, without tool, from vision to the sheet of paper.

Real perspective covers simultaneously:

- **A concept:** our environment is perceived through a cylindrical screen owing to the presence of our two eyes which permit us to see two times more in width than in height.

- **A technique:** for constructing a landscape with a sensation of relief, instead of using from the beginning a vanishing point for straight lines, it must use the curves characteristic of our natural visual perception - arcs, with which we are familiar, without realizing it.

- **An intuitive tool, therefore powerful, and total ease of use,** since it corresponds exactly to the function of our visual perception, that is to say what we see through a transparent plate.

  "Contrary to what romantics from Jean-Jacques Rousseau to Marx thought, the triumph of reason is not inescapable. It does not correspond to any genetic obligation. Faced with the durability of chromosomes think of the precariousness of civilizations." Jacques Ruffié, *Treaty of the Living*, 1982

Let us combine intuition and reason.

11.6 Decisive advantages of implementing

Real Perspective

1. The concept proves itself to be applicable by an intuitive technique, simple and powerful. Drawing in Real Perspective is easy for the artist.

2. The application of this technique is natural and immediate.

3. The application of this new vision of space brings fullness to volumes and contributes to giving them a life-like appearance.

4. The artist does not have to calculate or to reflect, he seizes things just as they are: the curvilinear world is natural for him.

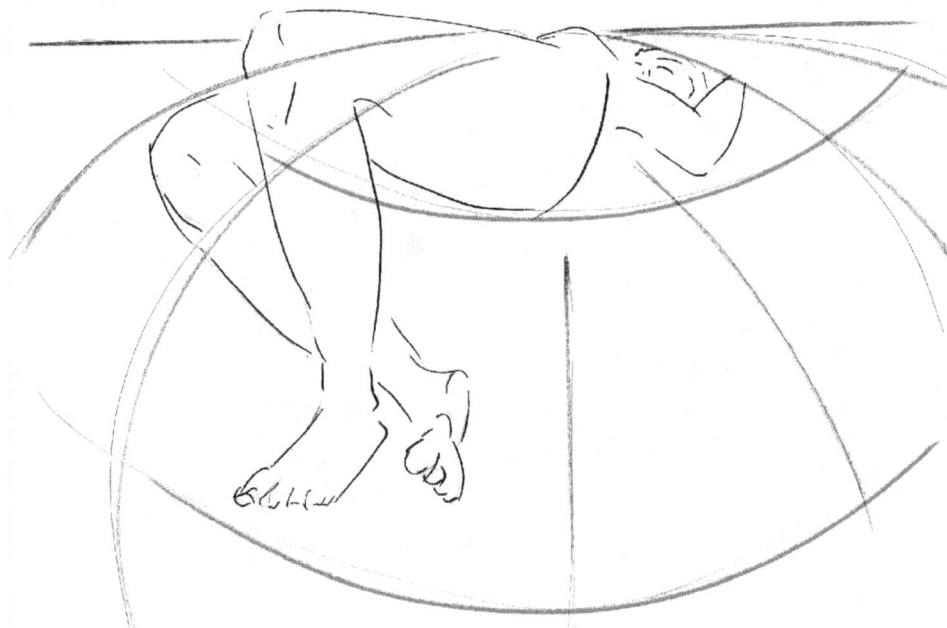

The schema done by the author shows a cylindrical space, the receding and contour lines around a vanishing point.

5. The artist profits from considerable saving of time in the sketching out of his drawing, freeing much of the flame of his expression.

6 The young artist takes his measurements of angles if he needs to, but avails himself henceforth of a new intuitive tool, which allows him to verify the coherence of his drawing without wasting time.

7 This technique totally secures the construction of the drawing.

8 One has a direct access to just lines, the only element from which the soul can arise.

Last but not least, let us bring attention to another important point: how to treat the background of the picture? The tool of Real Perspective proves to not only bring depth, but also the sensations of movement or of weightlessness, with a force that does not exist in classic Rectilinear Perspective. But this point is very rich, and will be treated in an other volume.

First Section

Rectilinear
and Curvilinear Perspective

History of a taboo

Introduction

Archimedes already left the beaten paths, he did not invent anything, he discovered what was and what is under the eyes of all of us, and he simply wanted to verify by measurements what he saw. In the same way Galileo, Vésale, Mariotte, Newton, Franklin, overturned habits. Gram is famous by error, Fleming by chance. But all of them took a step by ingenuously using the new tools available which enabled them to see better and by having the courage to believe just what they saw.

Laziness, social pressure, the established order, the stability of the lowest level of energy, replaced what man saw with dogma and, if it needed, of authority, as it was the case when Colbert gave to the Academy the monopoly of artistic teaching. Thus it is easier for us to believe what we do not see.

Neither has art ever escaped the fashion of the day; thousands of artists more or less pretend to be creators. Our artistic culture is such that we represent what would be strait in space by a line on a sheet of paper, although we know

1. our eye does not see a line but a curve

2. and that the drawing will have to note the transfer of this curve on a map in a manner that allows our brain to understand what our eye sees.

The definition of these curves is deferred to the Second Section dedicated to architecture but, before, the history of perspective will help us to a better understanding of the harness of our senses and our reason.

Let us retrace some steps of the epic efforts, of artists as well as scientists, in the search for mastery of perspective as first component of depth. The emotion brought by depth allows us in effect to transmit the living energy that we perceive. Our research in natural perception of depth will have as ambition to allow us to access more instinctively to life representation.

1.1 The Taboo

What is our natural perception?

Taboo

is the authority,

is death

is straight as an I,

it does not compromise,

one passes without daring to look at it,

it frightens,

like an empty fortress.

But finally

have you seen something straight on earth

that was not the fruit of your imagination?

What do you see in the following photographs?

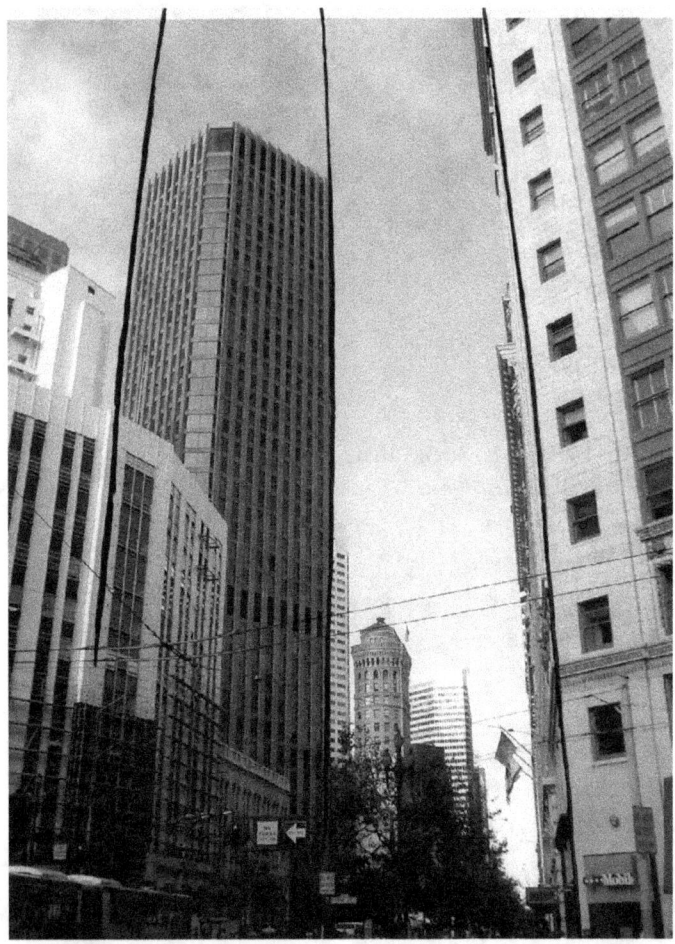

It is necessary to have several lines to follow the curvature of the edges of building that are close together. Even so in places we know that the edges are physically perfectly vertical. That is normal as one lens, of an eye or a camera, sees in degrees. But the photographs habitually enforce the erasing of this effect by a superposition of lenses or by corrective development.

San Francisco
Photograph by the author.

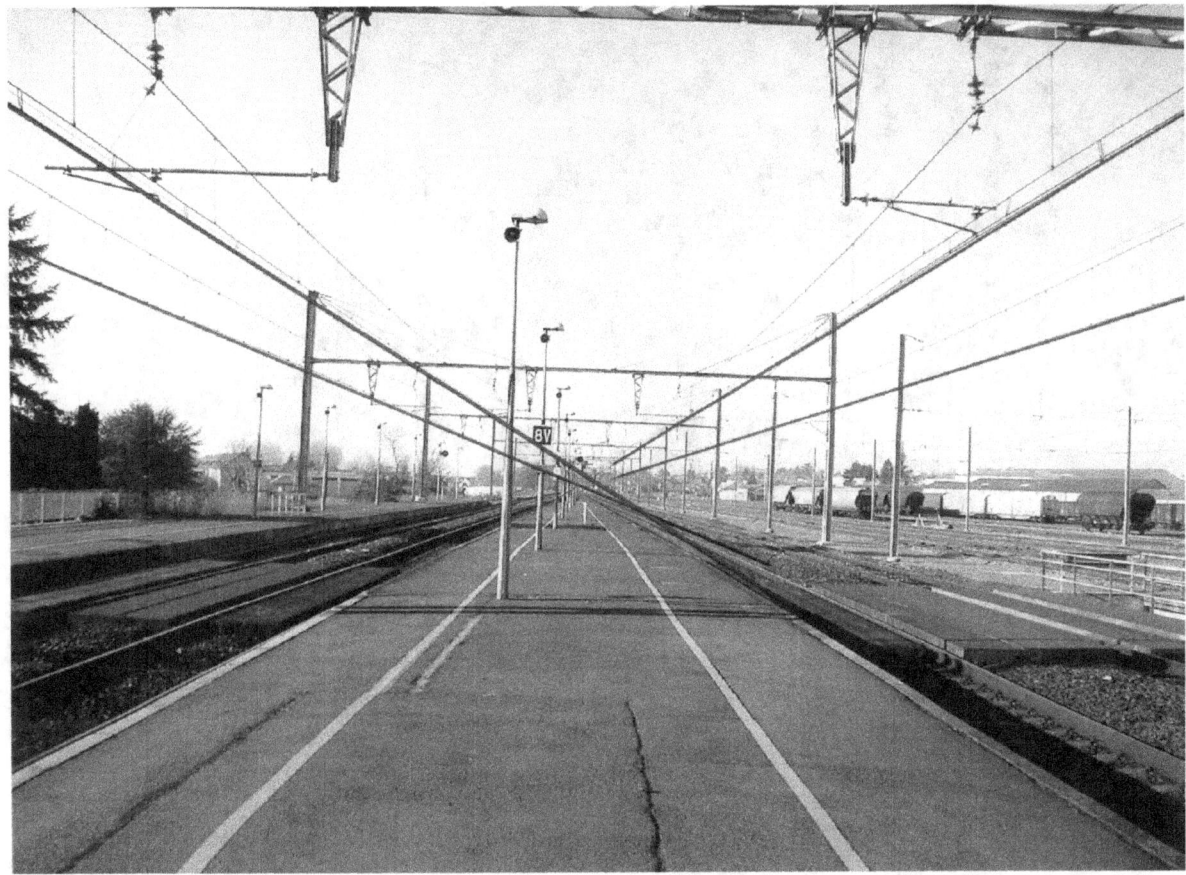

One can also see in this photo the following thing:

- on the left two catenaries part to cross on the track on the right

- While on the right tracks, a catenary passes under the other in place of staying in their horizontal level.

Therefore the lines do not make it possible to express the phenomenon of perspective.

Photograph by the author.

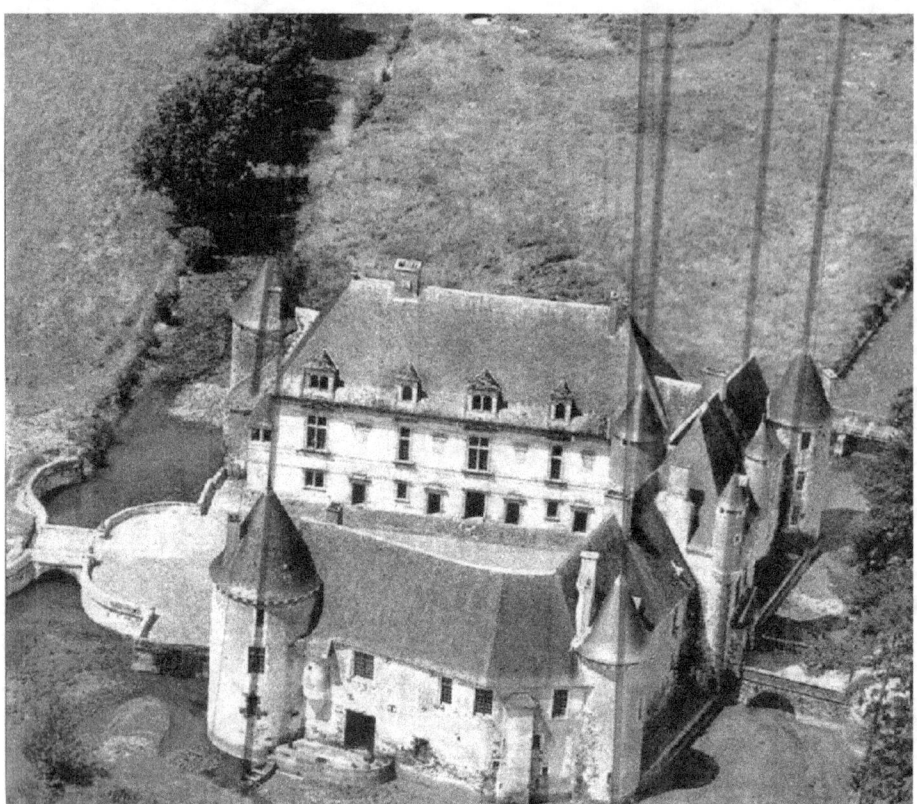

Moreover, in this photo, the towers on the right converge toward the bottom, while the towers on the left converge toward the top, whereas. . .

Boucard castel. La Nouvelle
République du Centre.
Photo Gérard Proust.

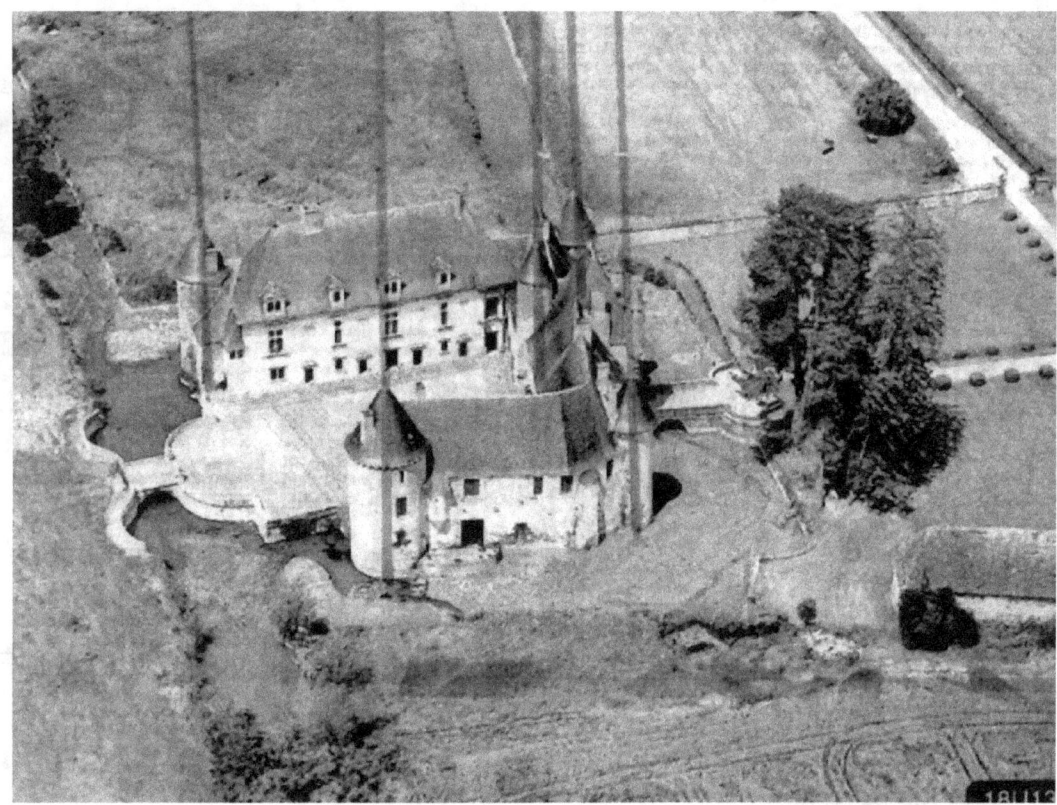

in this second photo it is the opposite.

We see therefore that the choice (by the artist) of horizontal line, of which the azimuth can vary between −90 degrees and + 90 degrees, is determinative of the orientation of the principle axes of a drawing.

Perceived reality also depends therefore on a decision.

Boucard castel. La Nouvelle
République du Centre.
Photo Gérard Proust.

We observe finally in this example of two types of curves:

1. **Receding lines** that come from the bottom of the street brush the top and bottom of the buildings. As their name indicates, the receding lines are lines that all start from the same distant point found at the far end of the street. One could say that they flee from the *vanishing point*.

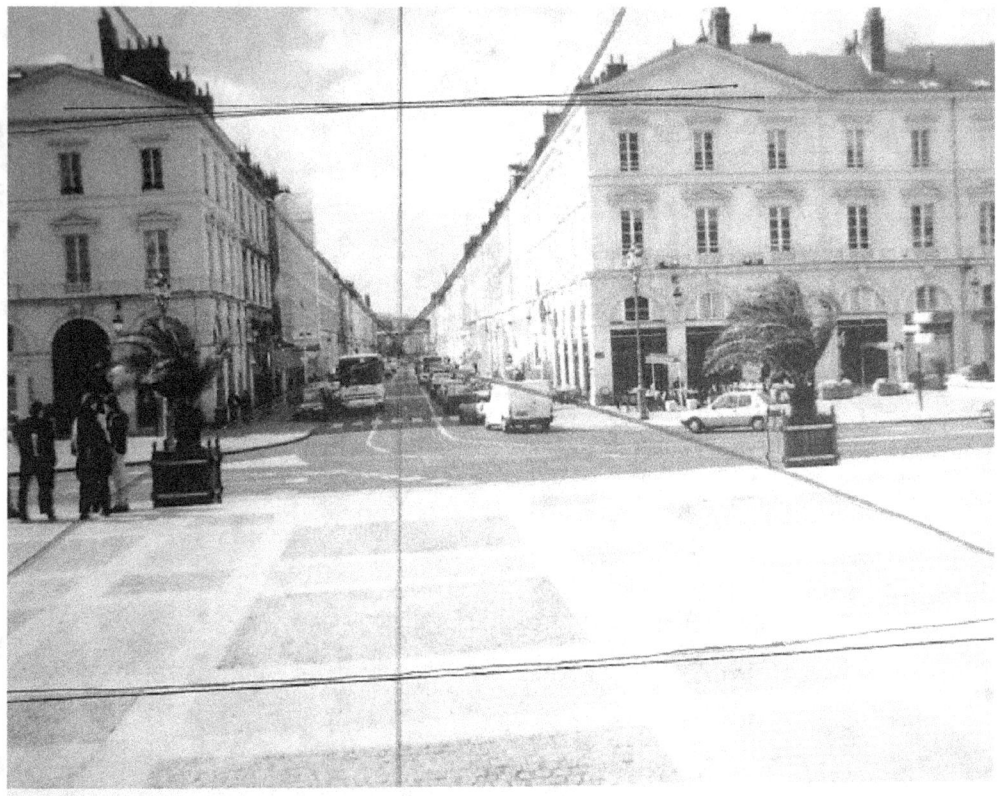

2. The **contour lines** cross the receding lines. By looking at the pavement in the foreground, one sees that these contour lines are perpendicular in space with the receding lines.

A contour line flies from the gutters of the building on the left to those of the building on the right. Another contour line in the foreground follows the checkerboard pattern of the pavement. One could also trace a contour line that runs along the foot of the building on the left to rejoin the building on the right. One sees that the contour lines allow us to see the enlargement of objects and for example that of the tiles of the pavement on the ground. Let us call them the *"contour lines of constant magnification."*

Orleans, France, Joan of Arc Street, viewpoint from the square of the Cathedral. Photograph by the author.

1.2 The Debate

Rectilinear Perspective imposed by the established order

INTRODUCTION

One sees in the caves of Eyzies in Dordogne, France (-15000) a cavity used to give the impression, lit by a torch, of a relief of a corpulent buffalo. The herd is shown in a view from above in what was already parallel perspective in order to arrange the animals on the prairie.

The Chinese used parallel perspective until the 18th century. There was neither a horizon nor a vanishing point; the drawing was indefinitely extensible. It's a matter of Rectilinear Perspective. In the 18th century the Far East adopted the occidental perspective, which is the rectilinear and converging perspective we know today.

The Egyptians used different effects of depth: profiles of people or three quarters point of view, value in the colors, when the subjects evoked permitted it. Their world seemed to be that of Rectilinear Perspective.

The Greeks invented geometry, the parallel lines that never meet, but paradoxically also receding lines in the first stage sets in theaters. Euclid managed this paradox. In a parallel manner, architects treated space by curving the floor in their temples and by converging their columns with *the objective* of giving them the aspect of strength the architect wanted.

The foreshortening of the mosaic of Alexander testifies a grand mastery of space that is not Rectilinear Perspective but free, in other words, curvilinear, whose structure remains to be defined.

Plato pondered on the perception of reality. Archimedes explained and measured appearances. The Greeks apparently managed these contradictions by adapting their tools of representation to *circumstances* and to *the objective defined beforehand.*

Several viewpoints existed on the plotting of a perspective.

In Rome, Vitruvius (90, 168) recommended the straight line. (*De Architectura,* book I chapter II.) But one pays less attention to the fact that the helical frieze of the Column of Trajan (113) is expanded to give the impression from the ground that all the personages have the same dimension according to a progression that is not arithmetic, and by consequence does not correspond to Rectilinear Perspective. This progression is in fact trigonometric. In that era Greek astronomers of Alexandria published a table of arcs and circles that we still use today under the name of the table of trigonometry. (See the little illustrated annex "What is trigonometry?) The viewpoints coexisting during this era, presented multiple races and multiple religions in Rome, provided that Caesar was respected.

We are aware of a debate nourished since the time of the Italian Renaissance. The debate has never ceased since then. The European Renaissance discovered the heritage of Antiquity in the framework of a debate. In effect, by drawing, theoreticians and artists quickly took consciousness of an important constraint: a picture corresponded not only to a precise position of the painter but also to a direction of a single observation.

An artist found himself prisoner of his position and the direction of his regard. Moreover, the central Rectilinear Perspective, the one with which we are familiar today, presented difficulties of reading to the great masters of the Renaissance.

Lanci, Vignola, Vinci and Dürer invented devices to project space on a plane. On this subject, the receding lines organized around a vanishing point were not, for everyone, lines. Cosme l'Ancien chose the Rectilinear Perspective of Giotto politically to mark the advent of the Medicis.

The culture of the established order, civil or religious, rejected the new destabilizing discoveries, in particular the idea that a line in space cannot be a straight line for our eye.

Note that perspective, or in other words the conception of space and of the world, is the fruit of a social organization.

In Europe two worlds of reflections were formed, that of engineers (Vinci) and artists (Uccello) on the one hand, which evoked the presence of curves, and that of theoreticians and architects (Alberti, Brunelleschi) on the other, who admitted only straight lines in a drawing to represent straight walls.

Nevertheless, the architect Vignola saw a floor rise at its extremities and the ceiling lower, so giving a confirmation of the tenth proposition of the optic treaty of Euclid: "it is evident that higher planes appear concave."

Lanci made a perspectograph with a cylindrical screen.

While tracing through a windowpane, Vinci and Dürer transferred onto the plane of glass the representation of their physiological perception.

Alberti, the theoretician who fathered Rectilinear Perspective, felt the difficulty and got around it by admitting that it is necessary to be limited to a narrow window in order for Rectilinear Perspective to be an acceptable approximation of reality.

Alberti recognized the limits of the tool invented by Brunelleschi: it acted as an admission of failure for the popular Italian technique that had not rediscovered the Greek knowledge.

Pierre Descargues made the remark "if perspective is a science, one understands poorly that the responses given by specialists of the era were so little precise."

The concession of Alberti reassured the established order, which accepted badly that a line in space is not a line in a painting. The world of illusions, like that of theatre, was out of favor. The troublemakers, partisans of

Curvilinear Perspective, were thus pushed towards oblivion. Their weak point was not having found a theoretician comparable to Alberti to give a definition to the curves they used. These curves, corresponding to our perception, were therefore ignored.

Nevertheless, in 1624, the scientist Wilhelm Schickhard, friend of Kepler, wrote in Tübingen in his Treaty of Optics:

> "I say that all lines, even the straightest, necessarily appear to curve. However no painter accepts it; to represent the rectilinear sides of a structure, they all use straight lines, even if this is false if one considers the true art of perspective. The sides should curve gradually like a paunch."

One imagines Wilhelm Schickhard leaving a tavern! This rural comparison is not surprising when one sees Dante showing in the *Devine Comedy* that the moon is not a cloud but a solid by comparison to a lean and fatty ham.

The controversy developed in France until the moment when, in 1683, Le Brun, discomforted by Bosse's criticisms, obtained through Colbert, conferral upon the Academy and the monopoly of artistic teaching. The paradigm was to be rectilinear, as that of French gardens. The Sun King established an imperfect tool as an absolute system. The Greek subtlety seemed definitively forgotten in France where Academicism still profoundly marks our culture.

The Diderot *Encyclopedia* recommends limiting a drawing to a narrow window, to avoid becoming confronted with difficulties of Curvilinear Perspective. The bourgeois revolution remained therefore artistically conformist. The 19th century had its grand masters, such as David and Ingres, who retained the methods of the Romans revived by the Italians. The academic painting was characterized the most often by an absence of depth, by coldness and by subjects subservient to the whims of princes or of conventional society.

In England, Robert Baker, presented in 1792 the first panorama of the

English fleet anchored between Portsmouth and the Isle of Wight, as a juxtaposition of windows.

This culture of authority was unable to be maintained:

1. Scientifics, taking into account their needs, recalled their perception of reality (parallel perspective, mass planes, projections on several planes). Monge invented, at the end of the 18th century, *descriptive geometry* and the method of the running point along two surfaces. The scientists of the 19th century no longer felt constrained by the Academy.

2. Parallelly artists followed their only inspiration in the world of the imaginary of which they defined themselves, content and form (Impressionism, Cubism, Surrealism, Hyperrealism etc.). They no longer felt concerned by the established order that sought to imposed on them forms and symbols of an official cult.

Rectilinear Perspective has therefore today shown its limits. New research into the representation of our perception is indeed necessary. We will see that Real Perspective corresponds to our natural mental process; therefore, it alone, contrarily to Rectilinear Perspective or to other Curvilinear Perspectives, can permit us to approach the living.

In this first volume we attempt to introduce the reader gradually to this perception of space by showing the different representations of depth since humans first appeared.

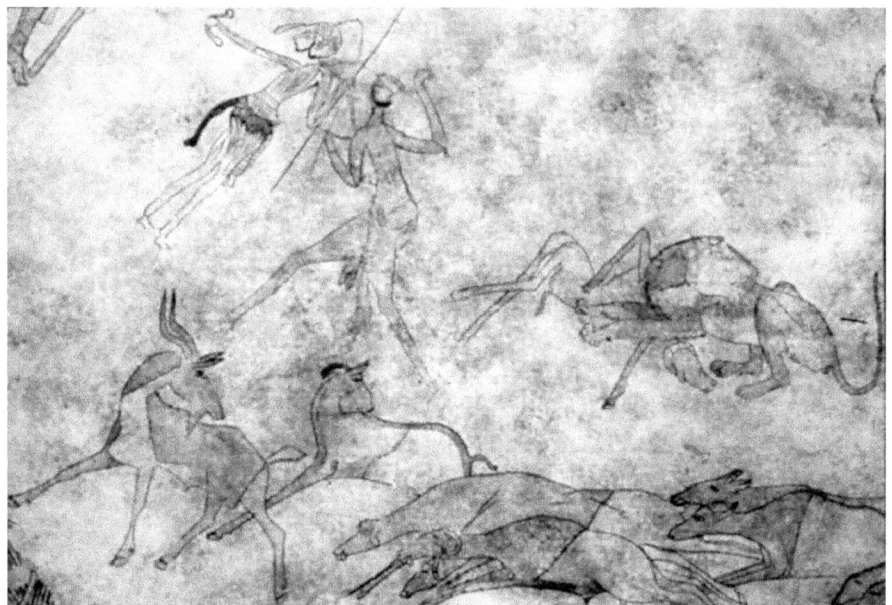

Sahara. Iheren. (Between 3000 and 300bce). Photo by Gabriel Camps.

Masters of the engraved drawing, figures and animals in three quarters. The view of three quarters testifies the mastery of depth and therefore of perspective. One also observes already such a treatment of the three quarter view in the panel of "Acrobats" in the cave of Addaura in Italy dating from the Epigravétien (-12.000).

This natural mastery of perspective did not await the principles of Alberti of the Renaissance that our culture tends to regard as an obligatory reference for discovery.

Tombe de Sennedjem, Thebes XIX-XX dynasty. Photo Yvonne Vertut.

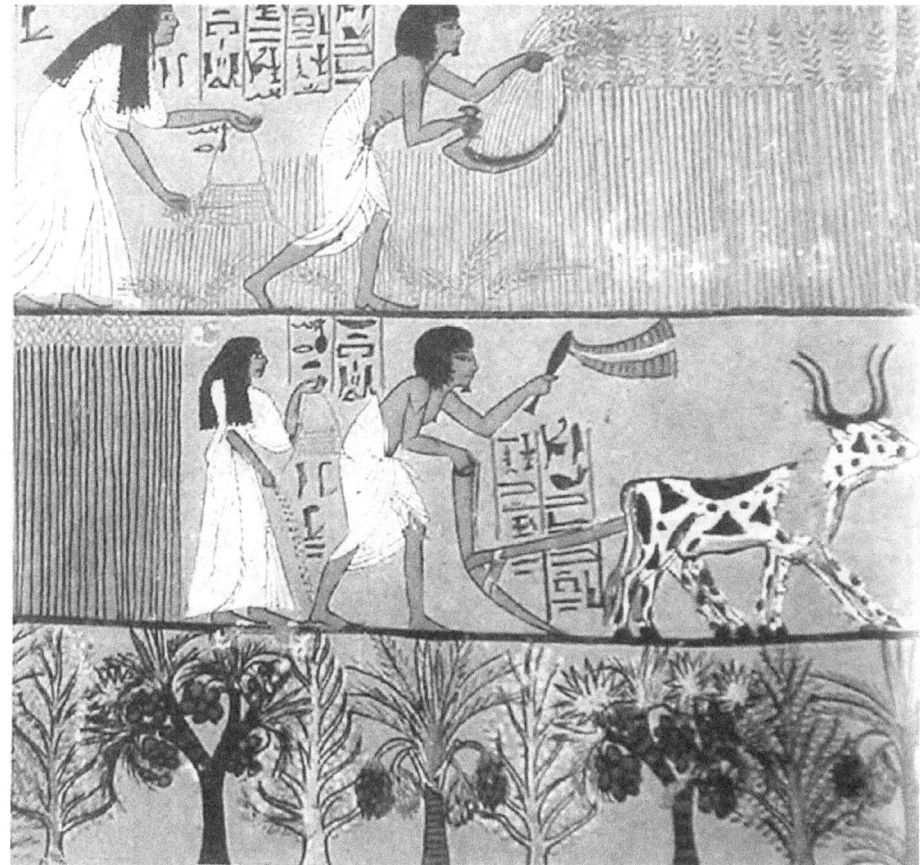

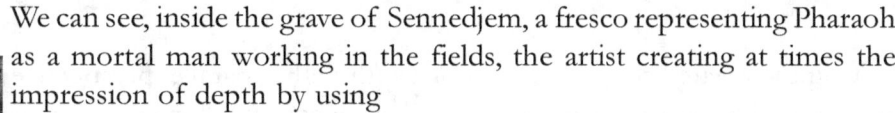

We can see, inside the grave of Sennedjem, a fresco representing Pharaoh as a mortal man working in the fields, the artist creating at times the impression of depth by using

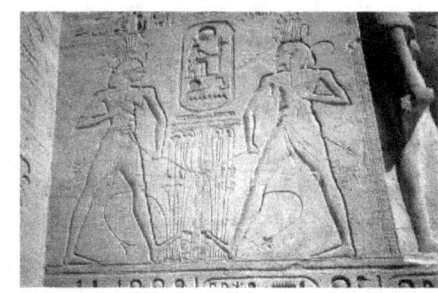

Abu Simbel.
Photo Catherine Brenner.

- Profiles of figures or in three-quarters,
- The repetition of a motif with two oxen dragging a plough,
- The color value in palm trees and trees with light green leaves.

This example is interesting as we are in the habit of seeing in Egypt representations of Pharaoh in official functions, shoulders facing and feet in profile.

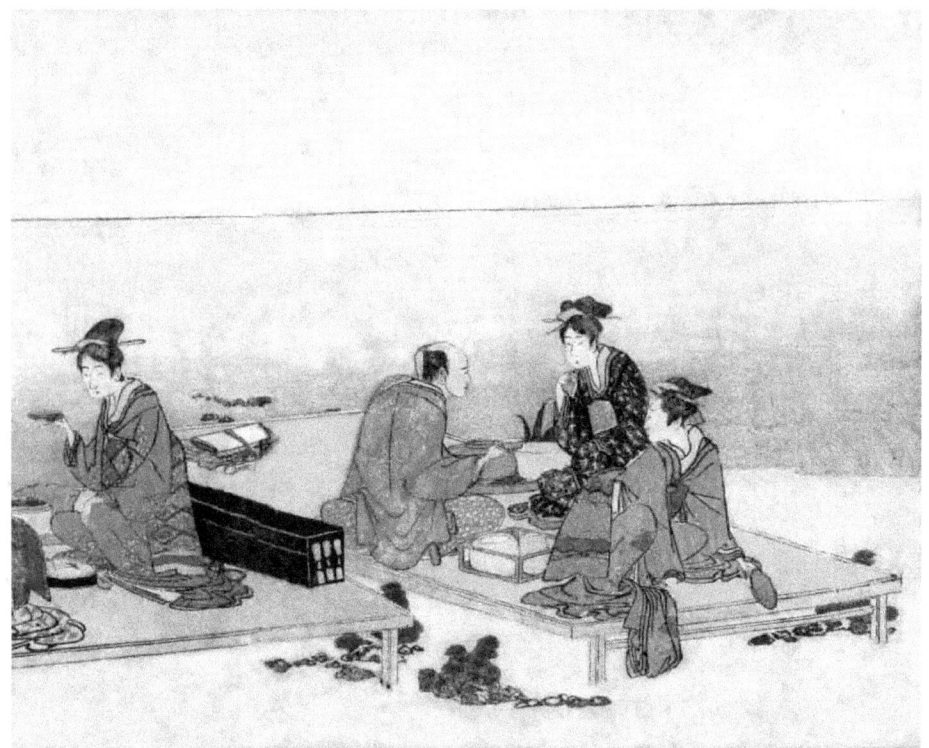

Eiri, 1790-1800. Japan.
Private collection.

The Chinese created the impression of depth with a parallel perspective associated with an view from above. This technique allowed them to arrange objects in a space indefinitely extensible. Japan did the same later.

This technique is called parallel because one sees in this example that the two edges of a table stay parallel. We have the impression that the side of a table the furthest away is larger than the side that is nearest. Upon the first table, the black box masks the fact that the two edges of the tables are overlapping one another.

Issos Battle between
Alexander and Darius.
Sopraintendenza Archeologica di
Napoli.

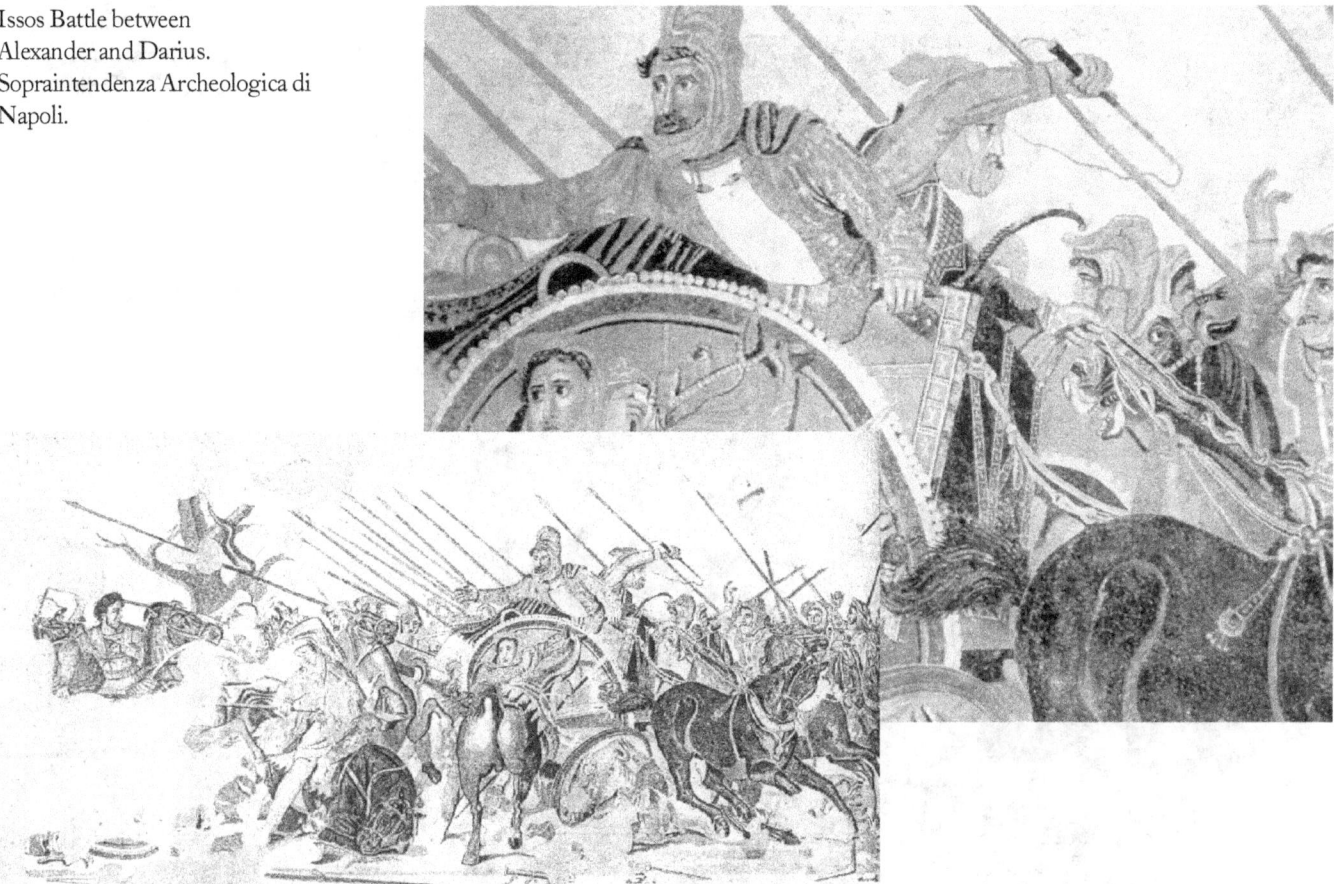

Eighteen centuries before Uccello the mosaic of Alexandria found in Pompei, displayed in Napoli, was probably a reproduction of a fourth century Greek fresco. The foreshortened views and three-quarters viewpoint were already mastered, they were laboriously rediscovered by certain artists in the Renaissance.

Notice in this mosaic the shadows, lights and values by colors. The first horse in front of the cart seen foreshortened from the back is of the same color as the chariot, which brings the central character closer, a Darius frightened by the progression of Alexander, who is approaching and dangerously near.

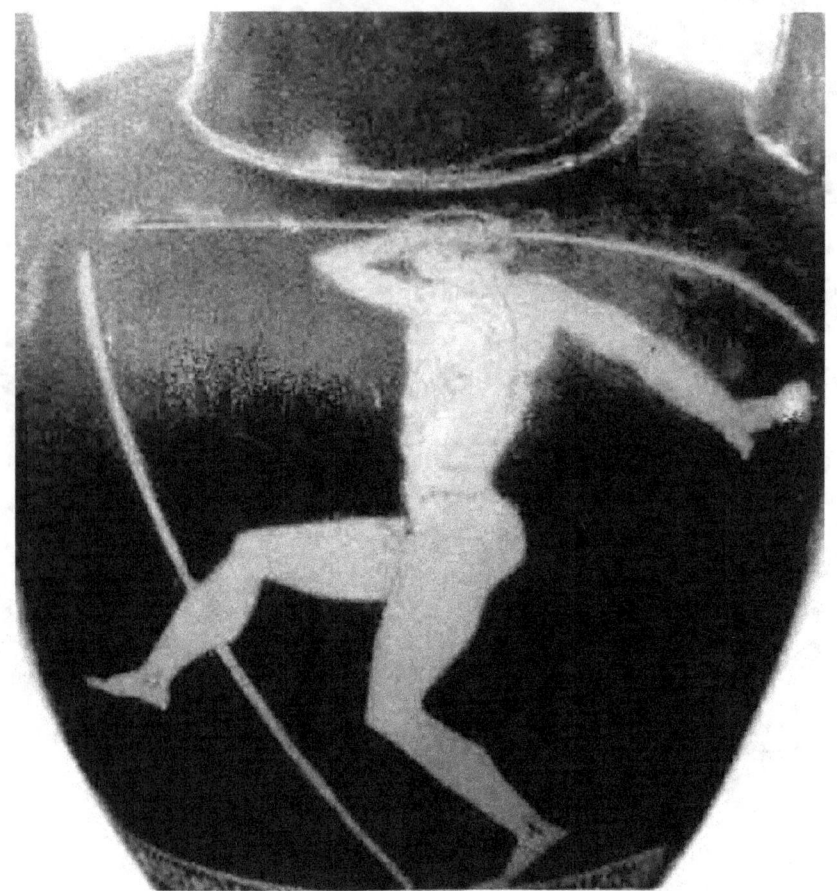

Villa Giulia museum, Castellani collection. Attic Amphora, dated 480bce, side 2.2 Pittore da Berlino, da Cerveteri.

We see on this Greek amphora an athlete throwing a javelin. The javelin is seen curved in the photograph made by the curvature of the amphora. But it is not the same for the line passing under his right leg, which can be interpreted as the side of the Olympic track.

Having examined the amphora in place, this line seems to have been intentionally traced as a curve. Why? Do we have here a testimony to a receding line of Curvilinear Perspective?

Villa Giulia museum, collection
Castellani. Attic Amphora, dated
480bce, Side 1.2 Pittore da Berlino, da
Cerveteri.

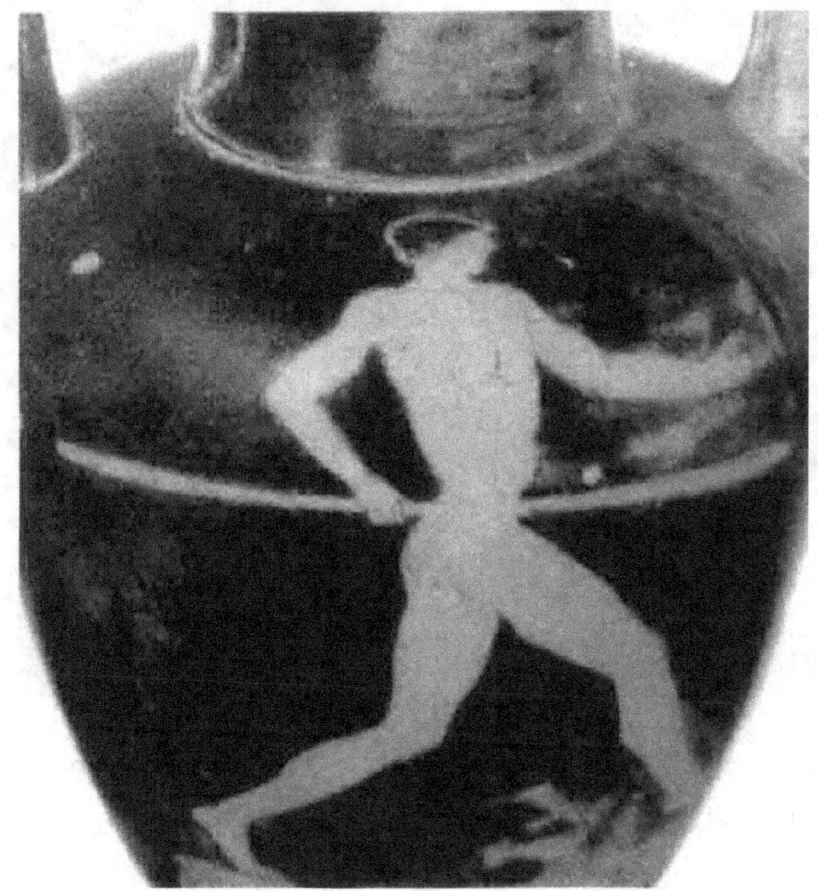

This side shows us an athlete holding his javelin horizontally before
throwing it. We see clearly that, in this case, the wish of the artist was to
show a rectilinear javelin and that the curvature seen in the photograph is
only due to the curvature of the amphora.

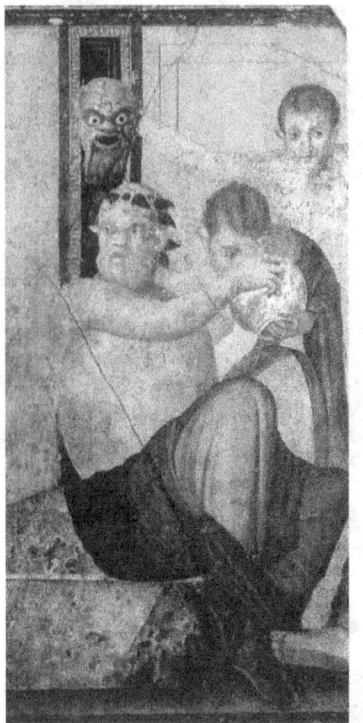 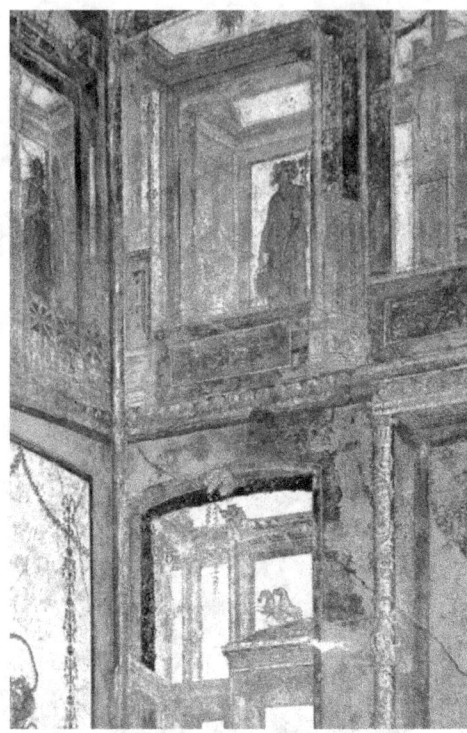

Casa dei misteri. Pompeï.
Sopraintendenza Archeologica di
Pompei.

The Romans endeavored to give the impression of depth in four processes :

- foreshortenings seen rather well done, in spite of the non-mastery of perspective, by a simple observation of volumes, one in comparison with another, allowed to overlap, almost adequately, the lines delimiting the volumes,

- light and shadow,

- values by colors.

- a rectilinear convergent perspective to an architectural background oftentimes without appropriately positioning of the vanishing point, this showed that the Romans did not understand the perspective of the Greeks.

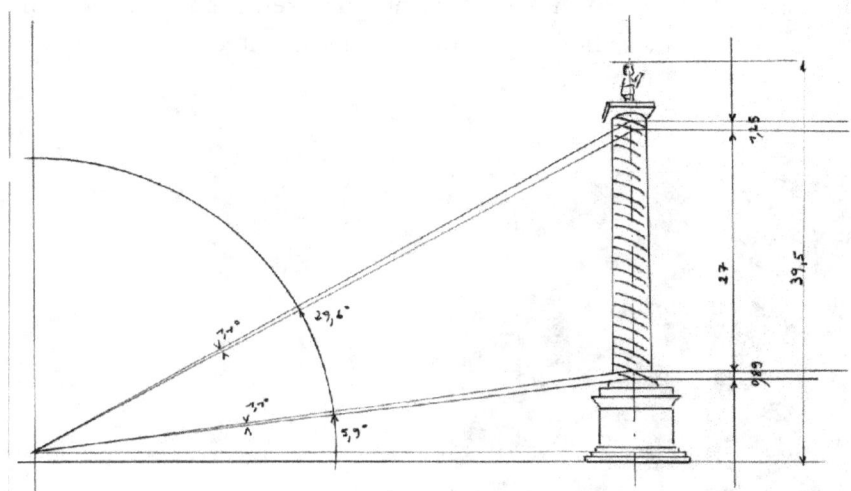

The Column of Trajan (113) is decorated with a helical frieze stepping up from 0.89 meters at the base to 1.25 meters at the top. As a result at 60m, in other words at the entrance of Trajan square, an observer sees the bottom and the top of the frieze under the same angle. This calculation was child's play for the architects who possessed a compass and a ruler. The column was built by a Greek architect, Apollonore de Damas.

Notice that a trigonometric table simply consists of noting, for each point on a circle located by its angle, the corresponding radius projected onto the vertical axis of the circle (called axis of the sines). See the little annex illustrated for my children "What is trigonometry?"

Ptolemy called this table the "Table of Arcs and Circles," in his encyclopedia known in Antiquity under the name *Almagest*. Ptolemy realized, therefore, a work comparable with that of Diderot in the 19th century. This encyclopedia gathered the information known for centuries, which is confirmed to us by the measurements of the bases of Greek temples built in 500BCE. These tables existed since the most ancient times used by astronomers and navigators on land or by sea.

We enter now into Modern Times. Albrecht Dürer returned from Bologne in 1520. His engravings show the apparatus he invented.

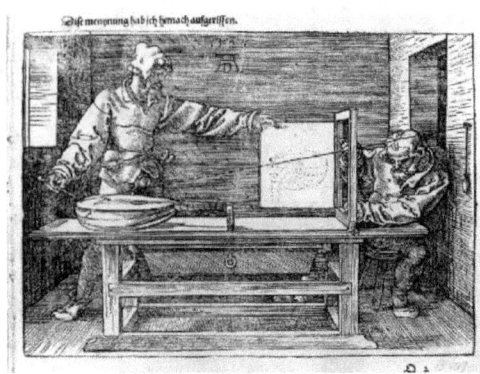

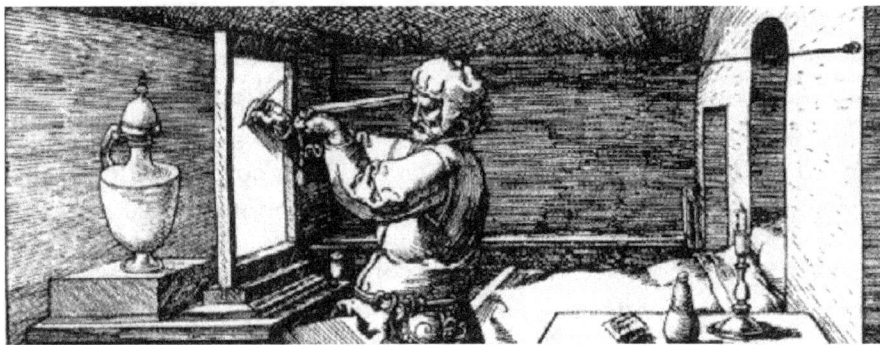

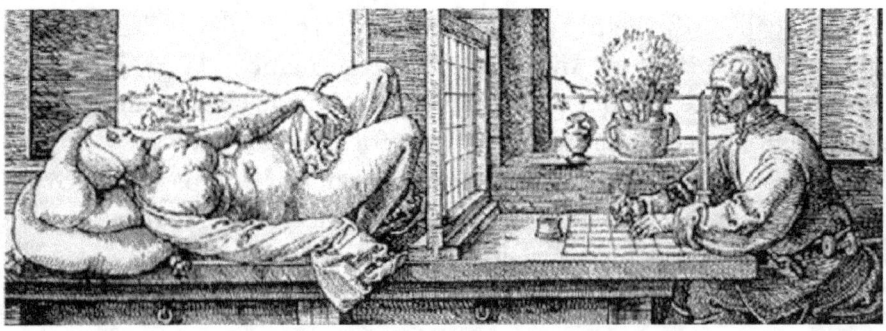

He presented his inventions five years later, in his book *Instructions for Measuring by Ruler and by Compass*. To master perspective projected on a flat surface, artists constructed point by point the projection of space on a sheet of paper. The men of the Renaissance therefore were not equipped with satisfactory theories and principles of construction for understanding their physiological perception.

The Renaissance was very laborious.

* * *

The Italians were naturally moulded by Roman culture. The Romans, powerful by their administration and their army, were rather loutish and did not understand much about Greek culture, which they invaded and pillaged.

One is convinced by visiting Pompeï where the works of art of the two civilisations are found juxtaposed.

The Italians of the Renaissance acknowledged the Roman architect Vitruvius as their spiritual father, who conceived space only in terms of straight lines.

One is not surprised then that the architect Alberti (1404-1472) issued his theory of perspective constructed with straight lines.

Alberti, by representing here, in the same drawing, a view facing a grid on the left and a profile view on the right, gives a method of constructing of the enlargement of the squares when they are closer to the observer.

This method presents many weighty inconveniences, which artists reject:

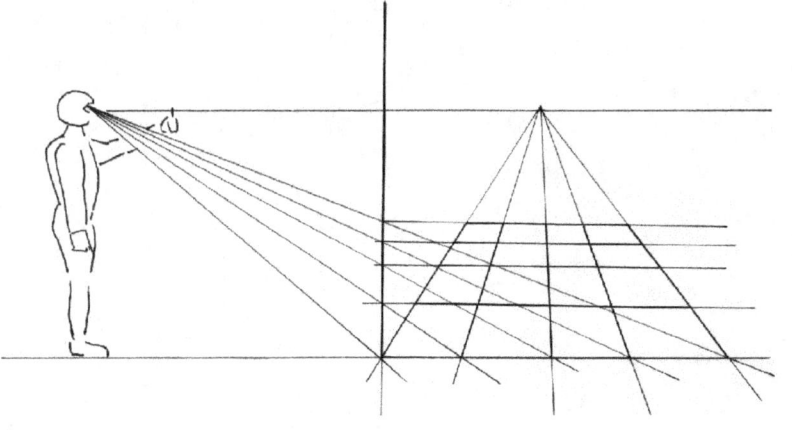

- It confines and reduces depth of drawing in a rigid system,

- To be an approximation sufficiently exact to reality, it implies working in a narrow window of 30 degrees,

- It advises drawing distant figures to avoid deformations,

- It is not simple to assimilate contrary to appearances,

- It is not intuitive since it frightened generations of artists.

- But on the other hand it pleases architects, who construct straight walls.

As a result, disputes rose from all quarters.

The theory of Alberti was in effect judged too simplistic to express natural perception, even if its author was justified in saying that he proposed a convenient simplification.

This method was therefore an acknowledgement of failure.

Paolo Ucello. *San Romano Battle.* Polo Museale Florentino.

The painter Uccello (1397-1475) was wary of the systematic mind. He was not satisfied with Alberti's insufficient propositions established as a universal solution. Uccello was an intuitive observer but also an artist of great freedom. Therefore, in *The Battle of San Romano (1456)* which we see here, he shows his mastery of foreshortening comparable with that seen earlier in the fresco of Pompei (500bce), for instance, a green horse whose color will be used again by Gauguin in his *Cavaliers (1901).*

Giotto painted a pink horse, in the sixth upper panel on the right in the Church of Assisi, by sections of colors, comparable from this point of view with that of Uccello; but his horse is treated in profile and is not foreshortened.

In such a painting, Rectilinear Perspective is of no help. To defend himself Alberti tried to denigrate Uccello who overshadowed him. Rectilinear Perspective penetrated with difficulty the ones spirit and was found to be an inconvenient instrument. One notes, indeed, when looking at the drawings of the famous architect Androuet du Cerceau, published in 1605, the strangeness in treating the staircase in the Fontainebleau Chateau or the view of the Vèves Chateau. This strangeness seems to be in fact, an anomaly generated by technical problems.

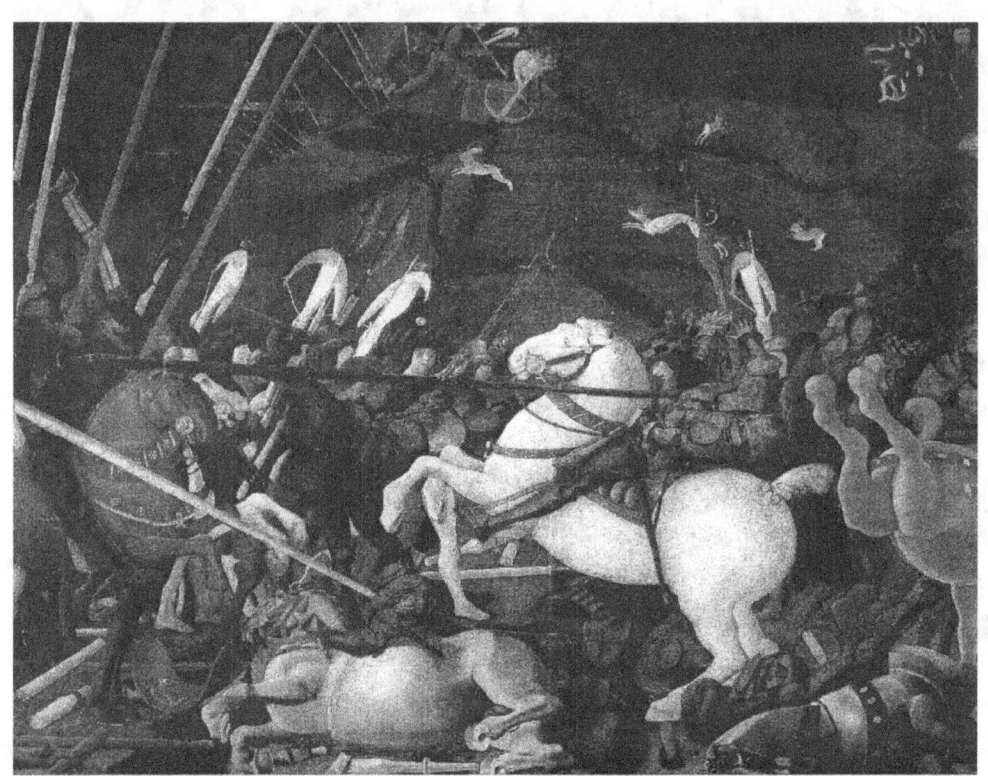

In 1523 Parmesan (1503-1540) presented his self-portrait in a convex mirror. The convex mirror intrigued classical painters because they found it a good example of treating an image not in Rectilinear Perspective. Nevertheless this exercise remained a curiosity, since it brought nothing to the debate of knowing if it were better to use straight lines or curves for spreading out figures in ambient space.

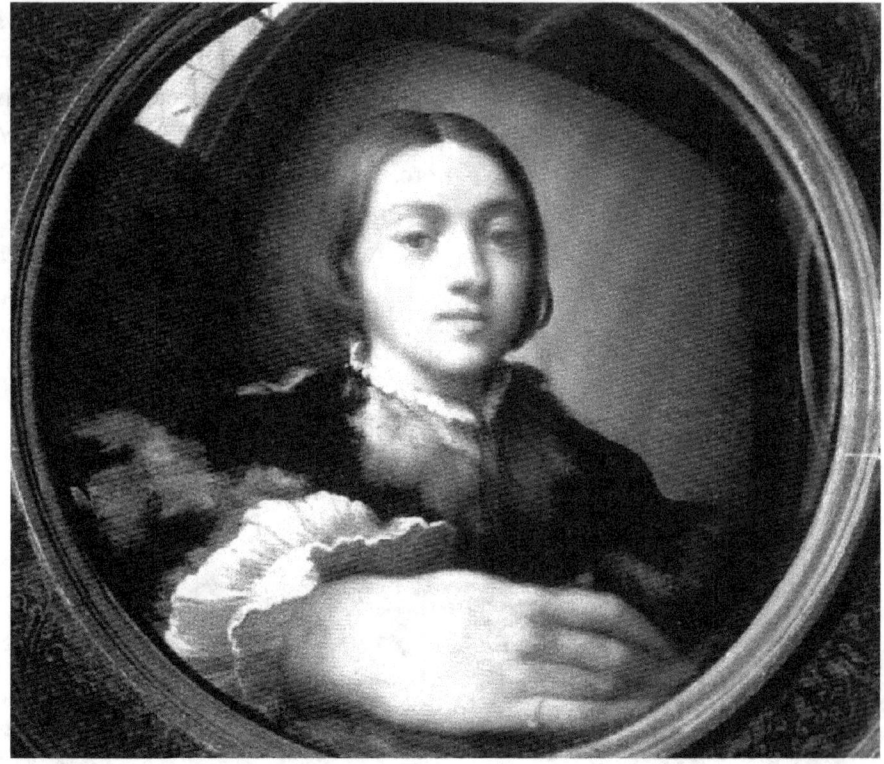

The image is in fact subject to the laws of a spherical space brought by the convex mirror, being spherical itself. If this marvelous painting brought an imaginary and vigorous world to life, it did not reproduce a certain reality sought at the time by established society. However, the presence of curves remains obvious for all painters who test the greatest difficulties in treating foreshortenings. We have for testimony, which are despite the work executed in the field widths of narrow windows, the two disproportionate hands of the pilgrim of Emmaus by Caravaggio (1573-1610), or better yet the ridiculously small feet of the dead Christ by Mantegna.

It seems that no artist or scientist of this period succeeded in identifying the nature of these curves. The astronomer Wilhem Schickard does not define either the nature of these curves that arc progressively, about which he spoke in 1624 in his treaty of optics.

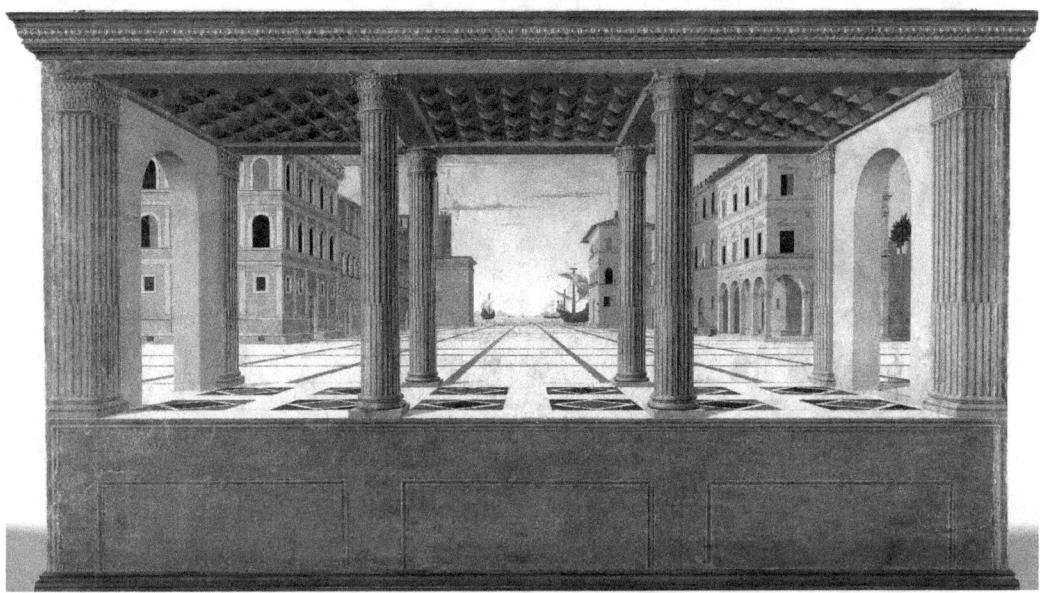

The architect Francesco di Giorgio Martini, 1439-1479, caused a sensation with the painting *View of Architecture* considered by his peers to represent technical progress in the mastery of depth.

It is understood that such an order pleased the despot Louis XIV who did not hesitate to bestow a monopoly of artistic teachings upon the Royal Academy in 1683, in order to save his friend Charles Le Brun, who was under fire from the satirical tract of the canon Abraham Bosse. The canon fought the royal painter's particular aesthetic views. The erroneous, cold and monotonous world of Academicism triumphed and became, for a long time, ensconced in European spirits.

The examples of the instrumentation of art by the powers are not lacking in history. Pharaoh or Inca alike left their stamp on artistic representation. Byzantine, Islamic or Roman, all made their art mere obedient works. Como the elder, in 1434 at the moment of his return to power in Florence, commanded Fra Angelico and Filippo Lippi, some of whose paintings were in central perspective, to mark the advent of a new era. Stalin and Hitler had their artistic schools impregnated with dogmas of power.

The Guidec House. Pietu-Bosredon
Architects. July 2004

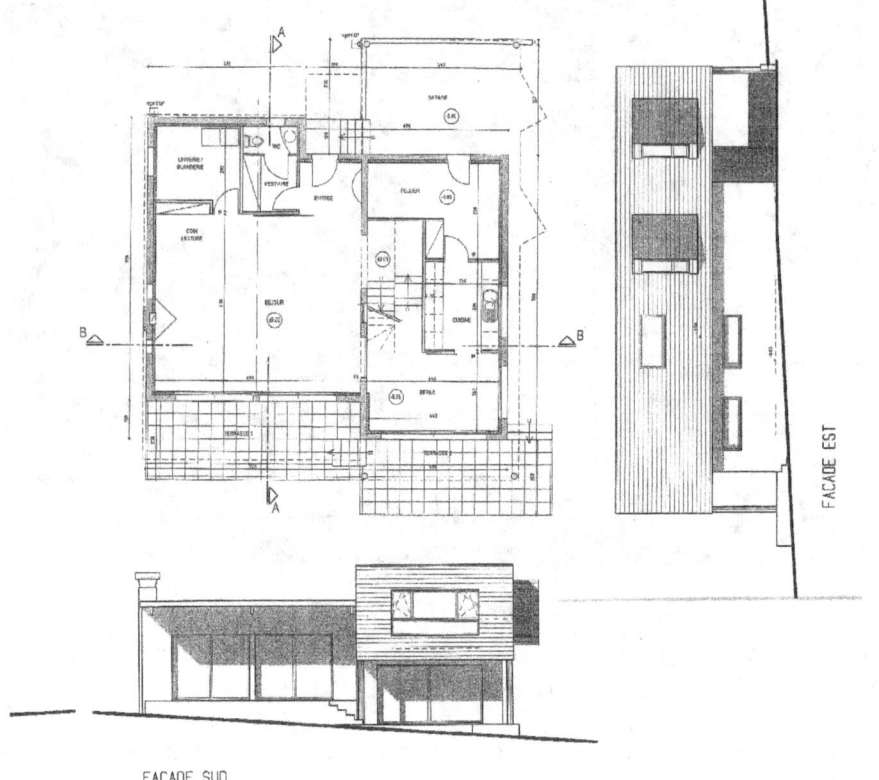

FACADE EST

FACADE SUD

Classic triumphalism had therefore some important limits for painters. But it met neither the growing needs of architects, nevertheless authors of the classical system, nor those of engineers who constituted a rapidly developing profession since the Age of Enlightenment.

Different techniques developed, and the academic monopoly of "seeing well" exploded. The technique of presenting a plane and its elevations is still used today.

Jean Hélion. *Fire at bottom*

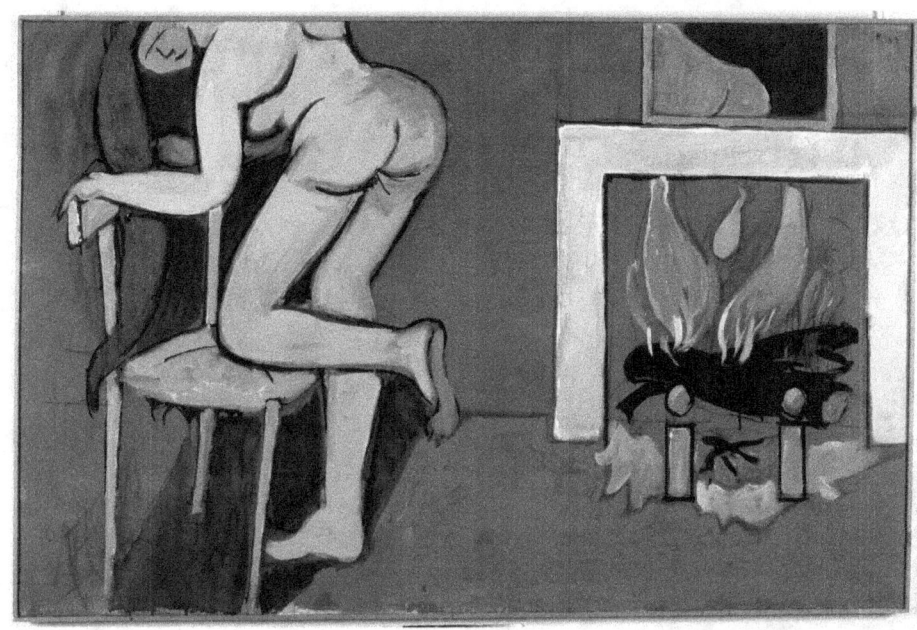

Paul Roche-Ponthus, *"6.4.62"*.

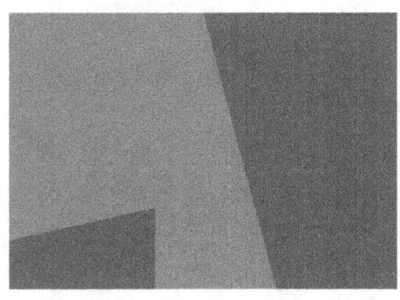

Artists became free to express themselves in their sometimes Dionysus phantasmagorias in the Nietzsche sense. Or in their Apollonian research of perfect aesthetic balance.

Painters were disinterested in academic rules and progressively created, from Turner to Picasso, new regards freed from classical traditions. Their success is certainly due to the force of the impressions that their paintings brought, at times disconcerting yet creative, to carry along the viewer in a wave of imagination. Paradoxically cubism and distortions were able to carry the force of emotion.

Perspective seemed forgotten. This technique had nevertheless carried the hopes of those who, rightfully, saw in the mastery of depth a life-like approach. Nevertheless, Curvilinear Perspective never ceased to intrigue the grand masters for whom it remained an object of research, the mastery of drawing becoming again an object of investigation today.

1.3 The representation of natural perception at a standstill

Successive attempts at sense and reason

INTRODUCTION

We noted that the Greeks curved the base of their temples to give a visual aspect perfectly quadrangular. One can see it everywhere, in particular at the Parthenon and at Egine. One observes it well from all angles when viewing the temple. That means that to give the illusion of a perfect rectangle, with rectilinear edges, the Greeks observed that a building had to undergo a curvilinear transformation to correct our mode of natural perception.

Moreover, the Greeks very probably understood the true nature of physiological perception. Indeed they used curves to trace the bases of their temples. According to this same understanding, most likely, they made their column converge. These curves became the subject of lectures around 1920 by Georges Gromort, professor of architecture at the School of Fine Arts in Paris.

What's more, we know that Ptolemy published in the *Almagest* around the year 150, a table of arcs and circles that is none other than our current table of trigonometry. This table was used for the column of Trajan in Rome; accordingly the helical frieze is dilated to give from the ground the impression that all the personages on the frizes are the same dimension.

The *Almagest* was a work, comparable to that of the encyclopedia of

Diderot, destined to assemble the sum of knowledge of the time. We know that the arcs and circles were used for centuries by navigators and caravans. We will see also that the trigonometric transformation is peculiar to our own physiological visual perception

Such as it is, the Greeks implemented a technique according to an objective, contrary to theoreticians of Italian Renaissance who went a different way, resulting in a dead end, that of the impossibility of treating large angles resulting in the magnifying-glass effect. As early as the Renaissance certain painters deliberately took the route of Curvilinear Perspective, drawing on their pragmatic observation of space.

Van Eyck presented in 1434, with the Arnolfini spouses, curves that appear in a convex mirror but also, curiously in the same painting, the rising sides of the window and the fall of the curtains. These latter are not vertical but, diverge upwards, lending space to the room in which they hold.

In 1480, Jean Fouquet presented in a large field width of a floor curved downwards.

Vignola wrote in 1583 *"Le due regole della prospettiva pratica,"* in which he presented a cursor machine whose results were transferred onto graph paper. He saw that for a wide angle the lines of the floor rose up and those of the ceiling descending, according to the Optics of Euclid.

The architect Lanci presented an apparatus for transferring, directly onto a cylindrical screen, a point aimed in space; but it was unjustly critiqued by Danti, who found the image deformed. But *"deformation compared to what?"* asked Corrado Maltese at the Milan assembly of 1977. The absence of an objective and of problems, before the construction of tools, is still today at the origin of scholarly debates.

Later, if certain classical artists took part in the game of representing space in a glass bubble or a convex mirror, it was but entertainment which did not lead them to scientific research. In fact our visual environment is not spherical, our horizontal field of vision, close to 180 degrees, is very largely superior to our vertical field of vision by about 90 degrees.

Our visual space, *the head fixed*, is therefore cylindrical. On the other hand, *by moving the head*, we shift the center of interest of the observed painting, we see the canopy of heaven and we are in a spherical space.

A drawing assumes a fixed position of the head directed towards a central point of the picture. The eye turns to observe by sampling the space that the brain reconstructs. The spaced observed is cylindrical because our two eyes allow us to see much more in width than in height.

It was necessary to wait until 1947 for an atypical artist, **Maurits Cornelis Escher**, and his mathematician interpreter **Bruno Ernst**, to attempt to explain Curvilinear Perspective in a cylindrical space. It remains to be known how to project a straight line on an artist's piece of paper.

Bruno Ernst evoked a sinusoid but without demonstrating it. *(The Magic Mirror of M.C. Escher* by Bruno Ernst – Taschen Creations). M.C. Escher became interested, with *High and Low,* in curvilinear receding lines supportive of his representations. He traced sinusoids without knowing it, according to his friend mathematician Bruno Ernst.

In 1963, **Albert Flocon**, published his calculations on spherical perspective. This interesting work produced a handsome technical result. The impression that resulted is that of a dreamlike world: the observer can see objects situated behind him. The technique was chosen before the objective.

Jean Mary constructed her curvilinear *curbiligne* perspective, starting with tomographic cuts of bodies to obtain impressive dreamlike effects.

In 1992 **David Hockey,** from a fixed point on the edge of the Grand Canyon in Colorado, took two hundred photographs and reconstructed a flat panoramic screen. Hockney supports that our visual space of perception is a cylindrical screen. That means that the photos perceived on this fictitious cylinder, and once unwound on the map of a table, are laid out according to a curve that is neither a circle nor an ellipse, but a

Parthenon Athena. Photograph from the author.

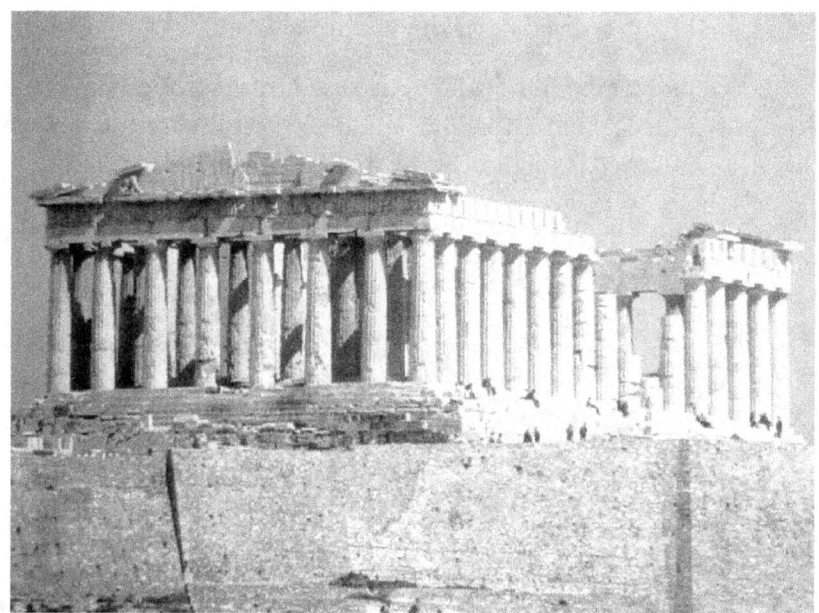

curve that he did not try to identify.

We are therefore today on the threshold of the rediscovery of "Real Perspective," which corresponds to our natural perception and therefore our natural physiology. We shall therefore have all of the elements to explain our Real Perspective and its advantages.

We will see that it corresponds to the proportions of the column of Trajan, to what Leonardo da Vinci saw through a windowpane and the magnifying-glass effect sought by Matisse. We will establish the mathematical structure of this particular natural Curvilinear Perspective.

The Parthenon has a convex base and columns convergent at the zenith. Around 1920 Georges Gromort directed on this subject several campaigns of measurements of temples to bring confirmation. The curvature does not seem obvious when one sees the Acropolis from the surrounding hills, the architecture being precisely conceived to correct the fact that a line would be perceived as a curve. Moreover the temple is observed and photographed from a distance in the picture above.

The effect of deformation of a line perceived as a curve could render its proportions noticeable in a foreshortened view, compared with how we will see it in Volume III, dedicaced to the magnifying-glass effect.

In the same way the steps of the Concord temple of Argigente appear curvilinear although his map is a perfect rectangle.

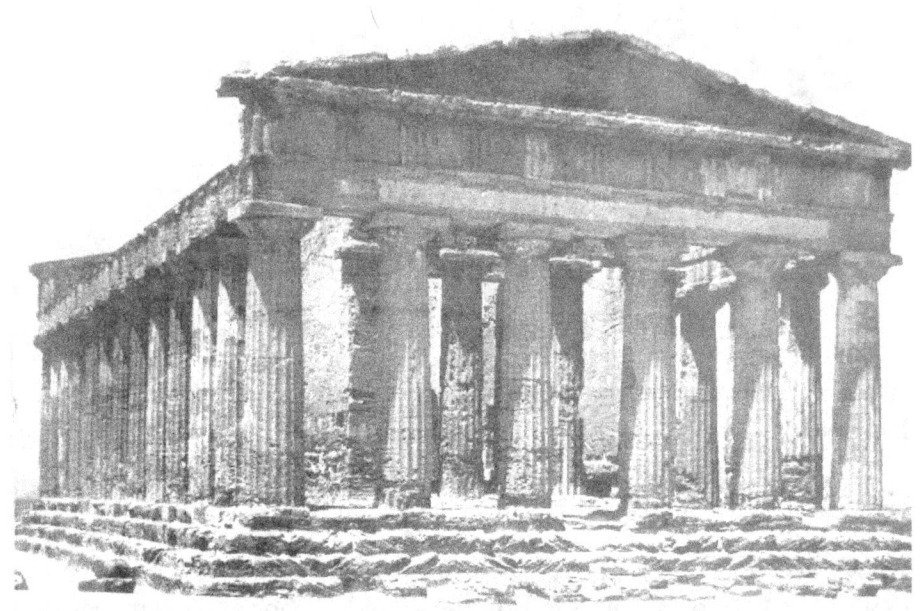

At a corner. Syracuse, Temple of Concord. Treatment of light helps to emphasize the curves. Photograph from the author.

Arnolfini spouses. Jan Van Eyck.
Photo The Nationale Gallery,London.

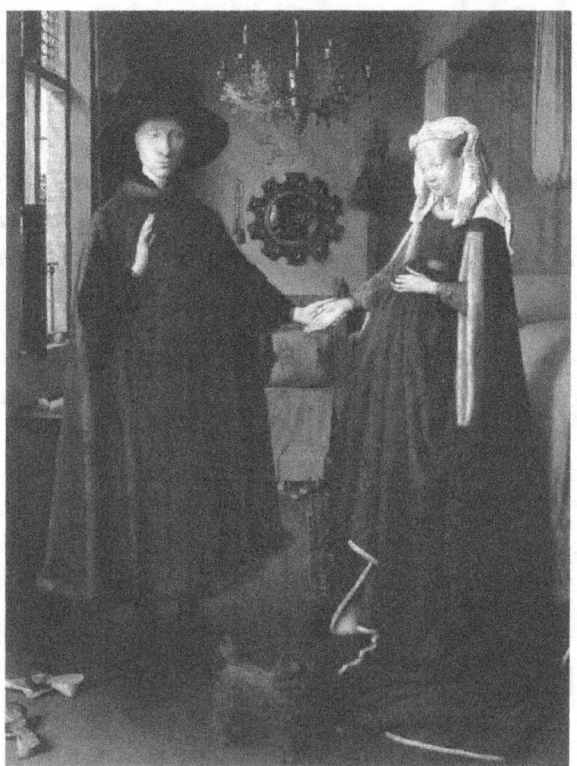

Jan van Eyck (1385-1441) showed us, in comparison with the axis of a candlestick, the slope of the curtain and a window frame diverging upward. This is not normally done, because our culture still remains impregnated with the classic belief that a line must be seen as straight line. Usually, one is drawn ro the convex mirror placed in the axis of the painting. But when tracing the rectilinear receding lines, starting from the center of the mirror, one notes that they do not correspond to the horizontal lines suggested in the room.

Jan van Eyck made us perceive another visual concept of space. Notice that Van Eyck did not confuse the rules of spherical perspective, which appear in the spherical convex mirror in the background, with those that he used to treat the volume of the room of the Arnolfini spouses.

We are convinced by comparing the treatment of the real window with that of the window in the mirror. The art historian Erwin Panowsky did not note these comments, when he approached this painting in *Perspective as a Symbolic Form*, for it is steeped in classic culture. He noted nevertheless *"space is in the room of the bourgeois home is represented in such a way that the plan of the painting does not seem to delimit, but rather select it (remark overall how the orthogonal timbers of the ceiling- you can see in the mirror- are stopped) so that one shows less space that it exist".*

In other words, he noticed that it serves as a close-up, without realizing that it induces a magnifying-glass effect having to be treated in Real Perspective, as we will see it in the third section.

Entry of the emperor Charles IV at the Basilica of Saint-Denis. (1460)

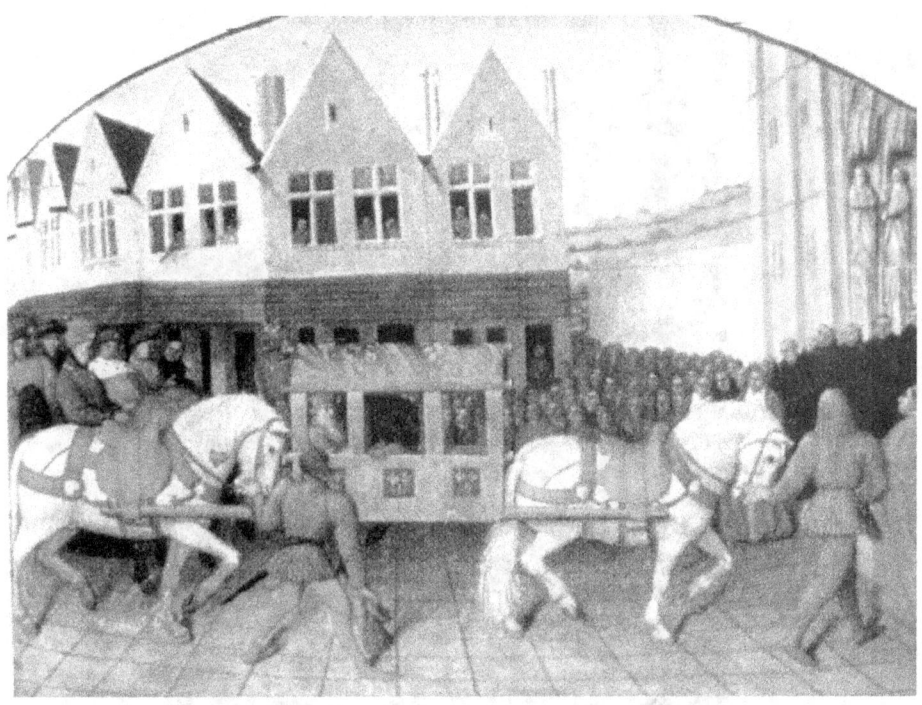

Jean Fouquet (1420, 1481) showed us a grid of curvilinear pavement, comparable to that of the photo of the Orleans cathedral square (shown at the beginning of the first section, *The Taboo*).

In fact, the artist did not represent his perception of space in just any grid: the receding lines on the right and left come to envelop the viewer, the contour lines resemble ellipsoids and not arcs of circles, conicals or quadrics.

Perhaps the verticality of the houses is due to their construction, of which we still have examples in our old cities. However one can note the skill of the painter in treating the ridges on the roofs. The edge of the tower of the cathedral does not seem rectilinear.

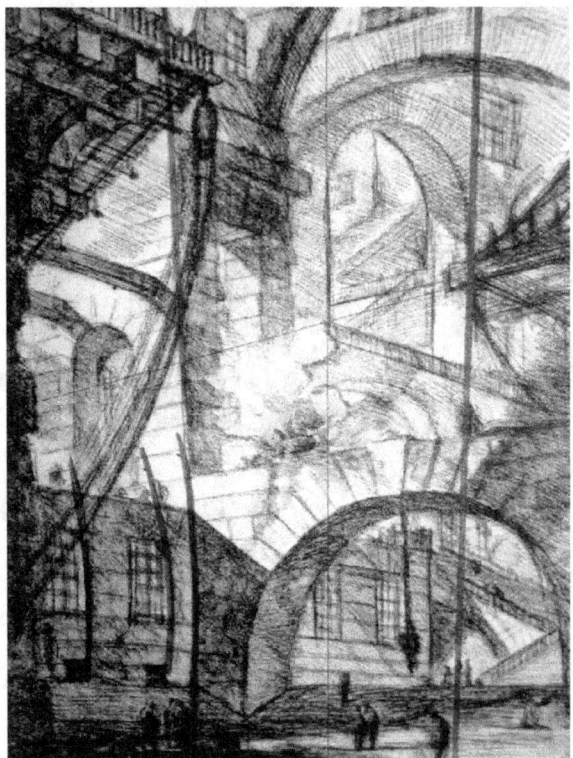

Piranese drew in 1760 his imaginary prisons to distract himself from the elevated architecture of Ancient Rome to which he devoted his life. These drawings are not the plans of an architect, leading to construction. Piranese offers us here a plastic vision of fantastic buildings by the sensation of immense spaces that they bring. He uses several vanishing points. Note that in order to do this Piranese leads to the following results:

- divergent verticals

- curvilinear ridges of walls and windows.

One cannot help but thinking of Piranese, descending, from the "piazza del Municipio" of Perugia, the western lanes bordered by very high thick walls connected by vertiginous arcades. All is curved, the exterior of the houses shaping the interior of the city in space already baroque.

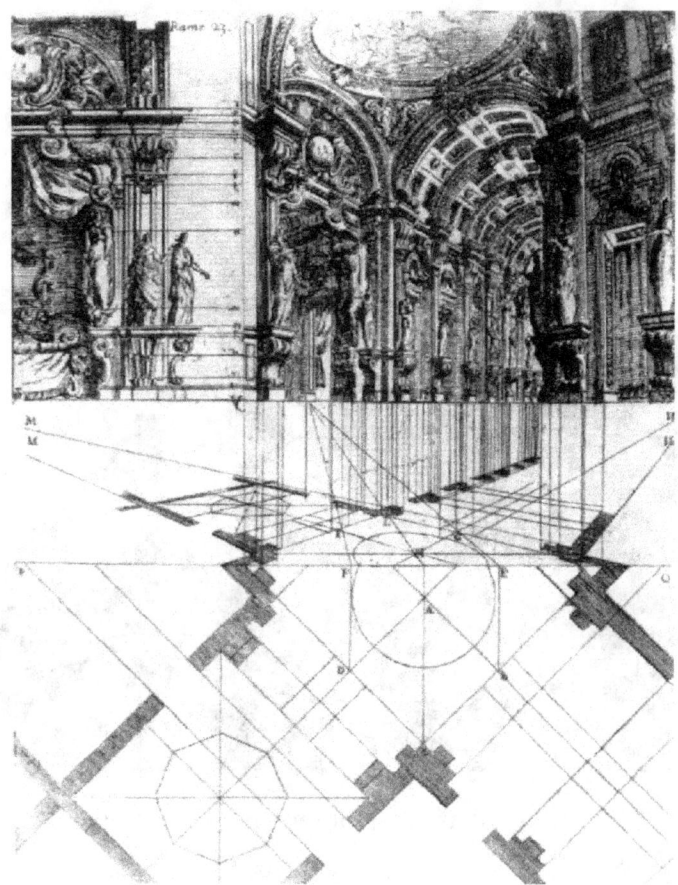

We see an architectural relief by Fernandino Bibiena (1711) drawn following the classical rules of Rectilinear Perspective. It makes it possible to lead a construction by simple and precise calculations.

In counterpoint to the plastic representation of Piranese we have the feeling of a tight space, whereas the technical drawing wants to present to us a palace. However Bibinea makes efforts to explore space in different directions with the help of different vanishing points.

Double vault. Holy Antoine Church. Parma. Ferdinando Bibiena.

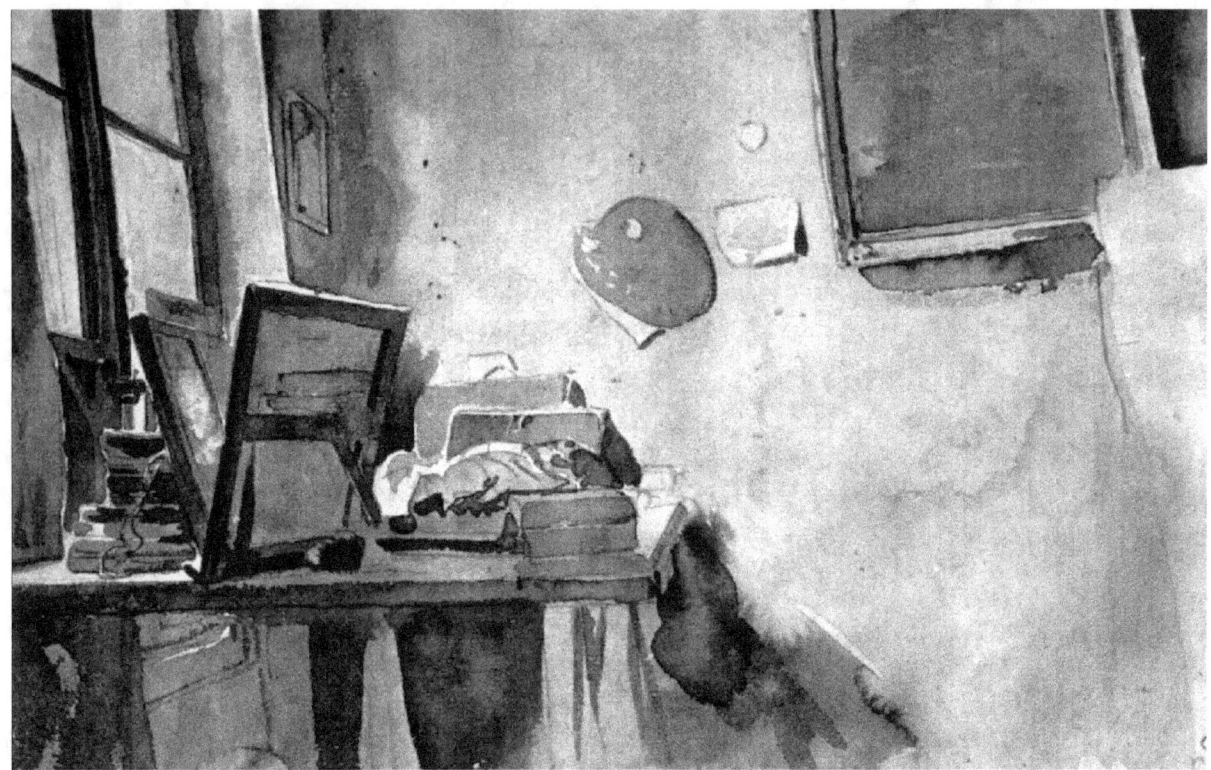

Eugène Delacroix (1798-1863) painted his workshop in Curvilinear Perspective as can be seen by the upright wall framing his window and his cupboard.

The corresponding curves seem to converge towards a vanishing point situated on the right, far under the painting. In this way the table seems to be perceived in a corner of the room by a displacement of attention towards the left, pulled towards this section of the workshop.

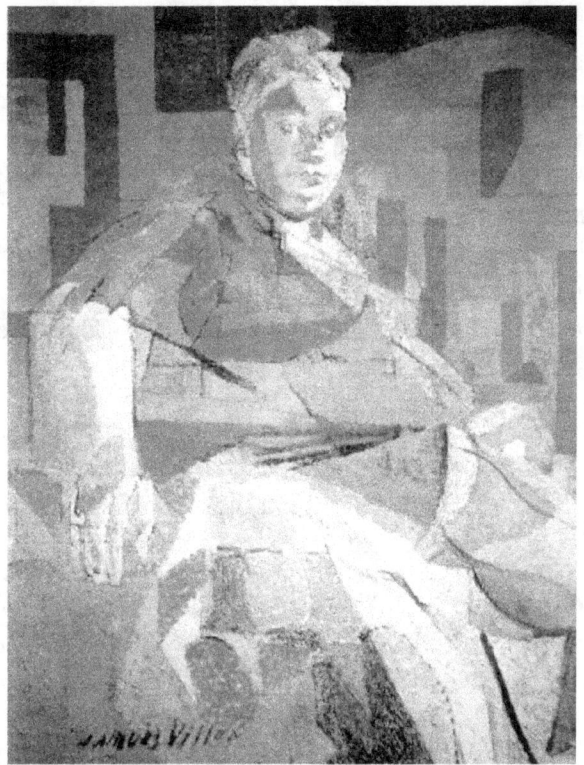

Jacques Villon (1875-1963) made a first draft of Camille Renault. The background of his drawings is quasi flat; the portrait is glued to a flat wall. Redoing the portrait as a painting you see here, he changed the treatment of the background, which gained depth by the placing of perspective, thanks to a vanishing point in the upper right of the painting, and two curvilinear receding lines on the border of the dark area at the top

- one towards the right quickly leaves the picture.

- and the other symmetrically prolonged by the right arm in the portrait to cross the upper left half of the painting.

Around 1930 **Barre** and **Flocon** methodically developed perspective in a spherical universe by proposing a process of construction with lines and large arcs of circles arranged according to a certain number of postulates. In this way the commentary of the authors concerning the schema of the construction of space presented in the top figure is as the following: "network of equidistant parallel lines cut at a right angle, parallel and vertical to the picture, their diagonals (dotted) align on the arcs of a circle receding to the first and third quarter of the horizon. This one is a diameter of the visual field of 180°."

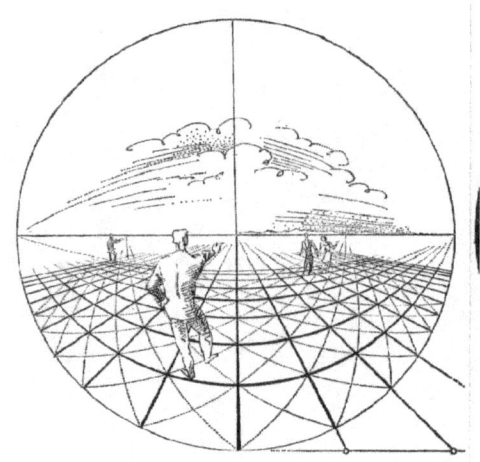

Impressive effects are obtained because in the lower figure one can see on the balcony in the foreground a table on which are placed a bottle and two glasses, knowing that the table is located behind the observer.

The picture below is commented on as follows: "*view from above, aerial view.*" *The horizontal frontals are preserved; the floor is raised by 45°; the vanishing point of the verticals to the floor is situated at the lowest quarter of the principal vertical. The observer sees objects located behind him (table, door, etc.).*

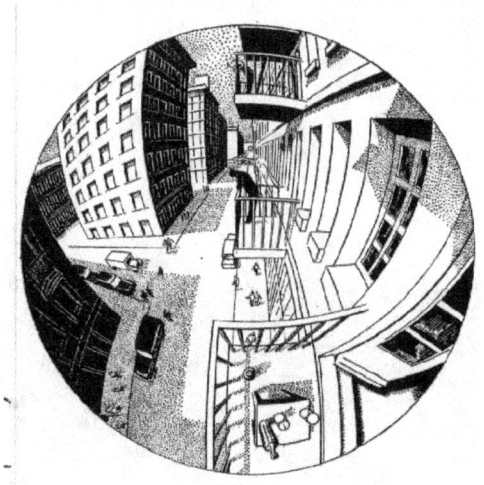

We are thus rather in a dreamlike world than in reality of life. Moreover, we have seen in the introduction that the horizontal lines of the pavement of the square of the Orleans cathedral are not preserved. *My final argument is:* we do not have the impression of living with a telescope before an eye.

The living therefore does not belong to a spherical universe.

Superette. Constructed Space. Jean Mary.

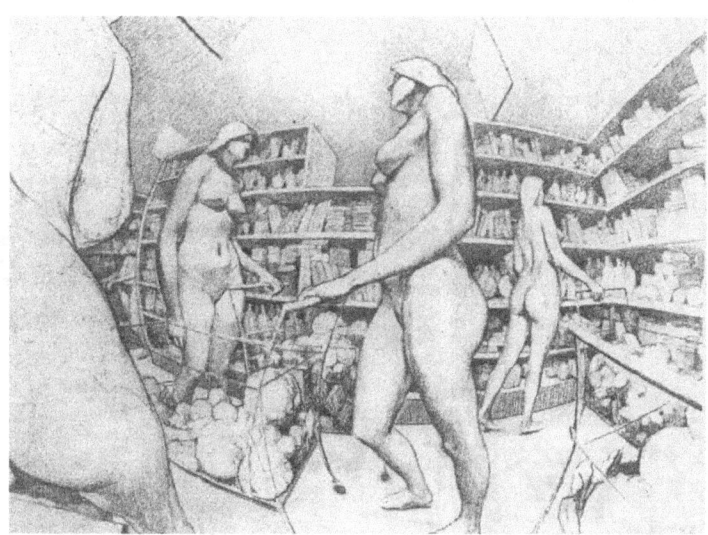

Nevertheless **Jean Mary** accomplishes striking volumes and spaces by executing constructed scenery and nudes at times obtained by studying their cross sections at different levels. We are in a dream world.

Interior Drawing on sight. Jean Mary.

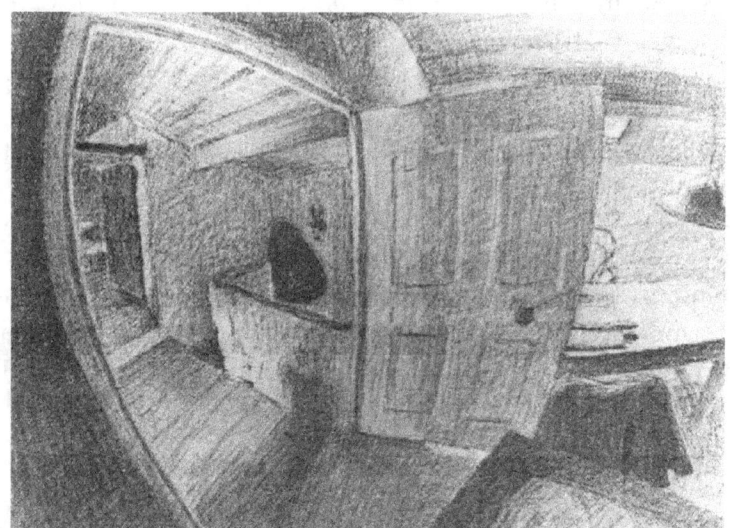

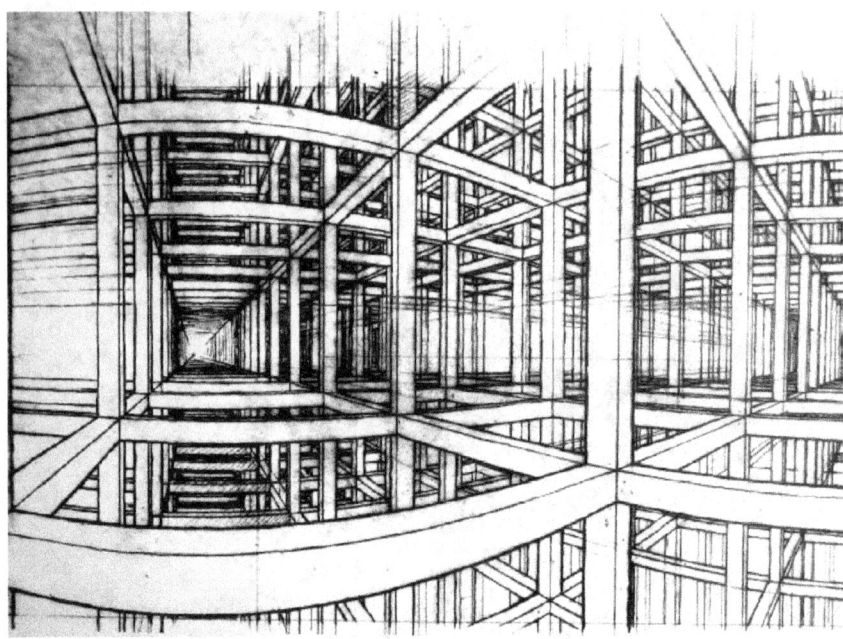

M.C. Escher drew in 1947 *"Cubic spatial equipartition."* Lines are curves. One observes that the receding lines, coming from a vanishing point located in infinity, curve progressively "as a paunch," according to the astronomer from the Renaissance Wilhelm Schickhard previously quoted. Engineers understand well that this curve is called a sinusoid. (1)

The mathematician Bruno Ernst, friend of Escher, proposed this hypothesis. Ernst visited Escher on numerous occasions in order to understand, in particular, his picture *"High and Low,"* on the subject of which Escher explained to him why the edges of a tower could not be straight. However, Bruno Ernst did not publish a demonstration of his intuition.

(1) A sinusoid has a familiar and characteristic aspect. It is neither a circle nor an ellipse. Practically rectilinear for weak values, they curve progressively and finally very rapidly to their maximum values. We have seen this idea of sinus by the way of the column of Trajan (First Section, Chapter 1).

We present a small annex, illustrated for children, on this subject.

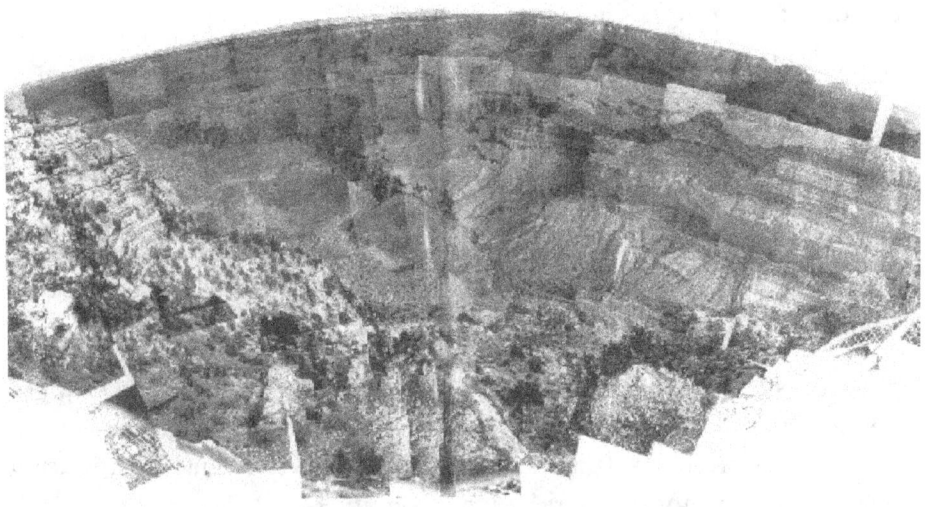

In 1992 **David Hockney** took two hundred photos of the Grand Canyon in Colorado and juxtaposed them. He noted that a horizontal line does not represent the higher edge of the canyon : rather, a curve does, said curve being neither an arc of a circle nor an ellipse. Hockney did not identify the curve but announced in his turn that our field of vision is cylindrical. We are on the right track.

David Hockney claimed that the notion of a single vanishing point was an invention adapted to Europe, of which the dimensions and the landscapes are small and narrow. This technique, according to him, was not adapted to American spaces that demand a particular vanishing point at each glance.

That is true, but intending to reconstruct a panoramic view by restoring the photos on a sheet of paper, one creates the *center of interest* of the picture on a plane.

The juxtaposition of the photos corresponds then to the habitual work of the brain, which reconstructs the space starting with a sampling around our vision's center-point of attention, looking for a position given by the head directed towards the center of interest.

The observer, at any given moment, is conscious of the center of interest, and will take into account the other zones of the picture, which stay on a fixed plane, either by moving the eye, or by a simple displacement of attention without moving the eye.

David Hockney mirrors, in fact, the technique of Leonard daVinci who traced his landscapes through a transparent plate, the fixed head directed towards a center of interest.

The photos of David Hocney are laid on a plane. When the head changes orientation as compared with the transparent plate, the vanishing point changes its coordinates. It is then spatial structure that changes, inducing the realization of another series of photographs.

Note that the edges of the canyon, on the right and on the left of the panorama, are kilometers more distant, than the center of the panorama. In fact, in the photograph presented by David Hockney the summit of the curve corresponds to a tree, for example, and this tree will go no longer be the summit of the curve once the head changes direction.

David Hockney follows, as Dürer with his optic device, the thread that goes from the nail in the wall to different aimed viewpoints. It is this nail that plays the role of the eye of the observer, the eye of Durer being only the trajectory of the ray to assure its aim. (See the illustration *First Section, Chapter 2.*)

Point of view on contemporary drawing

In France, since 1970, the fine arts schools withdrew the teaching of the mastery of material (drawing, ceramics, sculpture) for that of an explicative discourse of the work. An apprentice artist is not required to present a work, provided that he speak about it in a coherent manner. We are in the world of conceptual art that enriched and marked our era. In this context, drawing exists at best incidentally.

The conceptual wave, already forty years old, ran out of steam like its predecessors.

In Europe the form is conveyed by video, the tracing of projections, performances, the montage, installations, and once again drawing. The human spirit, in particular in the pursuit of abstract ideas, always grabs hold of simple mechanical images, or in its impressions, of real memories. The fairs of contemporary art multiply, testifying to a multiplicity of research.

The 1977 Milan congress of art historians, which united the biggest names, was remarkable by the expressed observations of Luigi Vagnetti, which we can translate and summarize as follows:

> "There exist a few structured and complete studies of art history and of perspective for there must be multidisciplinary knowledge in history, geography, archeology, optics, mathematics, philosophy, psychology, photography, computers, etc. Our era is that of the specialist who pain to communicate and therefore to finalize his research. This situation explains the stagnation of innovations in perspective. Artists do not control the mathematical tool and scientists do not pay sufficient attention to art history. We must pass beyond the state of non-communication of our era."

In the USA, San Francisco has been the place of new movements since the 1970s.

The American styles were born to pass, without having the pretension of discouraging innovation. One lives in a bubbling without complexes.

In Carmel, Allen Hirsch is a "neo-realist" who searches to know the living with his "black brain."

In Stanford, Deborah Butterfield presented a bronze horse, constructed from a gathering of pieces of deadwood found in the forest. One believes to see in three dimensions, a sketch of Delacroix representing the Arabic horse of a fantasia.

At the new De Young Museum of Golden Gate Park, Lewis presented an impressionist painting of a black family guarded by vibrant dogs in a light without shadows.

Claes Oldenburg presents a safety-pin ten meters high.

They, in fact, sought to translate beyond a form, the spirit of a form, the presence of a being, the life.

Artists remember the inspirations of Land Art.

The currents remain multiple.

One is far from the currents in the aspects of doctrines. Perspective is often present, as an integral part of drawing and painting.

REVIEW OF THE FIRST SECTION

1. We have, in the chapter *The Taboo*, shown the reader ordinary photographs, taken with an ordinary camera, which are not explained by Rectilinear Perspective.

One commonly attributes the cause of the observed curves to the camera, due to its lens. This is exactly the opposite of what is happening. The camera lenses are a succession of corrective lenses superimposed in a way that reduces the curvilinear aspect of the lines in space, for the buyer of a photograph does not understand, in our current classic culture, that a straight wall will not be straight in a photograph.

It's sufficient to see a photograph taken by stenope to be convinced. A stenope is a camera without a lens. In other words it acts as a simple box, provided by a small hole in one side, and equipped with photosensitive film on the opposite end. The result is that one sees on the developed photograph, a trigonometric arc representing the upright edge of a wall.

We will see two relevant examples regarding a cathedral in the next chapter. But the most realistic image provided by any camera, operated by any photographer, is still an image conceived by tradition.

For the objective of which is provided by the apparatus is precisely corrected in such a way so that a "normal" image appears. But this, after all is said and done, is nothing other than a constructed image according to Leon Battista Alberti.

> "We think that reality, even what is visible to a naked eye, gives, contrary to popular thought, multiple aspects which are still never placed in form."

André Barre and Albert Flocon, *Curvilinear Perspective, from visual space constructed the image.*

2. In the second chapter, we showed that the question of choice of a perspective has been the center of the evolution of the arts and that the acknowledgement of failure by Alberti had been established as a state system in France by Louis XIV, for lack of anything better. This limited system, in a rigid framework, went bankrupt. *"Put nature in a framework, the framework will burst"*, the French writer Audiberti said.

3. In the third chapter, we showed the recurrent research made by artists to identify another system of perspective that makes it possible to be freed from the restrictions of a narrow window.

Treading water was unavoidable because of a lack of objective research and of a scientific approach suitable for the construction of the structuring of space, only conductive to the transformation of three-dimensional perception onto a sheet of paper having two dimensions.

This accumulation of convergent results, of artists, of philosophers, or mathematicians and recently of physiologists, has indicated to us the way which we will now follow, that of *Real Perspective*, which is only one step in the prolongation of the precedents, but also the step that makes it possible to reach a scientific definition and tool of application. That's how it is in all research, which succeeds through repeated experiment.

Second Section
Real Perspective
Applied to architecture
Believe what you see

INTRODUCTION

We have rapidly retraced the epic efforts of artists as well as scientists, in the research of the mastery of perspective as the first component of depth. The emotion brought by depth allows us in fact to transmit the energy of life that we perceive.

But our current culture is such that we represent what would be a line in space by a straight line on a sheet of paper, whereas nothing is farther from reality. We will establish to the contrary, in the following pages, something strange for our culture, but which corresponds to our natural perception:

> A line in space is perceived as an ellipse, and its projection on the plane on the paper by the draughtsman is a sinusoidal arc.

We have already seen this last term with regard to the Trajan column or of M.C. Escher's drawing in the First Section. A small, illustrated appendix explains simply the origins of the notions of trigonometry and of sinus, which we owe to the navigators of Antiquity. But we do not want to believe what we see. Isaiah already noted in verse 42.20:

> "you have seen many things, but you did not go so far as to keep them."

After twenty-five centuries of mathematics we are, many of us, accustomed to distinguishing at first glance a line of a circle, an ellipse, a sinusoid or other usual forms. We are therefore ready to approach the notion of perspective in a cylindrical universe.

This technique is intuitive, for it corresponds to our mental process of perception. It returns to us space and depth. It can give place to calculations for engineers and to architects who will program their computers. This simple manner of seeing things is the first element of depth, so much so that line alone can do without the element of shade, too often used as a miserable hiding place.

Physiologists know today that our brain calculates volume and depth using different processes:

1. Contrast allows us to calculate the line,

2. Movement and stereoscopy allow us to calculate depth,

3. Volume is calculated taking into account these elements and "geon" which would be the elementary volumes catalogued in our memory.

But drawing, a single line allows the brain to exactly identify a form which will induce the impression of volume. A single line also allows the describing a space with the condition of using the right technique of perspective for a given culture. Now, our current occidental culture feels the limits of the technique of Rectilinear Perspective, that we have adopted since the Renaissance, and is in search of a new way.

What is Real Perspective?

Why is it inevitable?

What does this new technique bring?

We start from the contributions of M.C.Escher and Hockney who opened the vision of a cylindrical space. The Trajan column showed yet that the contour lines of this perspective are trigonometric. This work shows that the curvilinear receding lines of a perspective are sinusoidal arcs and endeavor to exploit the practical consequences: volume, space, depth, magnifying-glass effect, and large angle. It is the culmination of a long walk, described in the preceding volume "Rectilinear and Curvilinear Perspective, History of a Taboo," that had to be finalized.

This new technique of perspective is exploitable by means of the computer. This technique is especially useable without manual calculations by a simply being aware of the curvature of space. These magnifying-glass effects are very important, since we wish to embrace a visual field higher than 30 degrees, which occurs with broad landscapes or when close to a living model.

An artist will see naturally, without calculations, how, depending upon his position in space and the vanishing point he chooses

1. trace his receding lines by giving them a correct concavity,

2 position his constant magnification contour lines

It will be enough for him, in case of doubt, to take one or two directions with his pencil to set up the layout of his space. The result will be a great security in the placing of volumes and a considerable time saved. A simple awakening of new orders of grandeur brings the space that we are able of perceive and the emotion that arose.

Prepare your material

You will need

A plate of transparent plastic (instead a plate of glass that can break and be very dangerous), transparent sheets to put on the transparent plate, to protect your plate, clips, an easel, a black felt tip pen, a piece of wood 15 cm long and a squared section 2 cm on each side, tape such as Scotch tape, a folding chair, and some newspapers.

The transparent plate should have a dimension of approximately 50 x 65cm, that is to say large enough to not lock you in a narrow window of vision.

If you would like to keep your drawings to study them, I recommend a transparent sheet that you attach to your plate of transparent plastic. You can find transparent sheets in art supply stores. These sheets cost some money but have the advantage of being able to be scanned onto paper. You can find scanners in the dimension of 50 x 65cm in copy centers or office-supply stores.

The felt tip pen will allow you to draw on your plate or on your transparent sheet. Choose a felt tip pen able to write on plastic and without bad smell.

The piece of wood will hold your forehead at a fixed distance from the plate. The piece of wood must therefore be flat on its two ends to push in a stable manner on your forehead and on the plate.

The clips can be clothespins to hold the transparent sheet onto the transparent plate.

The tape will allow you to fix by the two upper corners your transparent sheet on the window of a store where you will draw a landscape in town.

A folding chair and an easel will serve you when you are outside.

When outside, or inside a church or a cathedral, you will need to be lying on your back on the ground. The newspapers spread out on the ground will keep you from getting cold and allow you to be more comfortable.

Your main tool is your sense of observation.

Why this material?

Leonardo da Vinci drew on a window to understand real space. We are going to do the same. We saw, in the second chapter, First Section, *The Debate,* the engravings done by Dürer who showed the apparatus that he invented to transfer what he saw onto a sheet of paper. But these apparatuses were inconveniently heavy and they were impossible to carry for drawing exterior scenes.

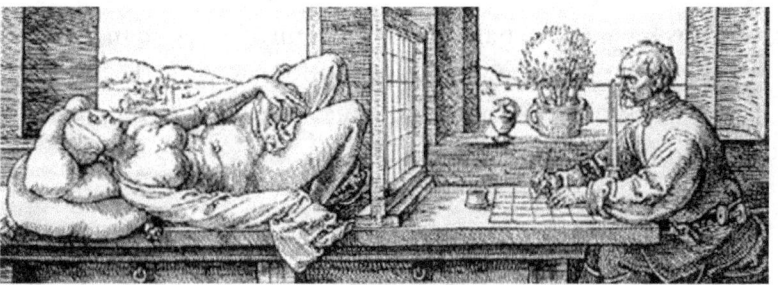

In this engraving we see what the painter sees on a vertical grid. He transfers some remarkable points of the model point by point onto his graphed paper. This paper carries the same pattern of squares as the vertical grid. Note that there is a viewfinder to fix the position of the observer's head. This is in fact indispensable, for a tableau cannot have but a single viewpoint at a time. We will simplify our material with the help of modern materials in the following way:

1. a transparent plate will replace the vertical grid;

2. a sheet of transparent sheet will replace the sheet of graph paper;

3. a simple pen will replace the aimed pinhole that we wedge between

our forehead and our transparent plate, to support our eye at a fixed distance of this one.

Our tool (transparent plate and transparent sheet) is light and easily transportable, in particular outside of the house. This is a bit Heath-Robinson but very interesting when one looks at what is obtained on the transparent sheet . There is no better method to understand space.

Our objective is not to recopy drawings, but to understand our natural perception of space, in a large window. Notice that when constructing a volume it is essential to deal only with its structure. Architects construct a model before passing on to the details; a dressmaker makes a frame to shape the form of a suit. An artist builds his volume before minding the details.

Later, when we will have analyzed the structure of space in our exercises, we will give up our transparent plate and draw directly on a sheet of paper. Let us present beforehand the structure of our perception of space and its representation on paper.

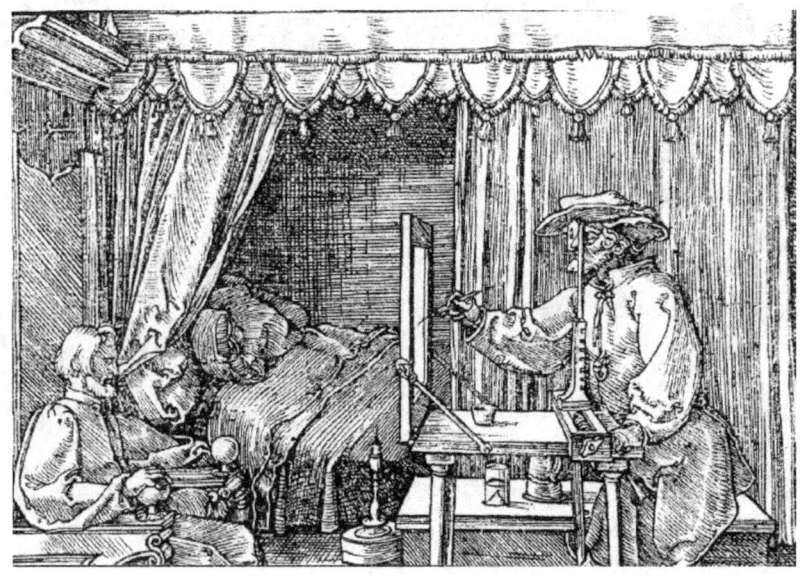

Etching of Dürer.
Example of use of a plate of glass.
The idea was from Leonardo da Vinci.

II.1 Cylindrical Space
The treatment of a line
Exercises 1-2

The important thing is to look at the drawings describing space. In addition, below, a little illustrated appendix for children explains the origin of trigonometric terms that date from the sailors of Antiquity. Mathematical demonstrations are gathered in annex.

INTRODUCTION

Let's revisit the explanation of Bruno Ernst: (1) our visual space is cylindrical, And we must determine three things:

- what exists in space,

- what we perceive,

- what we must draw to find on the sheet an object in space.

We will show that a line in space is perceived as an ellipse, which is projected in a drawing on flat paper as a sinusoid.

Bruno Ernst, in his work explaining the work of Escher, did not give a demonstration on the subject of the nature of this curve. According to Ernst, M.C. Escher did not know that he used sinusoids, but he said what he drew strongly resembled sinusoids. Curvilinear Perspective seems to have interested M.C. Escher only an instant in his life, which was otherwise incessantly turned toward searching for a new effect that allowed access to a surreal world.

(1) See annex: The Eye is Spherical. Our ancestor the fish.

The immediate demonstration of the presence of sinusoids that we give in this work is the following:

- an architect measures height of his building in meters,

- whereas the eye of an artist measures this height in degrees. (1)

The relation between the building in space and the drawing paper is therefore fatally trigonometric, *by definition* a trigonometric circle. (2)

To reassure the scientists we give them a second demonstration detailing the equations allowing to pass from a line in space to a cylindrical visual perception and its unfolding on the paper of the artist.

Now that we know with certainty the nature of these curves governing perspective, we can

- carry out some calculations, some measurements,

- redo some experiments from the Renaissance with a new eye,

- define the field of applications,

- and verify if this contribution is useful in our search of the apprehension of the living on a sheet of paper.

Observe your daily world, without moving your head, across a transparent plate, in particular under a field width greater than 30°: panoramic, magnifying-glass effect, shortcuts, monument, and a volume seen close-up. Trace on the plate what you see by turning your eyes, all the while keeping the head fixed.

The interest of knowing the nature of the receding lines of our universe of cylindrical perception is that of being able to calculate the proper contour lines magnification step suitable to our perception, which will enable us to restore the force of our impressions.

(1) See annex: The Eye is Spherical. Our ancestor the fish.
(2) See annex: What is Trigonometry? A small annex illustrated for my children

Field of Vision

The field vision, clear and colored is two degrees. It corresponds to what we capture with our fovea, rich in cones, which are sensitive to color. As this central angle is opened, the retina becomes less rich in cones but richer in rods, which are insensitive to color but more sensitive to the variations of light and movement.

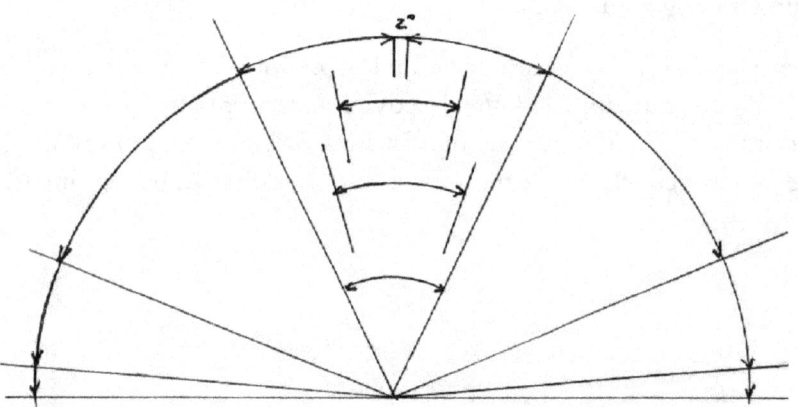

Let's start with a few observations, when we want to see a line.

I. The eye has a field of vision much wider than it is high

Without effort, thanks to our two eyes, we are capable of perceiving our hands when we have our arms spread out in the shape of a cross. In the vertical sense we perceive only a narrow band. Our visual space is therefore cylindrical. Of course, our cylindrical space decreases, on the left and on the right, to become a point on the horizon line.

2. We see two parallel lines as curves

Let's follow the reasoning of Bruno Ernst. Take the case of an observer lying in the grass looking at two power lines passing above him. The two posts are planted at the axis of his feet and his head.

At infinity on the side of his head the observer sees the two parallel wires meet, and it's the same on the side of his feet. Above his head the observer sees the two wires at an appreciable distance necessary to assure the security of transporting the electricity. For the observer will not see the wire forming an angle above him, he will see a curve.

This example shows us that our natural perception is not rectilinear but is found to be curvilinear. We discover a new problem: because by abandoning the well-known form of a straight line, we enter the immense world of curves where we must find the ones that translate our natural perception.

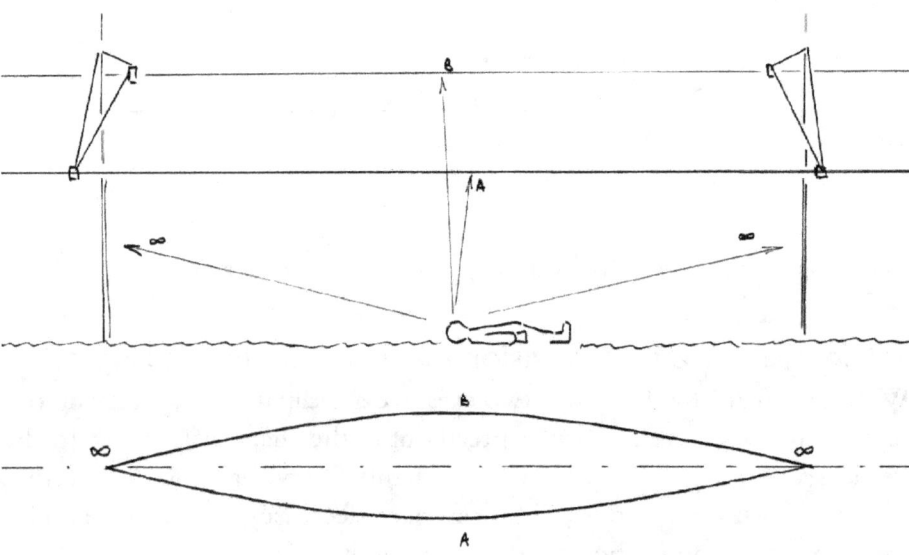

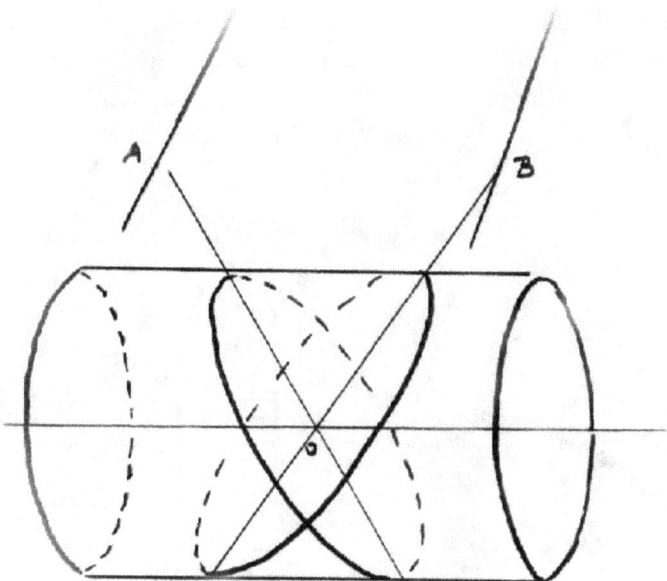

3. But what are these curves?

We know that the observer is in an environment of cylindrical visual perception: he sees indeed more easily from the side of his hands than from the bottom side towards his feet or from the the top side towards his forehead. The axis of the cylinder goes then from his right hand to his left hand.

Two electrical wires pass above the cylindrical screen of perception by going from the head towards the feet. Whereas the observer *perceives* these curves as meeting, the electrical wires *in space* are nonetheless the same straight lines. We are going to therefore discover the nature of the perceived curves.

In fact take the plane that passes by the eye of the observer and an electrical wire; it cuts the cylinder following an ellipse. (When you cut a sausage on the bias with a knife you in fact obtain an ellipse. When you cut the sausage vertically you obtain a circle that is the very particular case of an ellipse.) The curve perceived in space by the observer is an ellipse. There is an intersected curve for each electrical wire. In other words, *a line in physical space* is *perceived* by the observer as an ellipse *in visual space*.

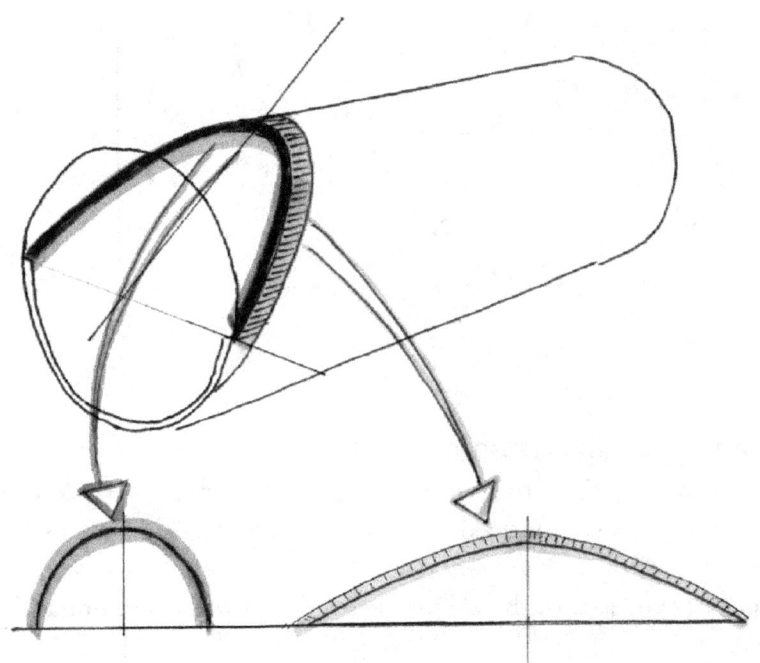

Now it is time to do a practical exercise

In fact Bruno Ernst seemed to stumble onto the following point: now that I know that a line in physical space is perceived as an ellipse in visual space, how am I going to properly translate my perception onto a piece of paper?

So take a cardboard cylinder (drawn above in the top picture) and paint green a section that I obtained before with a knife. *I apply* this section on a sheet of paper and I get the outline of a green ellipse. I have simply the confirmation that a plane cuts a cylinder according to an elliptical section. (Curve on the bottom left).

But what happens with the line that I get by *rolling out* the cylinder, like a rolling pin, on a sheet of paper to see what I must draw in the future on paper to translate the ellipse that I perceive in my visual space ?

I paint it then in red, not the cut section but the side of the surface of the cylinder. So I unroll the cylinder on the paper and I get a new curve. (Curve on the bottom right.)

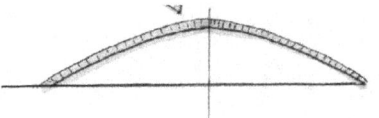

What is this new curve? Bruno Ernst said that it is a sinusoid, "but the demonstration would lead us away much too far." I take now one step farther beyond Bruno Ernst's premises, because there exist two demonstrations.

The first demonstration is very simple and immediate. We have already spoken about this with regard to the Column of Trajan. *When a line exists in space, an architect will measure it in meters, but our eye measures it in degrees, in particular on a piece of paper. The relation between a line and a circle is by definition a trigonometric function (for example a sinusoidal function).* See the small, illustrated appendix for my children *"What is trigonometry? "*

The second demonstration is given in the annex *For mathematicians Cylinder and Plane.* It must be done to convince them in our reasoning. I reassure the artists reading this that you will find a world without calculations drawing in a natural way!

Exercise 1

Whether you are scientist or artist, cut a large section of a vegetarian sausage or a saveloy. You will note that the **section** of the sausage is an ellipse, but the *skin* of the slice of sausage that you will **unroll** on the table is a sinusoidal arc.

Let us see the consequences for the artists

Sinusoids are projections of lines we perceive in space onto a piece of paper. Now these lines come from the horizon, they are thus translated on the sheet of paper by receding lines, which we now know are sinusoids.

In Rectilinear Perspective one uses straight lines as receding lines that converge towards a vanishing point, in cylindrical perspective one uses arcs of sinusoids as receding lines.

We also call this cylindrical perspective "*Real Perspective*" because it corresponds to our natural physiological perception. The grid in cylindrical space has therefore the aspect of the following figure for receding lines. To use a more poetic image than that of a sausage, let us say instead for

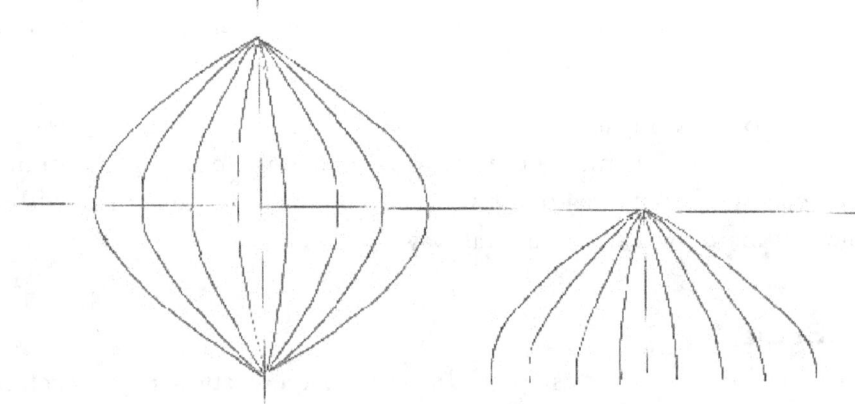

NB. The zenith is the vanishing point in the sky above our head. The nadir is the vanishing point on the ground below our feet, for example when we are on the top of a building.

Rectilinear Perspective a group of receding lines resembling arrows held in the hand of an archer, we would see in cylindrical perspective a shower of fireworks, which we will register in our drawings. Along a receding line, all points in space are equidistant from the axis eye of the observer —vanishing point he has chosen.

In cylindrical perspective a grid will therefore be drawn with these receding curves, as we have seen in the painting by Fouquet of the entry of the Emperor Charles IV at the Basilica Saint-Denis (see the First Section, Chapter 3).

But these receding lines only give us the two receding sides of a square of the grid. It is also necessary for us to know how to position the two sides of a square that are perpendicular in space to the receding lines.

We therefore need to know in Real Perspective:

1. The nature of the curves that cut the receding line perpendicular in space and on our drawing. We call those lines the *"contour lines of constant magnification."* Along a contour line the magnification is constant.

2. The distance between two sides of a square as it moves away, in other words the "contour-line magnification step."

Recall that Alberti constructed a method of progressively contracting squares as they move away in the distance. (See the beginning of the book *What is perspective? Technique of Rectilinear Perspective.*) In Rectilinear Perspective the contour lines are parallel lines for the observer and perpendicular to the receding lines in physical space.

In classical perspective, the contour-line magnification step acceleration stays the same at each step. In Real Perspective, the contour-line magnification step acceleration is progressive and accelerated. We will see some examples of calculation further, but in practice the artist will have only to check only one or two points with is pencil, as we will see very soon.

What are the curves of the contour lines in Curvilinear Perspective ?

1. In physical space.

They all act as equidistant points with respect to the vanishing point on the horizon. These points are found therefore on a circle in physical space.

2. Seen on our cylindrical screen of visual perception.

Given that a circle can always be inscribed on a sphere, we are therefore going to be interested in the intersection of a sphere with a cylinder.

Let us begin with a practical exercise.

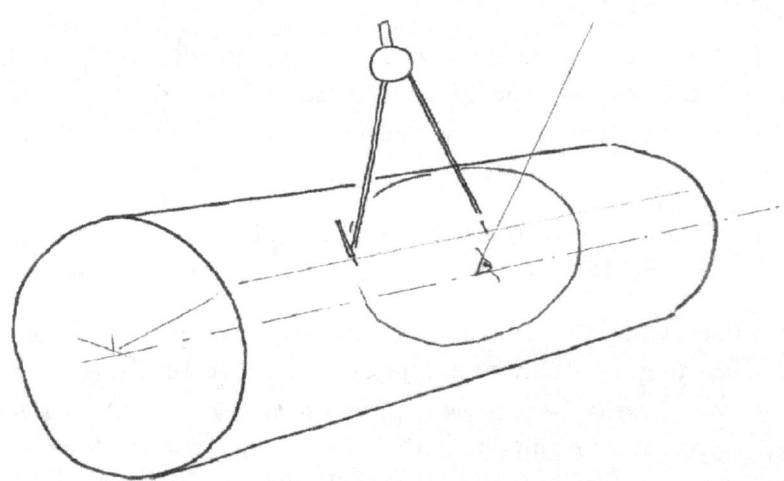

Exercise 2

Trace with a compass a circle on a cardboard cylinder, which symbolizes our screen of cylindrical visual perception. The top of the compass is placed on the vanishing point perceived on this cylinder.

Next, hold the cylinder with two hands and your arms stretched out. You will observe that the circle traced appears to be an ellipsoid, also called quasi-ellipse. You could also paint the tracing of the compass and unroll it on paper, as you would do with a rolling pin. You will see again an ellipsoid.

In other words, *in perceived space,* the contour lines are quasi-ellipses traced on our cylindrical screen of perception, perpendicular to the sinusoidal receding lines.

It remains to be known what takes place on our sheet of paper. In other words, what resembles the quasi-ellipse painted red when we unroll the cylinder on a piece of paper? We obtain another red quasi-ellipse on the sheet of paper, that will not be an ellipse but will look slightly flattened.

To reassure the mathematicians, is given in the annex "For mathematicians" Sphere and Cylinder Intersection description. It must be done to convince them.

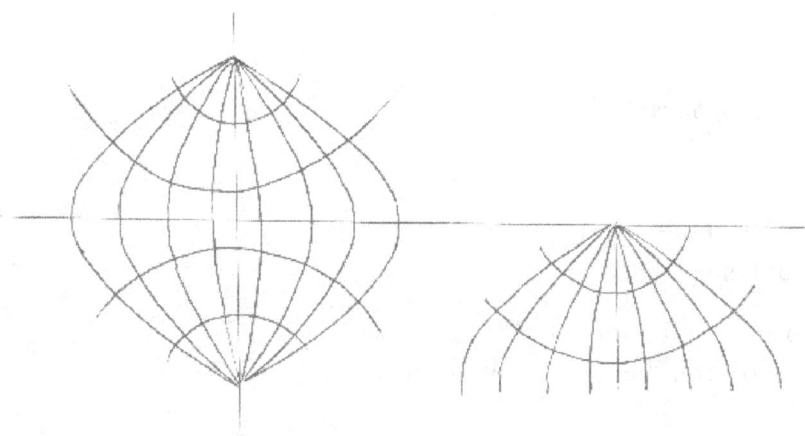

The horizon line is the extrapolation of the receding lines on the right figure, when we observe a horizontal plane, and the extrapolation of the contour lines on the left figure, when we observe a vertical plane.

As in a classic drawing we will see that the artist can use several vanishing points. With each vanishing point corresponds a grid enveloping the axis that goes from the observer to the vanishing point.

The lines of force of the grid will be consistent due to their cross checking at remarkable points on the drawing.

We shall see numerous examples of this in the final chapter dedicated to living models.

By using one or several grids, the artist secures his drawing in record time. Take this first example, which can be drawn up by hand without calculations.

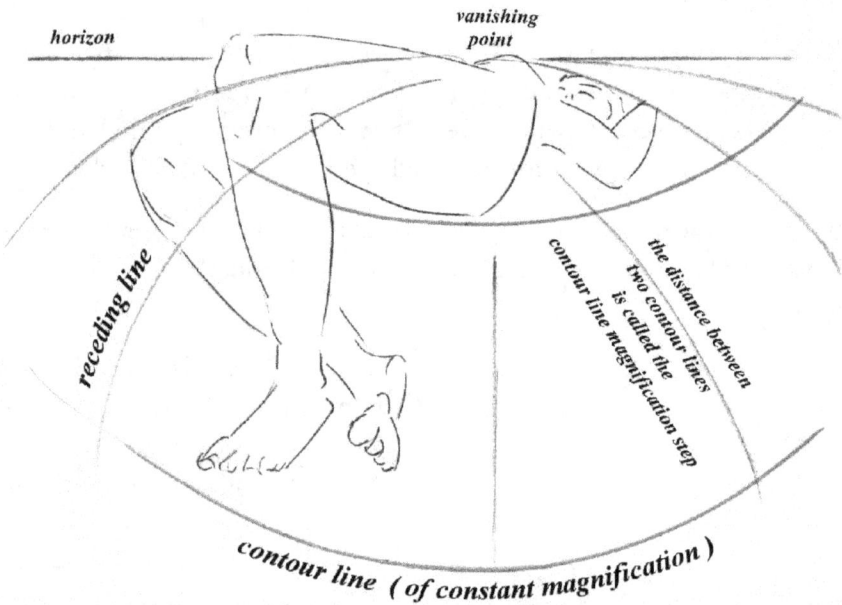

Let's take the example of a model, for the human form is known by everyone, and tolerates no errors without being noticed.

The vanishing point is chosen on the breast of the model, the receding lines are issued and descend towards the bottom, the contour lines form basins.

To position the contour lines it's sufficient to measure with your pencil the distance between the horizon line and the bottom of the buttock and the bottom of the feet. The rest of the construction of the drawing is completed by the curvilinear grid. We will study numerous examples in the third section of this book. There results a security in the setting up of the drawing and an impressive saving of time.

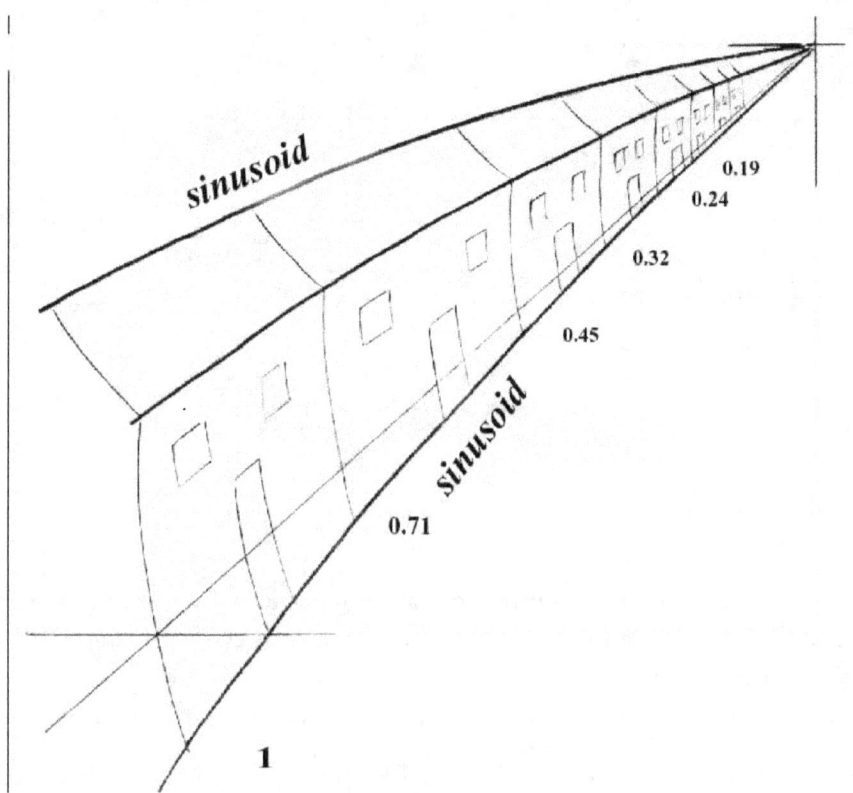

Houses the length of a street. Top view.

Now take the example of an architectural reading in Real Perspective. The observer is in this case situated, for a street of length L, at L/2 at the beginning of the street and an altitude L/2, the eye and the vanishing point are in the axis of the street.

We assume the houses have equal length along the sidewalk. We've obtained the measurements of distance on the paper between the houses with the help of the following schema.

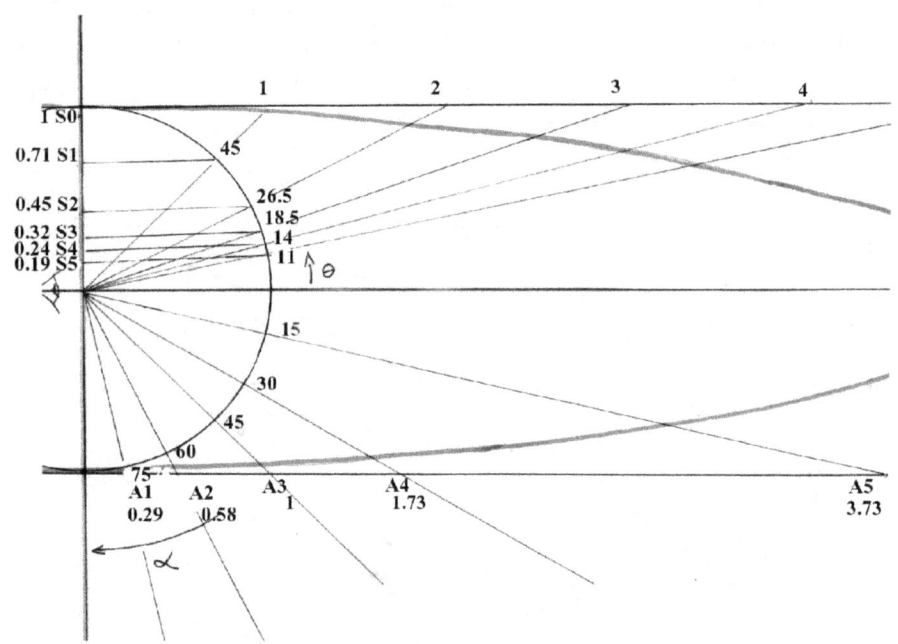

To have an idea of the magnifying-glass effect given by a trigonometric transformation we can draw the eye of the observer in the center of a circle and two parallel horizontal lines tangent to a circle. These two horizontal lines symbolize the edges of the pavement of the street.

We can then take equal modules on the upper parallel symbolizing the houses of constant width. The eye therefore sees these modules under different angles of variable importance.

By projecting the intersection of the lines that form the sides of the angles, with the circle, on the vertical axis of the circle (axis of the sinus) one obtains the proportions to be transferred onto the drawing for cutting the pavement.

On the down part we see how constant angles produce an accelerated increase length on segments from A1 to A5.

This type of exercise must be left to computers, which already calculate spaces fluently either in parallel perspective or in Rectilinear Perspective. These views in perspective are only a comfort for the architect with regard to ground-plans and elevations, which allow him to direct a construction with accuracy.

Now let's pass to the plastic art presentation of buildings, work which will be done by hand or by computers.

II 2
Plastic Art of Architecture

The perspective of living volume.

Exercises 3-11

INTRODUCTION

The perception of a building can be living. Again the right perspective must be used. We have described "Real Perspective" in the preceding chapter.

The use of trigonometric tables not being the favorite activity of an artist, the latter will use his intuitive knowledge of grids in the world of natural cylindrical perception.

As in classic perspective there exists:

- A viewpoint, that of the observer, in the interior or exterior of the volume studied,

- A horizon supporting one or more vanishing points,

- Receding lines,

- Contour lines,

- A center of interest of the picture.

The receding lines and contour lines of constant magnification make it possible to verify the coherence of the drawing.

The marking out of the contour lines depends on a number of parameters, which are spatial coordinates :

- The vantage point of the observer,
- The horizon line,
- The vanishing point,
- The distance of the observer from the center of interest of the picture/painting/drawing/tableau,
- The principle axis of symmetry of the center of interest.

But all this falls into place naturally since the artist has the diagram of the curvilinear grid of *Real Perspective* in mind. The grid is reminiscent of a shower of fireworks.

The receding lines are sinusoidal arcs and the contour lines of constant magnification are quasi-ellipses.

The laying out of the contour lines is done by measuring a very few points with your pencil (were is the middle of the image, the top, the bottom).

In the case of Real Perspective the artist will pay attention to the following facts:

- A sinusoidal receding line progressively curves "like a paunch," as W.Schickhard said, in other words by accelerating its curvature.

- The convexity of the receding lines envelopes the axis of the chosen symmetry.

- The contour-lines magnification step, that is to say the supplementary magnification obtained by going from one contour line to another, is much more important than in Rectilinear Perspective. It corresponds exactly to the measurements that the artist rigorously took with his pencil to obtain an accurate line, without leaving his "reasonable" brain freedom to recalculate a proportion conforming to his catalog of preconceived ideas.

Appearance of different classic curves

When comparing these curves, one understands that the classic Rectilinear

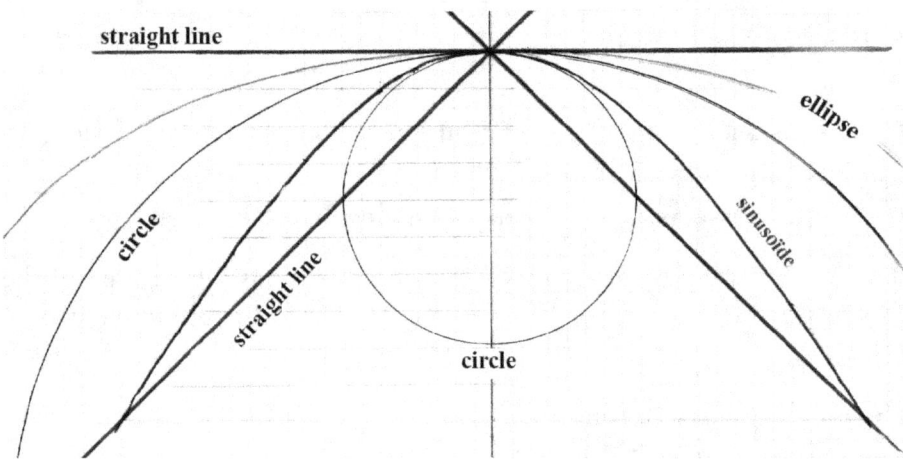

The sinusoid has a characteristic form

Perspective, which uses rectilinear receding lines and contour lines, totally erases the magnifying-glass effect and renders drawings flat and boring.

As opposed, the spherical perspective exaggerates the magnifying-glass effect, making drawings surreal, and embark us into an imaginary world that is no longer that of the living.

The sinusoidal arc is half way between the right line and the circle, it carries at the same time both softness and power to the drawing. Having assimilated these principles, the artist will be satisfied, after placing placed some points on his drawing, to locate

- the horizon line,

- the vanishing points,

- the curvilinear receding lines,

- and the contour lines, which are the equal magnification lines, in order to verify the coherence of his drawing.

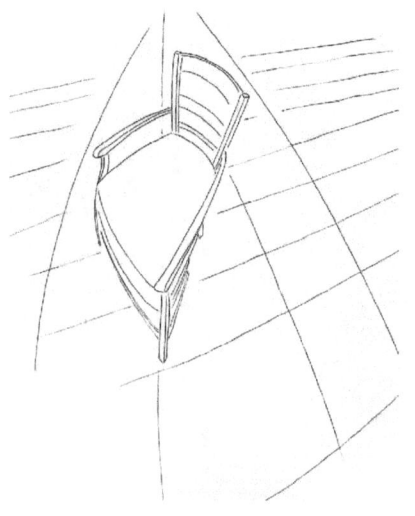

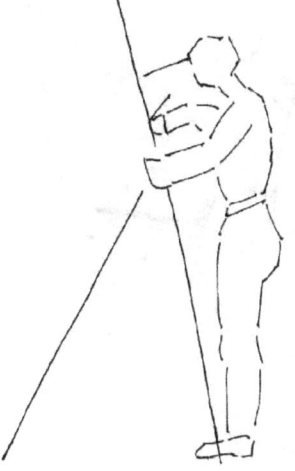

To familiarize the reader with the curvilinear grid, we present in the following pages some drawings traced through a window, as Leonard da Vinci did.

The device of the transparent plate will quickly become obsolete, when the structure of space has been perceived by the reader.

You can look at a book about Matisse and compare the example of a Venetian armchair painted by Matisse in 1942, and the drawing I did here of my armchair from a tracing with a transparent plate. You will see that Matisse understood our natural visual perception. Have a look also on his *Face of a Woman in a Starry Veil, 1942.* and to his *Branch of a Medlar Tree,1944*

Exercise 3

Set up your easel in front of an armchair positioned on large tiling. Set up your transparent plate on the easel. Attach your transparent paper to it. You are in front of your easel and you keep your forehead still by wedging a pen or a piece of wood between your forehead and the plate. You take a pen and you trace what you see. Turn your eyes like a chameleon, without moving the head.

Only trace the essential lines: the tiling and the contour of the chair. Follow the tiles as far as possible. Look the result on your transparency. When you have understand the structure of space, then draw the arm chair normally on a white sheet of paper. If you do not have any tiling at home you will find some at a friend's house.

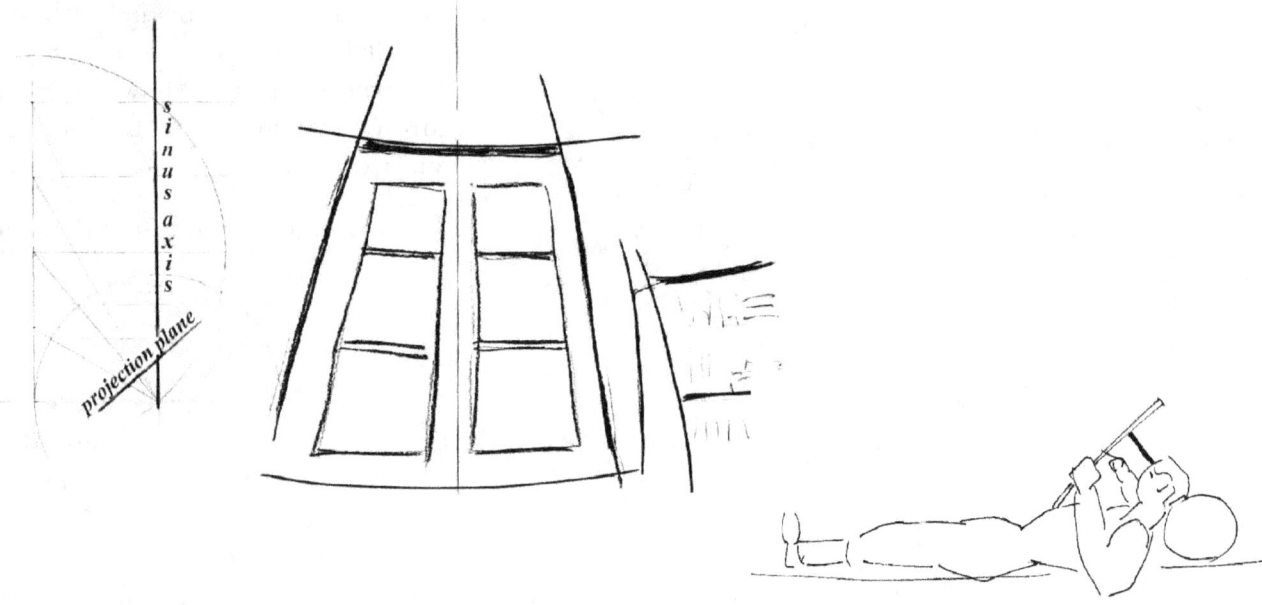

Tracing on a transparent plate a window in a room. Vanishing point on the horizon situated below the bottom of the window

The sides of the window converge towards the top. The concavity of the receding lines is symmetrical in comparison to the axis of the window. One distinguishes a concavity accentuated for the side of the bookcase situated on the right. One therefore guesses the rest of the "shower of fireworks" is falling from the zenith towards the floor. The contour lines are situated above and below the window and on the shelves of the bookcase. They correspond to the horizontals in space that act as reference marks for the artist. In the diagram on the left, the plan of projection indicated represents the inclination of the transparent plate, which has been used to transfer the landscape.

Exercise 4

Draw a window of your room. Take your transparent plate. Lie down on the ground on your back and place the plate on your chest.

Hold the plate with your left hand. Wedge a pen between your forehead and the plate to maintain a fixed distance.

Choose a vanishing point, this will be the top middle of the window, to frame your plate on this section of the window. The vanishing point will in fact be an extension of the pen that goes perpendicularly from your forehead to the plate.

Draw with your right hand what you see, *without moving your head*, only your eyes moving, like those of a chameleon.

When this is finished, measure the height of the squares that you've drawn, and you will see the curvature of the vertical lines of the drawing.

Note that the sides of the window cut at the *vanishing point* and that the horizontal bars of the window are the contour lines.

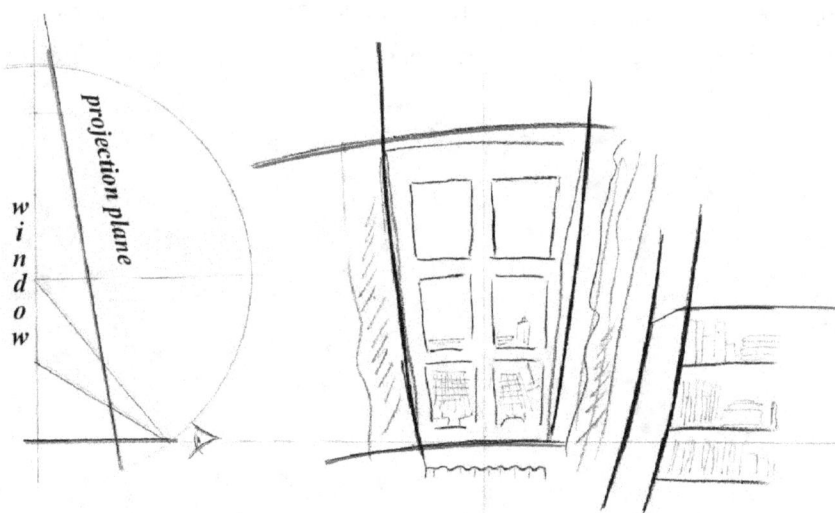

Tracing on a transparent plate a window in a room. Vanishing point on the horizon situated below the bottom of the window

This time it is the bottom of the window that is narrower than the top of the window. This was already true in Rectilinear Perspective.

The difference comes from the fact that Rectilinear Perspective is unable to render the reality of perception that we get having it traced on a transparent plate.

The uprights of the window are curves and the supplementary magnification step between the two contour lines are not constant but accelerated.

Exercise 5

Draw another viewpoint of the window in your room. Begin again, but this time you put yourself in a mezzanine in front of the window and aiming at the middle of the bottom of the window.

Observe that the outermost curves are the most curved and that the squares do not have the same dimensions. The vanishing point this time is at the bottom of the window.

Notice that the difference in height between the first and the second square is not equal with the difference between the height of the second and third square.

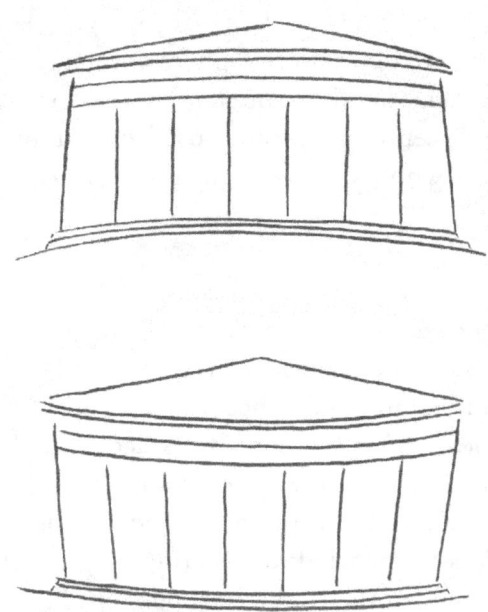

Regarding windows, next

The Greeks understood that they perceived their temples curved and convergent towards the zenith if they were at the bottom of its steps (top figure) and curved in the opposite sense if they overhung a temple from a neighboring mountain (bottom figure). This is why they gave their buildings an inverse concavity like of that of our perception so that these appeared perfectly straight and powerful.

By consequence if we are in an apartment located half way up the building from the other side of the street and that we take a horizon line positioned on the apartment across from us, so

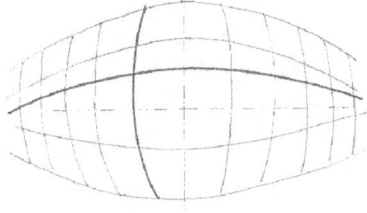

- the upper section will converge towards the zenith (the sky),

- the lower section will converge towards the nadir (the abysses).

We have the habit of seeing such presentations of cameras with wide-angle lenses. But these shock us because in everyday life postcard photographs are corrected by photographers with an apparatus, called a *camera lucida*, whose background can be manipulated. This is an apparatus known since the 17th century and often used by painters, among them was Jan van der Meer who painted *The Milkmaid (1668)*.

Exercise 6

Go to a friend's home that lives in a building on a large street bordered by buildings on both sides, and if possible regular bands of buildings. Ask his permission to glue a transparent sheet of paper on his window (which needs to have window panes big enough to accept a sheet about 50 x 65cm). You stand in front of the window fixing your eyes on the middle of the transparent sheet using a piece of wood wedged between your forehead and the glass of the window. You trace the principle lines of the facades of the other side of the street, starting from the extreme right go to the extreme left and do the same starting from the bottom to the top of the buildings. Your eyes turn like those of a chameleon.

You have traced the receding lines and the contour lines of the building in front of you. You have four vanishing points : on the left and right on the horizon, at the zenith and at the nadir on the vertical.

Photomontage by Jean-Louis Hamp.
Private collection.

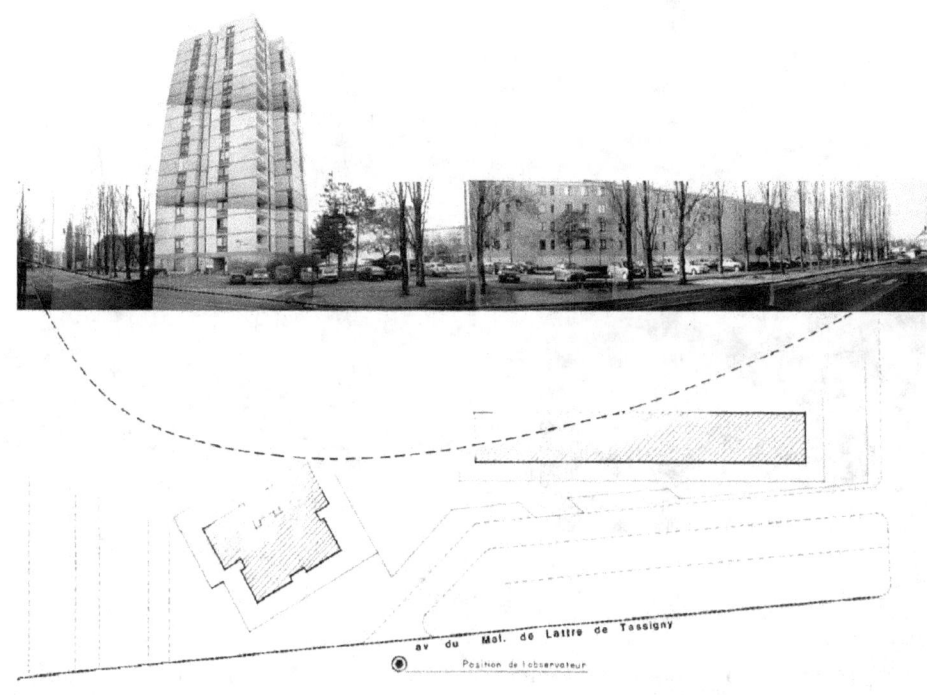

Regarding windows, continued and finished

The edge of a straight avenue, photographed on the opposite side, with a wide angle, or, in the style of Hockney, juxtaposing different points of views, will have the same aspect as the bottom of the preceding building. We have seen, in the explanation of Escher's cylinder, that a receding line that joins two vanishing points has the aspects of a sinusoidal arc, as drawn by M.C. Escher for his *"Cubic spatial equipartition"* that we have seen First Section chapter 3.

Painting by Livio Scotti (1952). The village of Courbevoie reflected in the glass façade of a building. The painter testifies that he treated the façade in Curvilinear We know now the nature of those curves. Perspective.

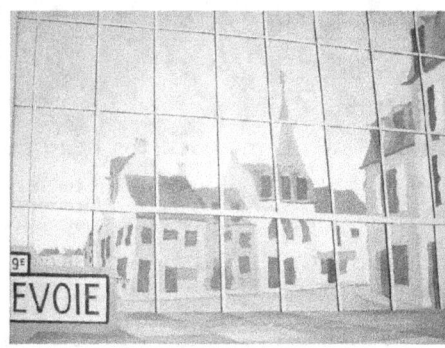

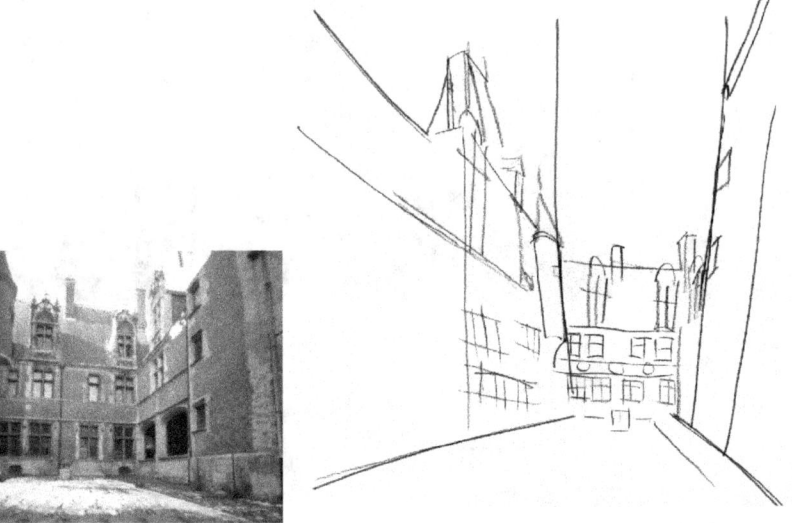

Stenope Erick Mengual.
Tracing by the author on a transparent plate. Cujas Hotel in Bourges, France.

A stenope is a camera where the optic lens is replaced by a hole. Consequently the rays of light that bring the image under different angles are projected on the flat surface of the sensitive film which is in the background of the apparatus. Space is thus projected in a trigonometric manner on the film.

This Renaissance hotel contains a courtyard of modest dimensions. The walls are raised which gives an impression of confinement. Drawing such a courtyard is quite simply impossible in Rectilinear Perspective. On the opposite here in Real Perspective the receding lines diverge, starting from the center of the ground floor of the building, giving a breathing room to this courtyard.

Exercise 7

I was lying on my back, my head raised up, with the transparent plate on my thorax and I aimed at the foot of the ground floor windows, opposite in the middle. The bar of wood wedged between my forehead and the transparent plate going thus in this direction. By extending the base of the left and right walls, which are receding lines, one meets the vanishing points. The vertical lines are the contour lines.

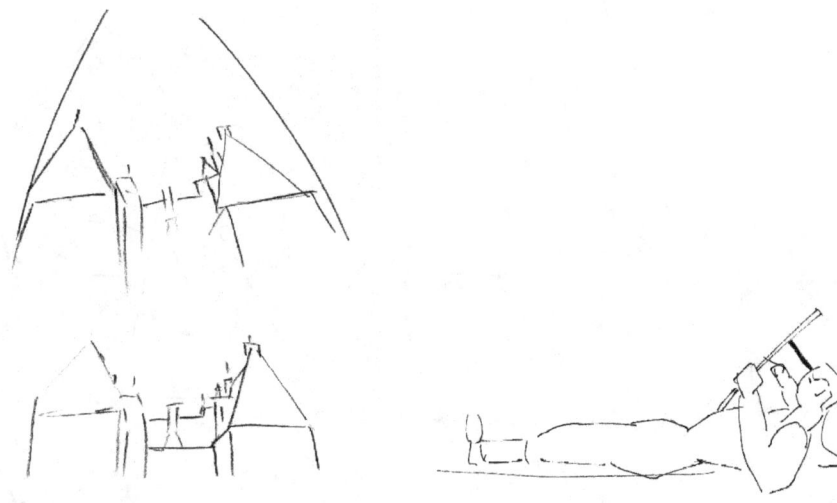

The gables of the palace of Jacques
Coeur in Bourges, France.

Tracing a landscape onto a transparent plate

Find a courtyard of a building and do the same. The gables of the palace
only offer little interest for they were not decorated. It is for this reason
that the view is pulled toward the roof, that is to say towards a vanishing
point near the zenith.

The upper drawing corresponds to a vanishing point more elevated than
in the lower drawing. You can see the curves changing with the position
of the vanishing point you choose.

The magnifying-glass effect is not corrected here by the brain of the person
drawing because it acts as a simple transcription onto a transparent plate.

Find the back of a garden at the foot of a house.

1. Lie down on your back on the ground and get settled in. This is the
    easiest way to vary the vanishing point. Make an initial tracing by
    choosing a low vanishing point, then a second tracing by choosing a
    high vanishing point. Observe the difference.

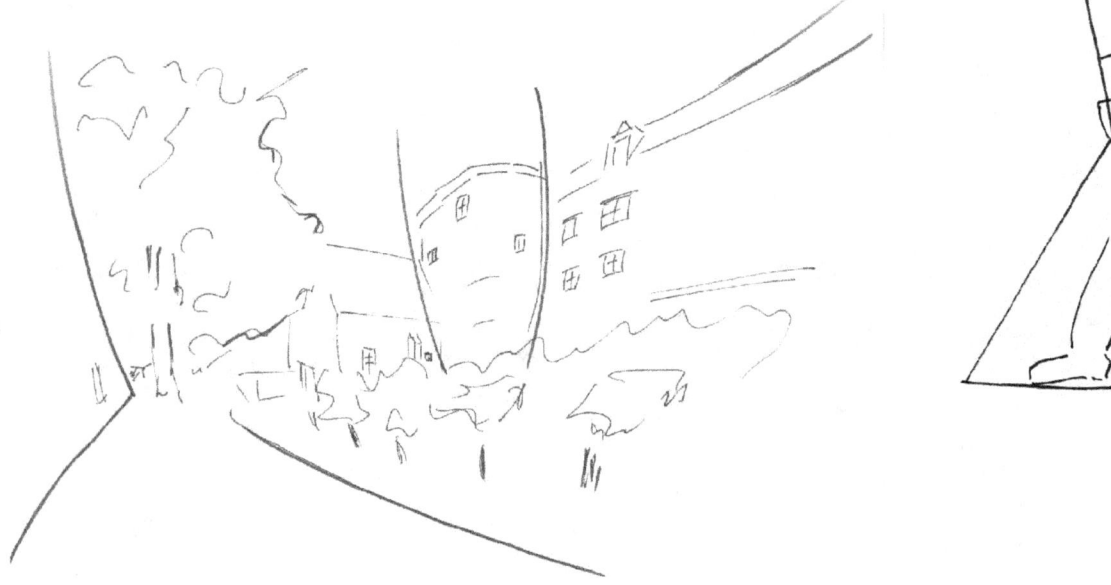

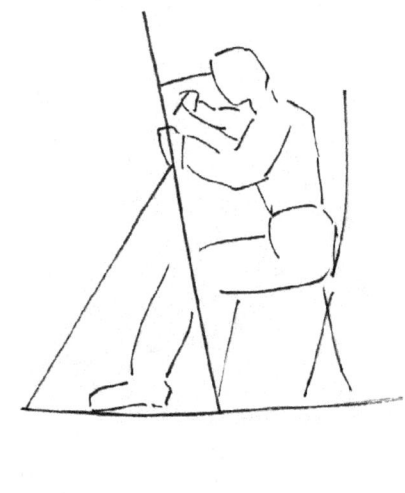

Footpath along the ramparts in Bourges

2   Trace in the both cases, on your two transfers, the receding lines and the contour lines.

3   Now you have well marked out a vanishing point at its receding lines, redraw the house, without the transparent plate, directly onto a piece of paper in the same format as that of with the transparent plate. Trace first the receding lines along which you will make run the edges of the house, next trace the contour lines at each floor. With your pencil measure the proportions of height and width of the house. Mark out the middle of the house. You will note that your vanishing point may be located somewhere other than in the middle of the house.

The center of interest of the tableau is the tower. The vanishing point is located at its foot. The observer is in the middle of the alley, at a third of the drawing coming from the left. He is outside the tower. He is also on the exterior of the garden.

This explains that the straight edges of the path have a concavity that envelops the tower. It also results from it that the vertical receding lines diverge upwards with their concavity enveloping the tower.

If the vanishing point had been at the foot of the tree, the concavities of the edge of the alley would have enveloped the observer and all the spatial structure of space would have moved.

Exercise 8

I have taken a chair and my easel to settle myself in this tranquil location. I held a pen with my forehead against the transparent plate. I chose the base of the tower for the vanishing point. My eye turned to embrace the maximum amount of space. When the sides of the easel obstructed me, I

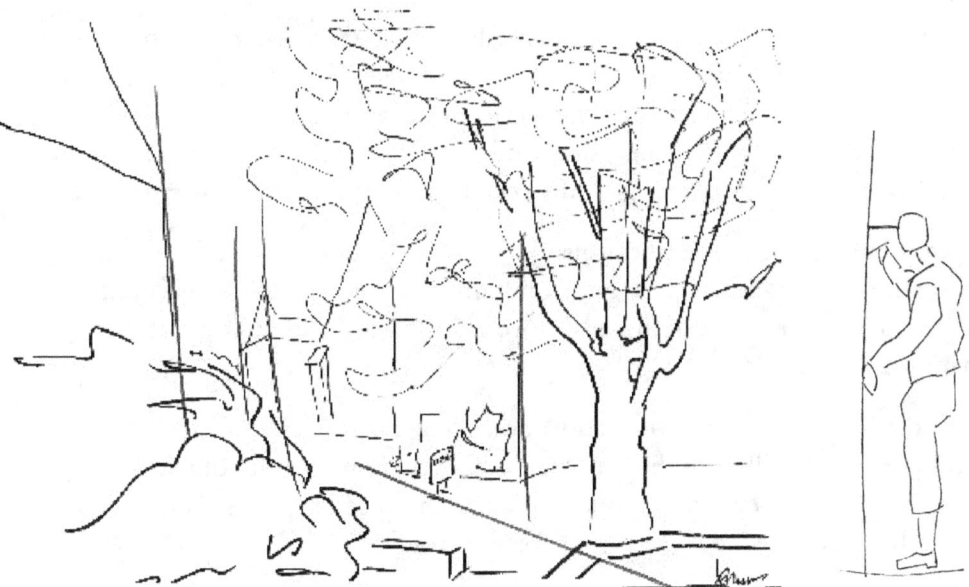

A passage the length of the ramparts in Bourges.

moved the easel without displacing the plate and my forehead.

Find an alley in a park, or a pedestrian walkway without cars so you are able to settle yourself in. This type of location is interesting for it shows us a volume with a great field depth. In this case the volumes delimit space. Choose a vanishing point.

Trace the space, drawing only the principal lines of this space, that is to say the texture of the space. Our intention is not to draw the details.

Draw then the receding and contour lines, and be assured that your drawing is coherent with the shower of fireworks, constructed starting from a vanishing point. The vanishing point is at the foot of the angle of the house opposite the observer, slightly left of the tree. We note that no straight line in space is vertical on the transfer.

On the left three angles of the house are highlighted: their concavity envelops the vanishing point.

Exercise 9

I had located the waiting room of a medical analysis laboratory whose glass wall gave onto a walking path of the city. I glued a transparent sheet onto the window, at man's height and I traced the landscape while holding a pen with my forehead against the window. When the nurse started to worry I had finished my tracing and I could show her that all was well.

It is easy enough today to find walls of glass in commercial locations, in administrations or newly laid out companies. I have always been well received. The operation doesn't last more than a quarter of an hour at the maximum.

1 Find a sympathetic location and trace. Analyze well after your transfer. You will note that you can have vanishing points outside your transfer: they are at the intersection the receding lines which are the vertical edges of a house for example.

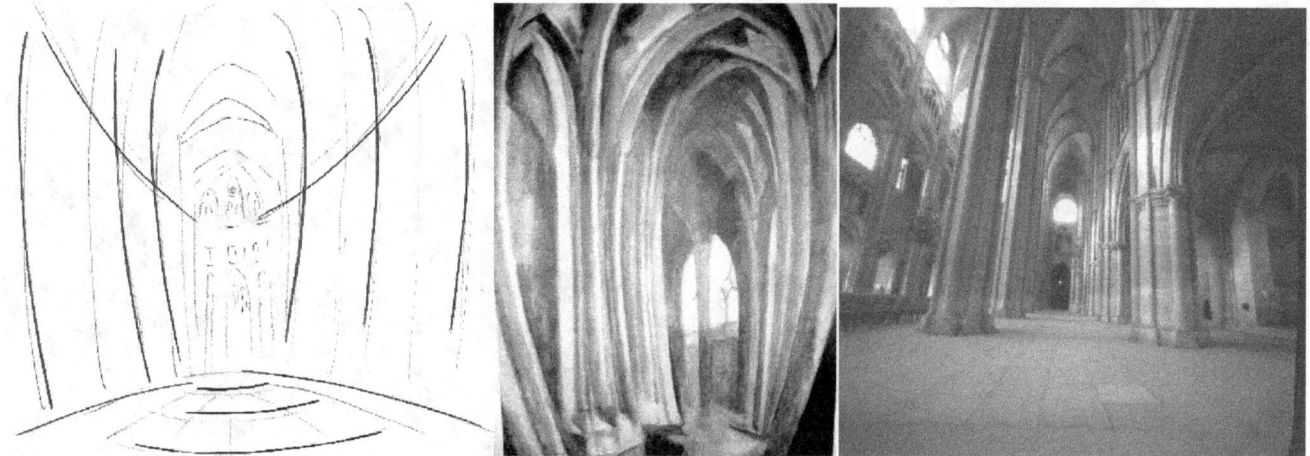

2   Now take a sheet of paper. Do not be afraid to attack a white sheet. Note your receding lines, your contour lines and carry out the drawing of the passageway. In other words, you follow in the opposite direction the procedure of the preceding run, you trace first the firework shower before drawing. This firework shower will help you to set up your drawing.

This cathedral has five naves; the central nave is 38 meters. It serves as the nave of the Bourges cathedral. The view is naturally directed towards the light of the choir and I fixed my gaze on the keystone of the choir. I have noticed that the pillars diverged upwards. I've attributed this phenomenon to the push of the ribbed gothic arches. I went into the lateral naves thinking I would find an incline of the same type, which I imagined, were definitely stopped on the outside by the buttresses. To my great surprise there was nothing and I discovered the same outlines of curves that were in the central nave. I searched for an explanation.

I consulted local architects, took myself some measurements and some photos. A photographer told me how the post cards of the cathedral were made: the photos are passed through the clear chamber to straighten the pillars. I then made this tracing on a transparent plate to have confirmation of Curvilinear Perspective, which appears.

Tracing by the author on a transparent plate (2003).
Stenope Erick Mengual (2003).
St Severin Paris Robert Delaunay (1909).

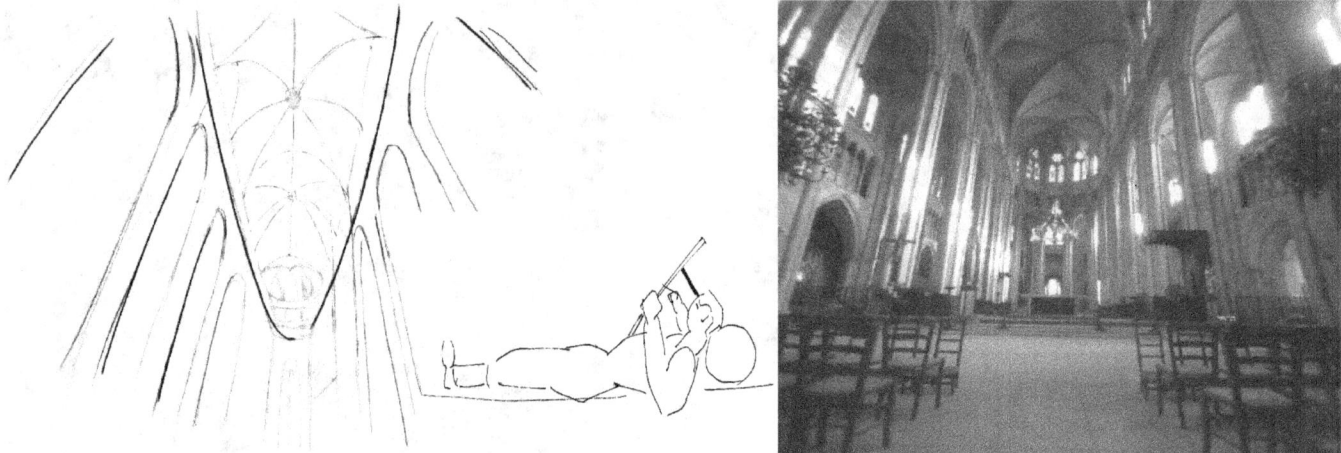

Robert Delaunay, would have observed in 1909 the same phenomenon in the ambulatory of the church Saint Séverin in Paris. Whichever technique used to make his picture, he followed natural perception.

I made a second tracing and changed the vanishing point, which is now found above the pillars in the middle of the choir. You can see all the structure evolving like a shower of fireworks that move from the centre.

Exercise 10

Lie down in a place, on the ground, opposite the choir of a church, or find an equivalent large public building. Newspapers will insulate you from the cold.

1. You have your head elevated as much as possible and you aim as low as possible across from you. You trace.

2. You start again this time by aiming as high as possible, either the high choir in a cathedral, or the top angle of a ceiling opposite if you are in a public building.

3. Compare your receding and your contour lines. It's while forging that one becomes a blacksmith.

Tracing by the author on a transparent plate. *Stenope* Erick Mengual.

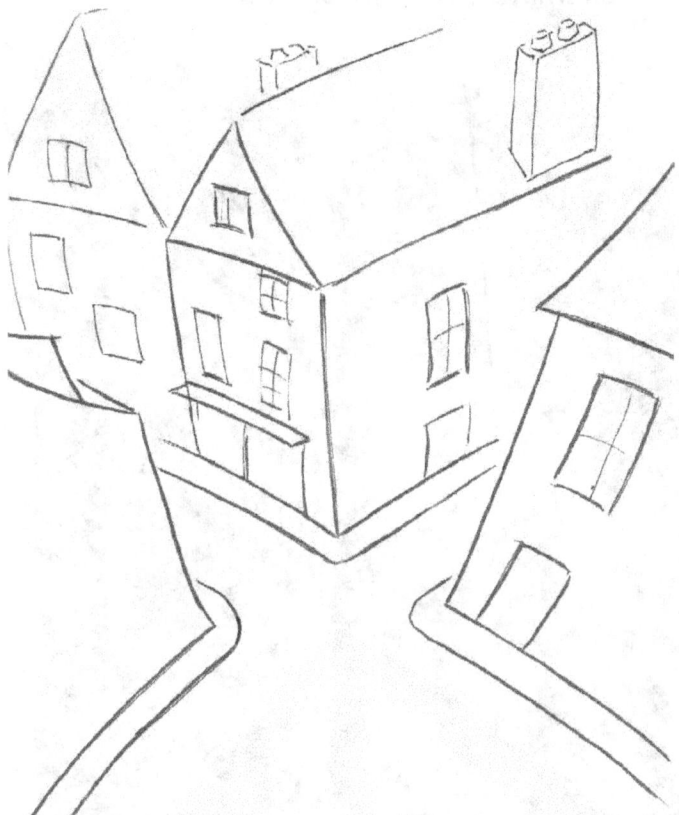

In all circumstance the concavities envelope the principal axis from the subject to the vanishing point. It is the case of a crossroads that the observer hangs over.

Exercise 11

Climb up some terraces and now choose a plunging view. Lean against a railing. Take your sheet of plastic, hold it with one hand so as not to let it fall in the street. Aim at an intersection or a garden at your feet. Trace the principal lines. Observe your copy. Notice that the receding lines of the arch of fireworks come out to wrap around you.

Now let us examine two photographs

San Francisco
Photograph by the author.

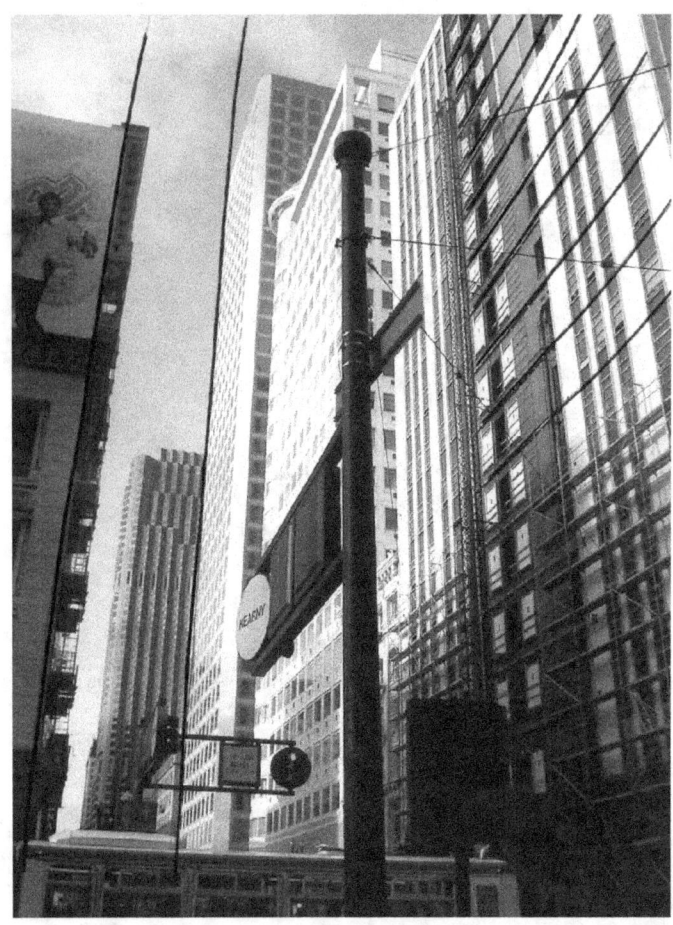

The vanishing point is towards the zenith, consequently one observes in this photo to the right the curved contour lines, and to the left two quasi linear vertical receding lines, slightly curved towards the right, that embrace the central post. The quasi linear aspect of those three lines indicates that the photographer was located in the middle of the image.

San Francisco.
Photograph by the author.

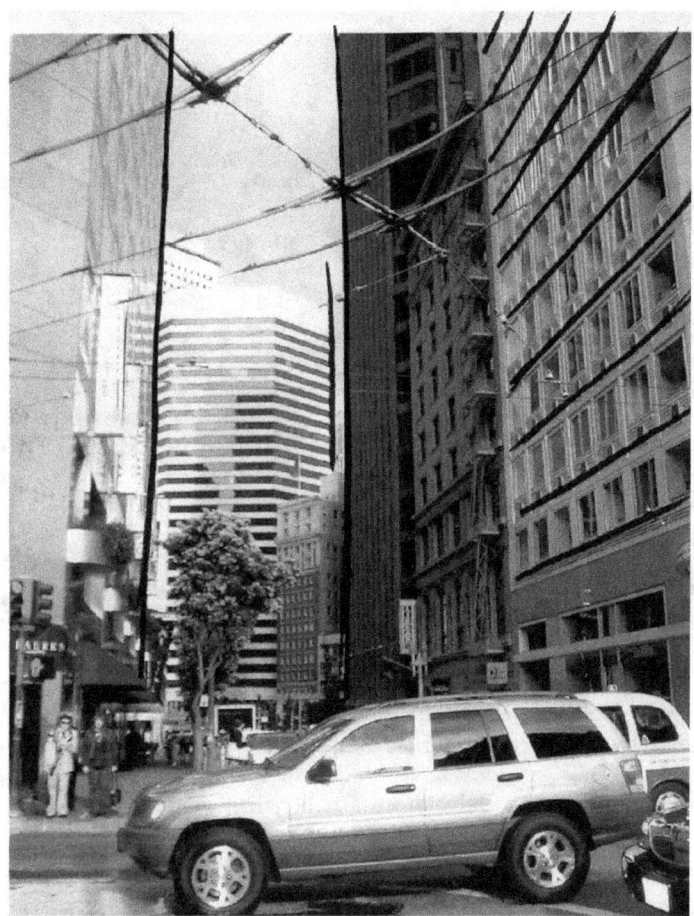

The vanishing point is still towards the zenith, consequently appears

- on the right, the contour lines, which look curved,

- on the left, two vertical receding lines that wrap around the left side of the photo which indicates that the photographer was located to the left of the scene.

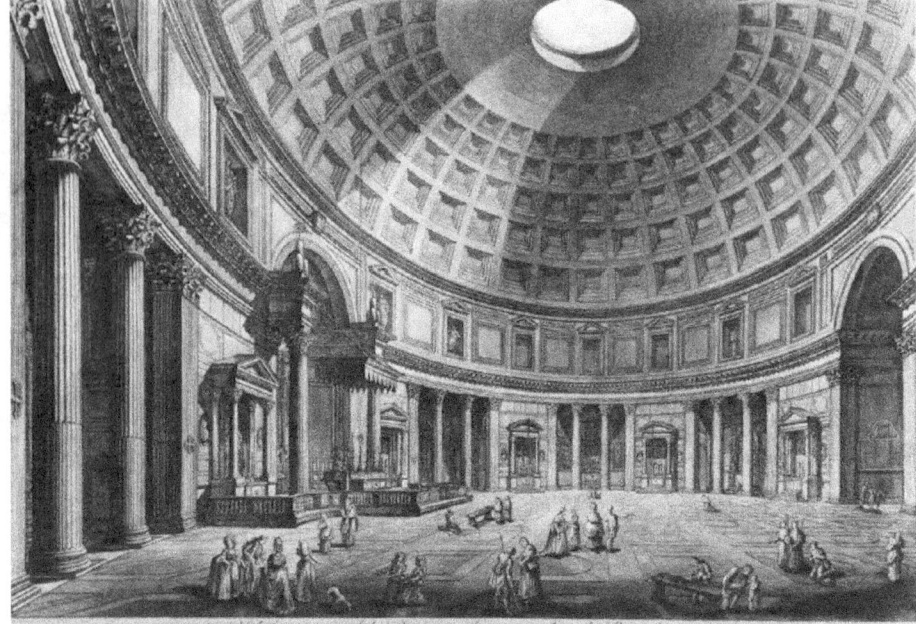

Piranesi. Cupola of the Pantheon of Rome (1750). Library of the Four Pillars.Bourges, France.

The cupola introduces the space of the meridians and parallels lines that are for the two categories inscribed circles on the sphere of the cupola.

For a sphere cuts our visual cylinder following a quasi-ellipse.

We have seen that the unrolling of quasi-ellipse inscribed on a cylinder is another quasi-ellipse.

The meridians and the parallels of the cupola seen by Piranesi are therefore quasi-ellipses. It is definitely what Piranesi saw before the theory of perception in a cylindrical universe was established today.

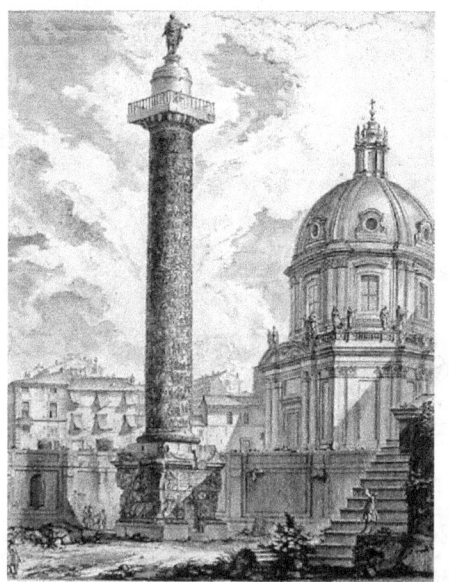

Piranesi. The column of Trajan (1751).
Bib. Mun. Bourges.

The column of Trajan (113CE) carries a helical frieze illustrating the victories of Caesar on the Dacians. The height of the frieze is 87cm (34.25 inches) at the base of the column and 127cm (49.99 inches) at the top.

At 60 meters (196.85 feet), which is the length of the Trajan marketplace, the eye perceives the base and the top of the frieze under the same angle of 1.1 degrees, giving the impression that the width of the ribbon is constant, and by this method, the impression of the column is strong.

Trigonometric table in hand, we note therefore that this column was constructed following the trigonometric perspective suitable to a cylindrical vision of space.

The Greek architect Apollodore de Damas, of the Roman province of Syria, understood the Greek heritage published by a table of arcs and circles at the same era in the Almagest by Ptolemy.

This information is supplements by the works of Georges Gromort on the convexity of Greek temples, made to straighten the concavity of our natural vision, leaves us to think that the Greeks mastered what we today call in this work Real Perspective. Such is the heritage lost and rediscovered today.

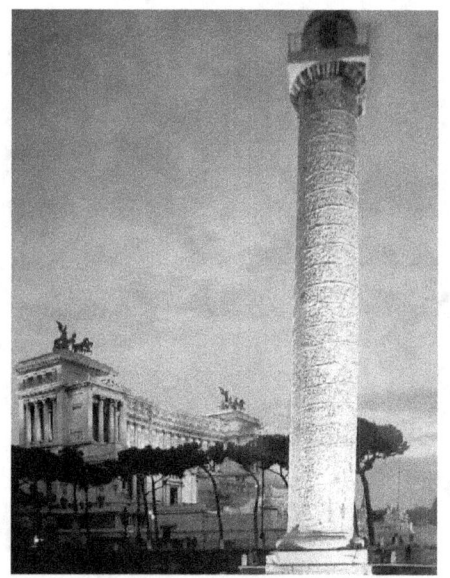

Photograph Aurélie Constant.

REVIEW OF THE SECOND SECTION

1. In the first chapter we entered into the world of cylindrical space, because it corresponds to our visual space. We have drawn from it all the mathematical results that allow us to define the structure of space.

The non-mathematician took the same path by cutting a slice of sausage and unrolling its skin on a table to discover the form of a receding line on a sheet of paper.

On the whole the criss-cross pattern of space in Real Perspective is like that of a shower of fireworks starting from a vanishing point chosen by the artist. Any spray is easy to draw and one could trace as many of the branches of the shower that one wants to construct a drawing.

2. In the second section we applied our new understanding of space to the practice of drawing buildings. We began with buildings for they consist of straight lines and levels, which are the simplest forms to draw.

To take our first step we operated in the fashion of Leonard de Vinci, by simply tracing what we saw through a transparent plate. The tracing made, we set out to closely observe what we drew.

We observed the convexity of curves.

We located the vanishing points that we chose.

We noted that the receding lines intersect at the vanishing point. We have seen also that the contour lines are perpendicular to the receding lines in space.

If the vanishing point is located on the horizon, it merges with receding lines as the edges of sidewalks and horizontal gutters, then the contours lines of constant magnification are, for example, the descents of vertical gutters.

If the vanishing point is at the zenith, the receding lines are vertical and the contour lines are horizontal.

After having traced a landscape on a transparent plate, we redrew directly onto a sheet of paper the same landscape, beginning by marking on your paper the place where is found the vanishing point, to make a shower of fireworks flow in which you inscribed your buildings, in the form of lines, those which were sufficient to put volumes in place.

Third Section
The Real
Magnifying-Glass Effect
Application to close volumes,
a living model

INTRODUCTION

The term perspective, makes us think of remote objects, the term magnifying-glass effect, of close things. But in both cases our visual perception is practiced in a cylindrical universe, our two eyes are able to detect a presence in a horizontal field width of 180° and of 90° only in a vertical field width. This is definitely the height and width of a field that we arrange after fixing a vanishing point in a picture.

In both cases, we subjected to an organization of space represented by a shower of fireworks which corresponds to our physiological perception and which we call for this reason Real Perspective.

We have shown (Second Section "Real Perspective applied to architecture") that our universe of perception leads us to the following observations:

- a straight line in space is for the observer a perceived ellipse that he translates by a sinusoidal arc on a plane of drawing paper,

- receding lines coming from a vanishing point are therefore sinusoidal arcs on the drawing

- the contour lines of constant magnification are quasi ellipses on the drawing,

- the enlargement between the two contour lines accelerates gradually.

We have also underlined, and we confirm it with examples in the present section, that Real Perspective is intuitive, simple to use, without calculations for the artist who will be content to get accustomed to the orders of magnitude of the magnifying-glass effect which nature offers.

The artist will have to stand in his rightful place in our culture of Rectilinear Perspective, which was the object of debates since the Renaissance, to be thereafter imposed in France, and finally contested by the artists of the 20th century. (First Section "Rectilinear and Curvilinear Perspective, History of a Taboo ").

The form is inherent to the living and our perception renders the magnifying-glass effect inevitable. This magnifying-glass effect corresponds to features of a landscape traced onto a transparent plate. For a single line, if it be accurate, restores depth to volumes and from it emerges the living form.

We must be aware of the fact that it is easier for us to believe what we do not see, rather than in what we do.

Thus the concept of Real Perspective, by its approach without concessions, opens for us new plastic spaces of architecture and new volumes for our representations of living models.

* * *

In the first chapter we will try to locate the appearance of the living and of the magnifying-glass effect. We will see that, since the first drawings that we have known, Homo sapiens have shown their fascination for the living.

Later the first preoccupation of artists seemed to be the evocation of the Gods, men and animals of the Nile, of Asia or Olympus. The surrounding space remained little represented.

During the Renaissance the backgrounds of paintings were juxtaposed, whereas the landscapes in the background remained at times treated summarily. It is therefore not surprising to see the grand masters make crude mistakes of perspective on the figures that they represented.

Academicism had the merit to bring a certain mastery to perspective in the representation of landscapes and figures, even if we critique them today for having imposed a limited window of narrow vision to avoid facing the difficulties of Curvilinear Perspective.

However, at the same time that academicism triumphed in France, one saw artists who were fascinated by the living. They attempted to enter into this world by using the grand plan and the magnifying-glass effect. Then, the established order having been shattered into pieces, artists no longer hesitate to leave to the discovery of new representations at the risk to sail in an unreal dreamlike world.

In the second chapter we will see that this technique of a single but accurate line can, without shading, represent depth in a series of drawings of hands.

We will next give some examples of advantages brought by Real Perspective: correction of classic drawings, coherence of a drawing, how to seat a model, how to emphasize all the parts of a model as belonging to a whole.

We will finish with some free drawings, which I carried out in a studio in a few minutes, of which the reader will be able to imagine the new receding lines and magnification step.

III I
The fascination with the living

A short history of the Magnifying-Glass Effect

INTRODUCTION

This chapter does not claim to present an exhaustive work of an historian, but to simply make some notes. In Antiquity, the mastery of space did not seem to have been the first concern for artists. When the environment was evoked, it was only with the minimum of necessary elements for the understanding of the message. Close exterior space wraps man and animals that appear in an elaborate manner in the frescos of Egyptian mastabas, for example.

The magnifying-glass effect was not used in Europe during the Renaissance, the era being attached to the representation of heroic dreamlike worlds, divine, historical, religious or symbolic. The irruption of the living appears in prosaic scenes, translated by a very foreshortened view of the subject, an exaggeration or a magnifying-glass effect, as was done by Claes van Swanenburg.

Academicism was anxious to restore a perfect perspective in its eyes, but nevertheless in windows too narrow to represent a strong and present nature. In reaction, the grand plans, from Rembrandt to Lévy-Dhurmer, became increasingly daring at the risk of flowing over into a fantastic universe.

In their search for the use of the magnifying-glass effect, Degas (1834-1917) and Matisse (1869-1954) made life emerge, in a methodical effort that showed the richness of this new way.

The first artists seemed more interested in the living beings that in their environment. Landscapes are absent. But examples of the mastery of volume in three-quarters view are numerous, as in this chariot or in the attitude of giraffes. One used an instinctive perspective, that of our natural perception.

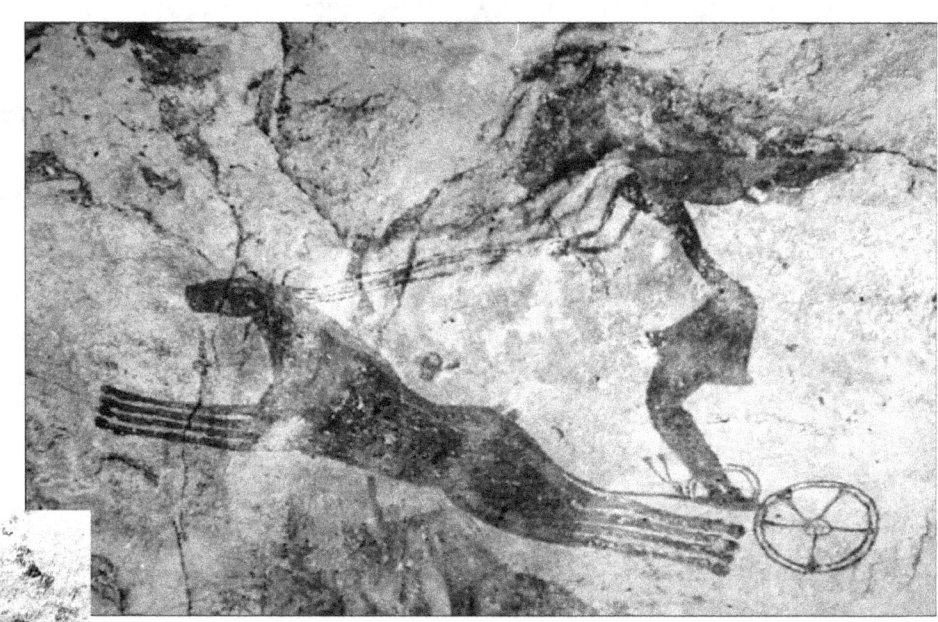

Sahara. Photos by Gabriel Camps.
Chariots of Tamadjert.

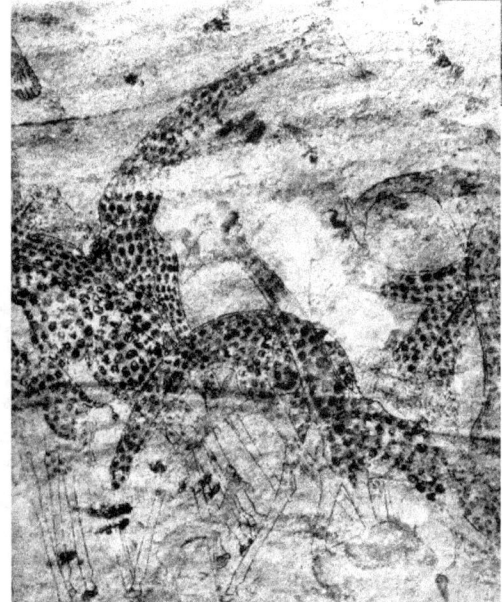

Sahara. Tassilin'Ajjer
Photos by Jean-Dominique Lajoux.

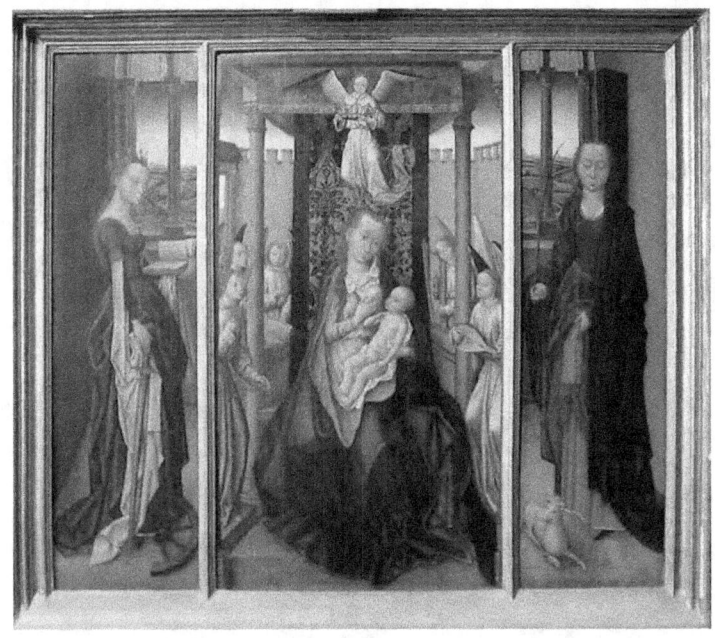

Unknown of the fifteenth century.
Museum of Bourges.

In the Middle Ages, the representation of space presented difficulties

One observes a decoupage of a painting in several scenes, certain landscapes show the mountains treated with steps of a staircase, the walls or curtains act as the background. During the Renaissance one transferred a landscape onto a window to understand the placement of a setting brought by a landscape or the nearby environment.

Furthermore one observe that the feet and the hand of personages are in the same level. The Great Masters usually practiced fluently this stratagem, as Le Titien (1490-1576) to *Young Girl in the Mirror*.

This difficulty of treating the limbs is expressed by Léonard de Vinci (1452-1519) in his Treaty of Painting:

"Sketch figures quickly, do not push the execution of the limbs too far, but content yourself to indicate their placement; next, you will be able to finish with ease, if you like them."

In his painting, "Nathanial presented to Christ by Saint Phillip", Jean Boucher (1548-1645) gave the same weight to all the extremities. Traditionalists preserved these practices until the 19th century.

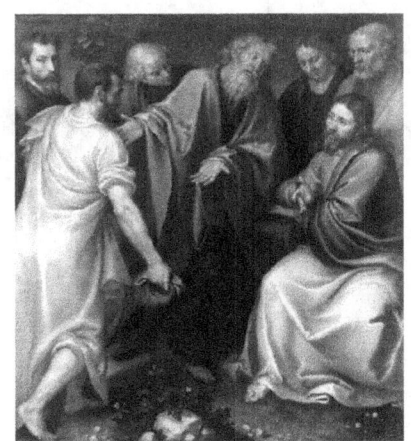

Jean Boucher. *Nathaniel presented to Christ by Saint Phillip*. Museum of Bourges, France.

Even Simon Vouet (159001649), in an allegorical painting, gave an impression of perfect mastery of space, worthy of the grand classical era, always presented hands and feet on the same level.

A portrait in three quarter conducted here by the artist, who has taken the risk, with some enormous errors of perspective : the right hand, which is the same size of the left hand, appears monstrous.

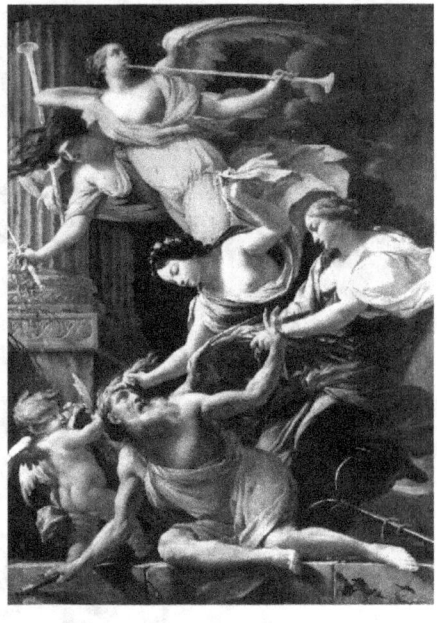

Simon Vouet. *Saturn conquered by Love, Venus and Hope*. Museum of Bourges, France.

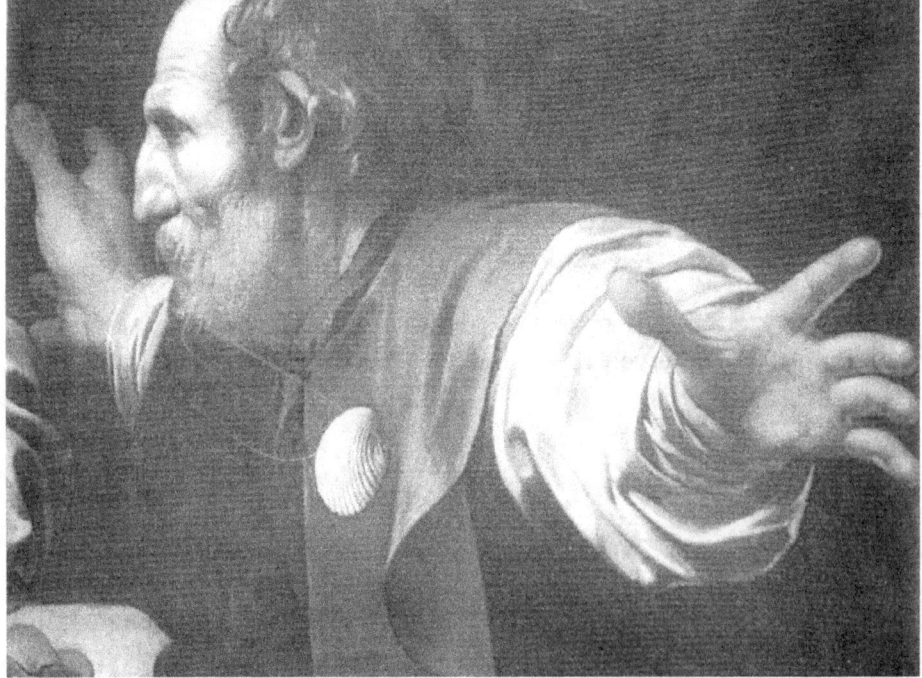

Caravaggio (1571-1610) *The Pilgrims of Emmaus*, detail. (1601) Village of Loches, France. Photograph by Jean Mercier.

Mantegna (1431, 1506) presented "The Dead Christ" in 1465. All the foreshortened proportions are false: the pelvis is mid-height on the paper instead of being in three-quarters, and on this horizontal body the feet should be much larger and the head much smaller.

One could explain this picture of Mantegna by saying that the painter made a didactic effort to show the hands and feet wounded by the nails, as well as the suffering of the face. But this interpretation does not hold up when one knows his pencil sketch, kept at the British Museum, "Man lying on a stone slab," the subject of which was not tortured and which presents however the same errors of perspective.

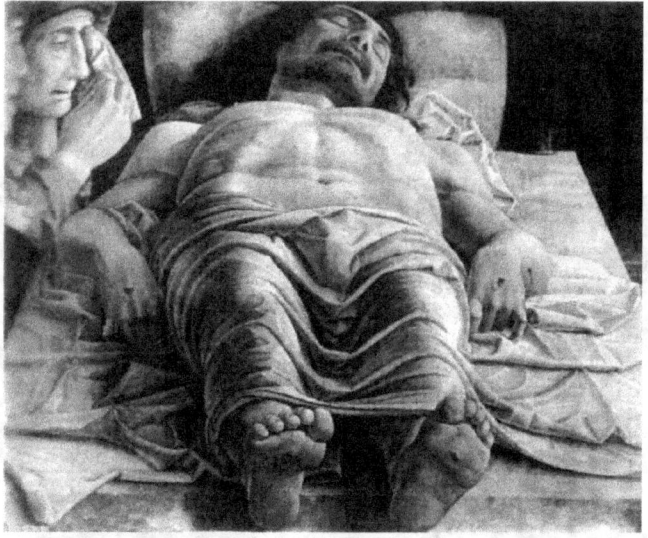

Su concessione del Ministero per i Beni e le Attvita culturali Pinacoteca di Brera. Andrea Mantegna Il Cristo Morto (1465)

Michael Angelo (1475-1564) familiarized us to disproportions, which disappear behind the athletic and masculine morphology of his figures. We see, in the Sistine Chapel, for the "Sybille of Eritrea" (1508) a left hand and a right foot disproportionate with the right hand.

On the ceiling in the "Last Judgment" (1575), one sees the feet of a damned soul, from which his head is hanging between his legs, located in the foreground, are too small in relation to his head, tilted back into the background. All this occurs as if a photographer had taken the scene of the ceiling at a distance with a telephoto lens, which would have had the effect of crushing the distance and effacing the effect of perspective.

This treatment is not awkward for a ceiling, but it shows among other examples, that the effects of perspective only formed a relative part of the concerns of the master.

In Northern Europe, the living being fascinates by the attempts of large close-ups and scenes of daily living. If the perspective of the background is rectilinear, it is not certain that it will be in the foreground. Indeed the wooded loom on the left is not in the axis of the perspective in the foreground.

The dresses and the arms of the two workers could not be treated in Rectilinear Perspective neither with the vanishing point in the background nor with a nearer vanishing point.

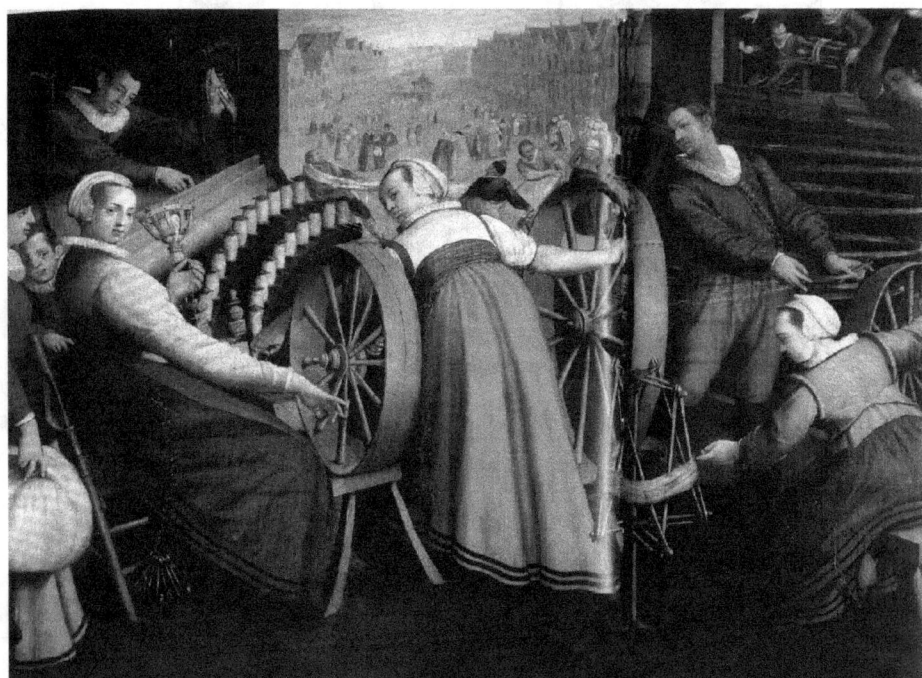

Isaac Claesz van Swanenburg.
Manufacturing of cloth at Leyde in 1450.
Interim photo.
Stedelijk Museum De Lakenhal,
Leiden, Netherlands. Oil on wood,
137.5 x 196 cm.

Self-portrait with Eyes Wide Open
(1630). Strong water 5 x 4,4 cm
Collections artistiques de l'Université de
Liège, inv 919.

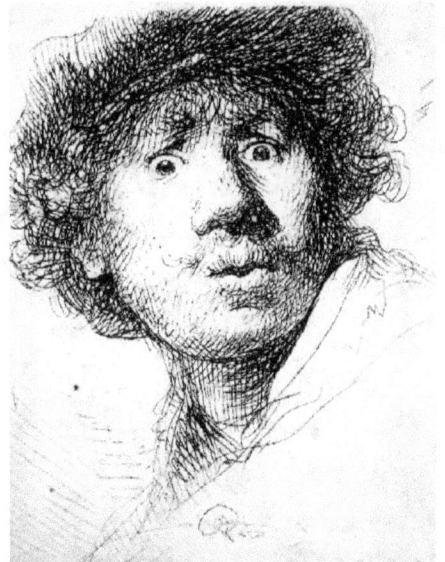

Rembrandt has a breakthrough. The force of a living being is such that the doors of hyperrealism are open. The magnifying-glass effect used to treat the face gives this impression.

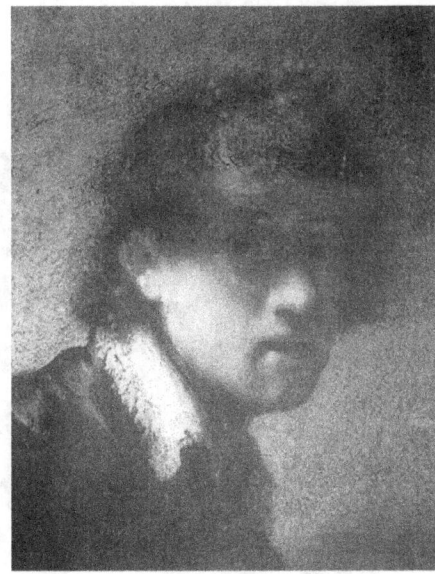

Self-portrait of Rembrandt in a painting embarks us this time into the domain of a dream.

Jugendliches Seldstbildnis
Eichenholz 15.6 x 12.7 cm
Bayerische Staatgemäldesammlungen,
Alte Pincoteck, Munchen.

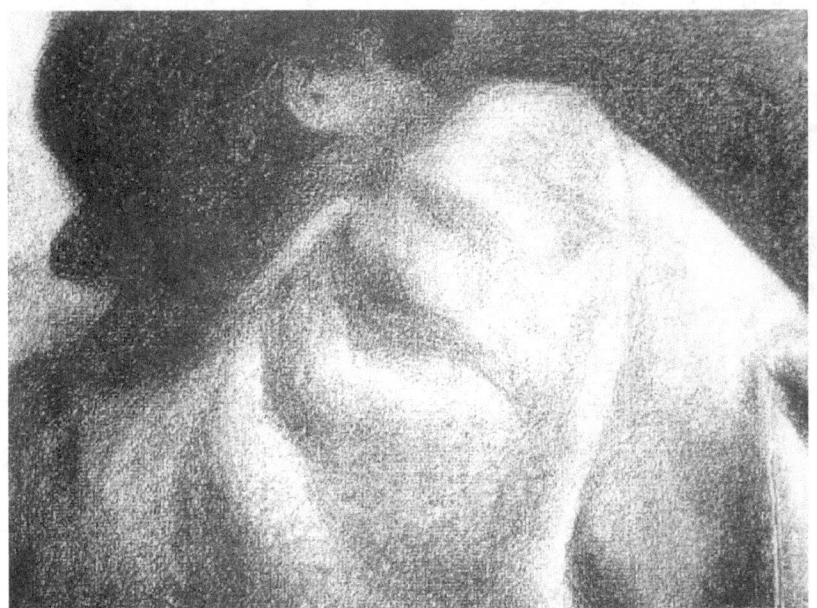

Seurat (1859-1891) *Man in a Bowler Hat, Study* (1883).

The close-up can approach any part of a scene under any vantage point. However the painter rightly choose a characteristic volume in the expression of the force of the figure.

The studies of close-ups seem to be too few, however, and limited to dreamlike worlds, as in Seurat (*Madame Seurat Mère,* 1882), or phantasmagorical, as in Lévy-Dhurmer (*Nocturnes*, 1896, or *Silence*,1900).

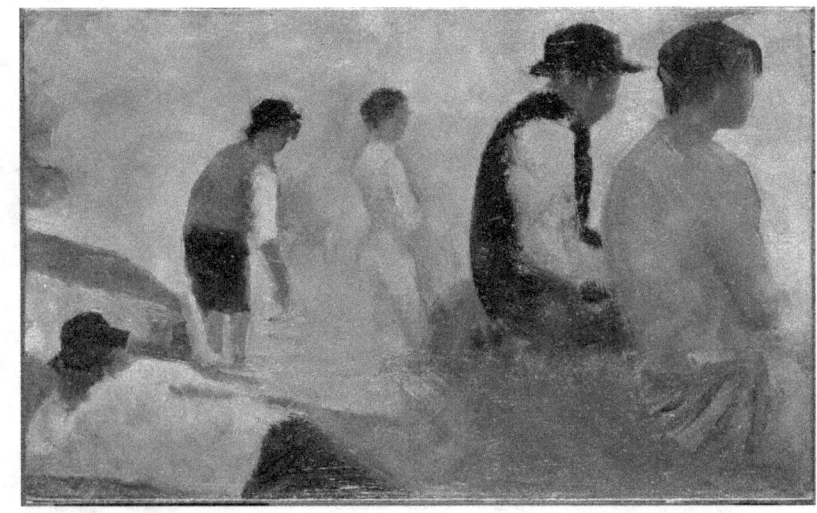

Study for 'Bathers at Asnières'

Félicien Rops (1833, 1898)
Woman with a Black Veil (1880)
Félicien Rops Museum, Namur.

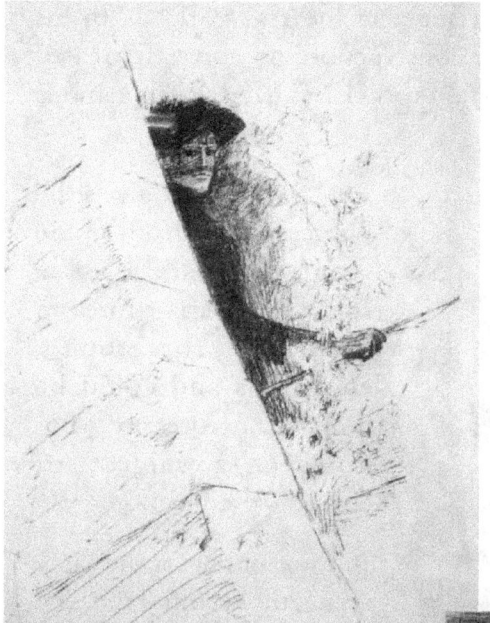

The close-up puts Curvilinear Perspective of the buttress in an obvious place, with undeniably curvilinear aspects.

There remained only an ethereal style of representing women in the 1900s.

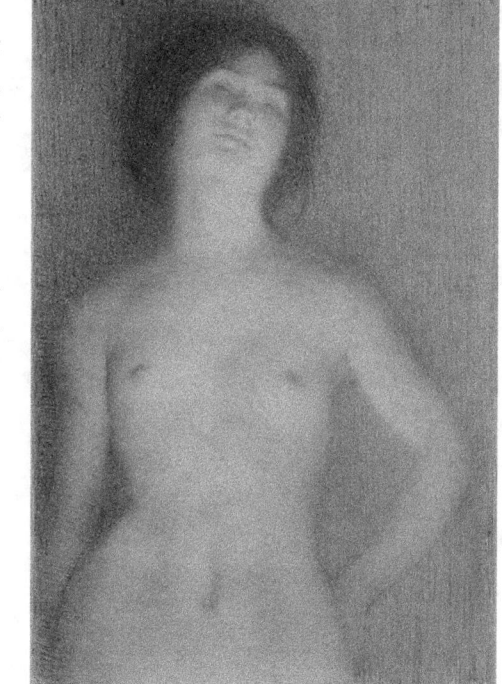

Léandre. Private collection.

On the contrary, one sees Degas remain in the real world. With his solid training and his concerns for construction, he correctly treated the right hand of the bather in relation to her left hand. in his famous painting *The Tub* (1886)

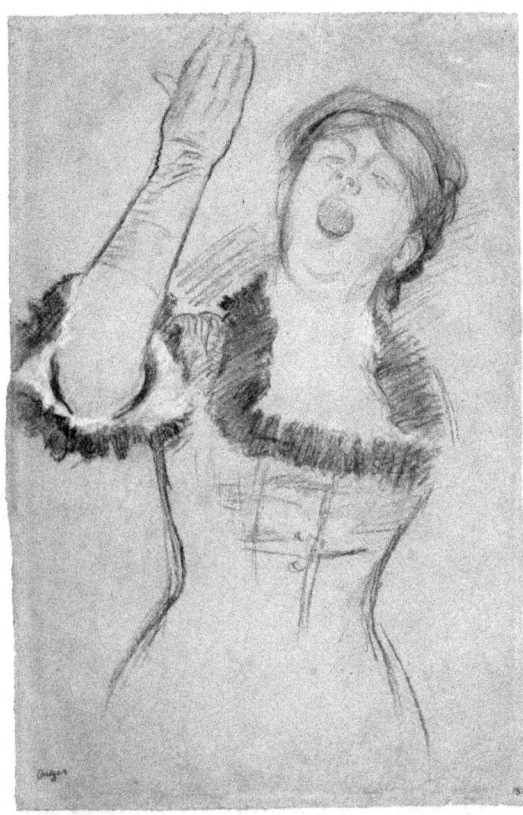

The foreground gives the impression of depth to the scene consisting of a solitary figure. The forearm is in the foreground, enormous and could be more so. A forearm is not however a subject of classical predilection.

In the painting of the same scene, the face and the bust of the singer express all the force and vibration that she transmits. The vertical colored band of the curtain behind the right half of her face is five times less broad than what is behind her forearm, to confirm an effect of depth where the vanishing point would be lost in the black space on the right.

Look at the drawing *The Singer* at a Cafe Concert (1878)

Finally, Henry Matisse (1869-1964) showed us that a deliberate magnifying-glass effect is a door with access to living beings.

His results are not the fruit of chance as is testimony to his methodical work for the portrait of *Lydia Delectorskaya* (1935) during the course of which the painter progressively accentuated, in six preparatory pictures, the close-up, until he made spill over the frame.

Matisse began the same type of work again in 1937 for his self-portrait, showing that this way of researching living beings is rich with meaning.

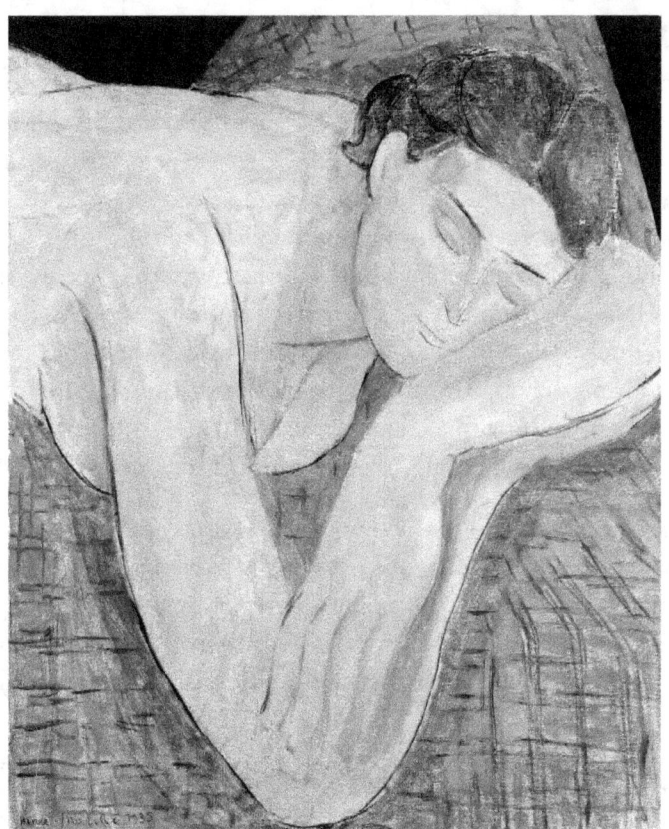

The Dream *(1935)*

III 2 Application to a living model

Believe what you see

Exercises 12-22

INTRODUCTION

Cylindrical space is that of our perceived world. But our reasonable brain permanently corrects what we see by saying: "If this wall is straight, I must draw a straight line in my drawing" or "the eyes are not in the middle of the face" whereas they are. Our reasonable brain is authoritative and does not like to take a new look at generally accepted ideas. When we see a curved line, our brain seeks standard diagrams that are in our memory to conclude a construction which it considers logical. On the whole the drawing, which has not escaped from all these reasonable imprecations, is disappointing, having been incapable of transmitting the living. On the contrary, when we reproduce exactly what we see and we correctly project it on the plan of the drawing, we have a correct line.

Obtaining the good line is nothing extraordinary because it is sufficient, for example, to trace what one sees on a transparent plate. One could also obtain a correct line on a sheet of paper by taking care to recall that space is a grid in the manner of a shower of fireworks and to assure the placement of a drawing with the help of one or two measurements with one's pencil.

A correct line alone, without supplementary artifice, carries depth and the life of a subject. The impulse of a line then makes it possible to transmit all the personality of the artist in symbiosis with his subject. A just line does not need shading and light to express its volume. It's the line that expresses the pronounceable goal of the artist, and the transfiguration of the soul, with which he communicates. Some drawings of hands are used as an illustration in the following pages.

Next we give some examples of the implementation of Real Perspective by showing, with the aid of some diagrams, how to :

- correct an erroneous academic drawing,

- seat a model in space,

- emphasize all the parts of a model as belonging to a whole, in other words to verify the coherence of a drawing.

We will do some exercises which will demand that you find living models. It is not question here of passively copying drawings, for you must learn how to see in space.

Seeing is a voluntary and active step to appropriate space

I present at the end of this chapter some free hand drawings in which the reader will find the reference marks of the structuring of space. I carried out all these free hand drawings in five minutes. It is within reach of everyone and I assure you that one gets used to the practice very quickly. To increase the time devoted to a drawing does nothing but spoil the drawing.

Launch yourself; do not be afraid to "break the paper." If you have fears, tranquilly take your measurements before starting your drawing: locate the middle, the horizon line, the middle of the middle, the right, the left, the top, the bottom, the axis that connects you to the vanishing point, the axis of the body of the model. Really look at the angles of the feet and the hands. Verify the coherence of your drawing with the grid of a shower of fireworks.

PREPARATION OF EXERCISES
OBJECTIVE

Aim to set up on your sheet of paper some volumes in space. What counts is to obtain a true volume, with the right proportions. You will reach that point with a good understanding of space. The details, the shading, the well-smoothed lines do not interest us. The more you work on a false drawing, the more it will be ugly. You must learn to have reference marks and points as crosschecks, so as not to see the next day that your drawing is unsound. We will concentrate then on the placement and the correct line.

REFLEXES TO TAKE UP

1. Work regularly, without getting discouraged. Work everyday, even for just a little while. A change of culture represents work. Reflect, the drawing is not a simple catalogue of cooking recipes, it's a voluntary reflection on your manner of seeing space.

2. Carry everywhere with you in your bag a small wooden board on which you hold with a clip some papers 21 x 27 cm in size. Draw all that you see: in a waiting office, at a café, at a concert, animals in the countryside, but never forget to *construct* your drawing.

3. Leave your eraser to the side; you do not need it, all the lines are interesting, they translate your emotion and the exchange of the living with your model.

4. Correctly take your pencil in hand: place it on a table and take it between the thumb and the four fingers. This grip will allow you to see the point of your pencil in place of working in the dark with your hand hiding the pencil.

5. Draw standing up! When you have the occasion to use an easel. All of your arm will be free.

6. When you want to horizontally hold your pencil when checking,

take it by two hands. When you want to have the direction of a body part, take this direction with your pencil and without moving the inclination of your pencil, carry it to your paper.

7. Limit the number of your measurements. Content yourself to locate the middle of the volume, in the direction of the height, in the direction of width, and report the overall dimensions onto your paper. The more measurements you take, the more they will be false, for each time the thickness of a finger on your pencil introduces a supplementary uncertainty.

8. When you draw a contour, make it with some segments of lines, go from point to point of the volume, by locating well each time the direction taken between each point. Locate the positions of the key points, on in relation to others, crosscheck, without stopping, the elements that must be on the vertical, horizontal, receding, and contour lines.

9. Do not listen to your prejudices, draw what you see: the eyes are in the middle of the face, the distance from ear to eye equals the distance from the eye to the chin, the crotch is mid-height on the body.

10. Go quickly. Set yourself a limited time. Do not drag it out. Concentrate. Enter into the line. Let go of the shape you draw. Start again. Do not be afraid to damage the paper.

WHAT DOES CONSTRUCTING A DRAWING MEAN?

Constructing a drawing means to not launch randomly only to perceive afterwards that the paper is not large enough or that the head is not in proportion, etc.

1. Choose a vanishing point. This is your decision. The vanishing point will be the point of convergence for the picture. For your

first drawings, take for a vanishing point the middle of the volume, which will be the middle of the picture.

2. Choose your vantage point, on the side or not, higher than the model to have an aerial view, lower than the model to have a counter-aerial view.

3. The axis of the vanishing-point/eye of the observer will probably be different than that of the axis of the body. You will be able to construct some contour lines on the axis of the body and on the axis of the vanishing-point/eye. For beginners, work only on the axis of the vanishing-point eye. We shall see some examples.

4. The receding lines issuing from the vanishing point wrap around the observer. The contour lines are positioned by choosing some focus points such as a knee, a chin, etc.

5 Locate the high and low, left and right extremities that must have a global volume. Make the extreme receding and contour lines pass by the extremities of the volume.

PRESENTATION OF THE EXERCISES

We will now familiarize ourselves with drawing volumes with rounded contours.

We will take successively as models:

1. Hands, *exercise 12,*

2. A round chair, *exercise 13,*

3. A man lying down, *exercise 14,*

4. A woman stretched out, *exercise 15,*

5. A couple, *exercise 16-17,*

6. A woman under different azimuths, *exercise 18, 7 diagrams,*

7. True proportions, *exercise 19-20-21,*

8. The set-up of a living person, *exercise 22, 8 examples.*

METHOD OF WORK

We resume with the method followed for architecture

Step 1 – Tracing on a transparent plate

1. Choose your place and your subject and settle in.

2. Frame a subject with a large field width that will be a landscape or a foreshortened view to profit from a magnifying-glass effect.

3. Trace.

4. Locate and trace on your copy the receding and contour lines.

Step 2 – Draw on a sheet of paper.

1. Choose your vanishing point.

2. Trace an outline.

3. Set up on paper the structure of space, which has just been drawn.

4. Draw by successive oriented segments.

5. Control the coherence of the drawing while following the axis and the curves by crosschecking.

Exercise 12
Objective: Draw a accurate line that does not need any shading

Draw your hand. Follow the method in two steps as indicated above.

If you would like to draw your right hand, replace it by the view of your left hand in a mirror.

Settle yourself in your work spot. Wedge your transparent plate with some piles of books. After a construction as described above, you will be able to recommence your drawing, your free hand drawing by following the details of the contour of the hand.

VERY IMPORTANT FOR PROCEEDING FURTHE.

1. Correctly pick up your pencil. Do not hold it like a pen. Pose your pencil on the table and take it firmly between the thumb and the other aligned fingers. You will have the advantage of seeing the point of your pencil.

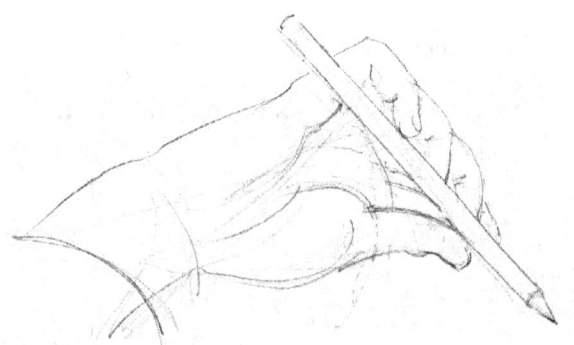
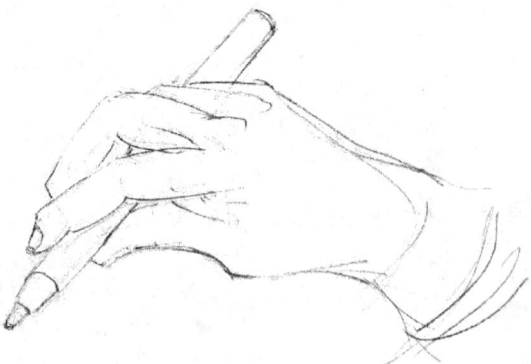

2. Draw standing up. Doing the drawing standing will give you multiple advantages you have a more dynamic attitude, your entire arm is free, this allows you to draw more supply and on larger dimensions, you move, that's indispensable for understanding a volume, for our brain needs movements of our body to calculate a volume, you are not subjected to a pose, you go in front of the model, you can choose an interesting angle, at a shorter and more interesting distance, you have a better connection with your model.

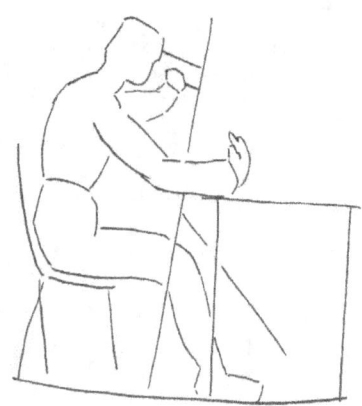

3. Choose some models that are truly energetic. Do not keep models who get bored or who come just to make money. A model must concentrate on his pose, for if he thinks about an interrupted

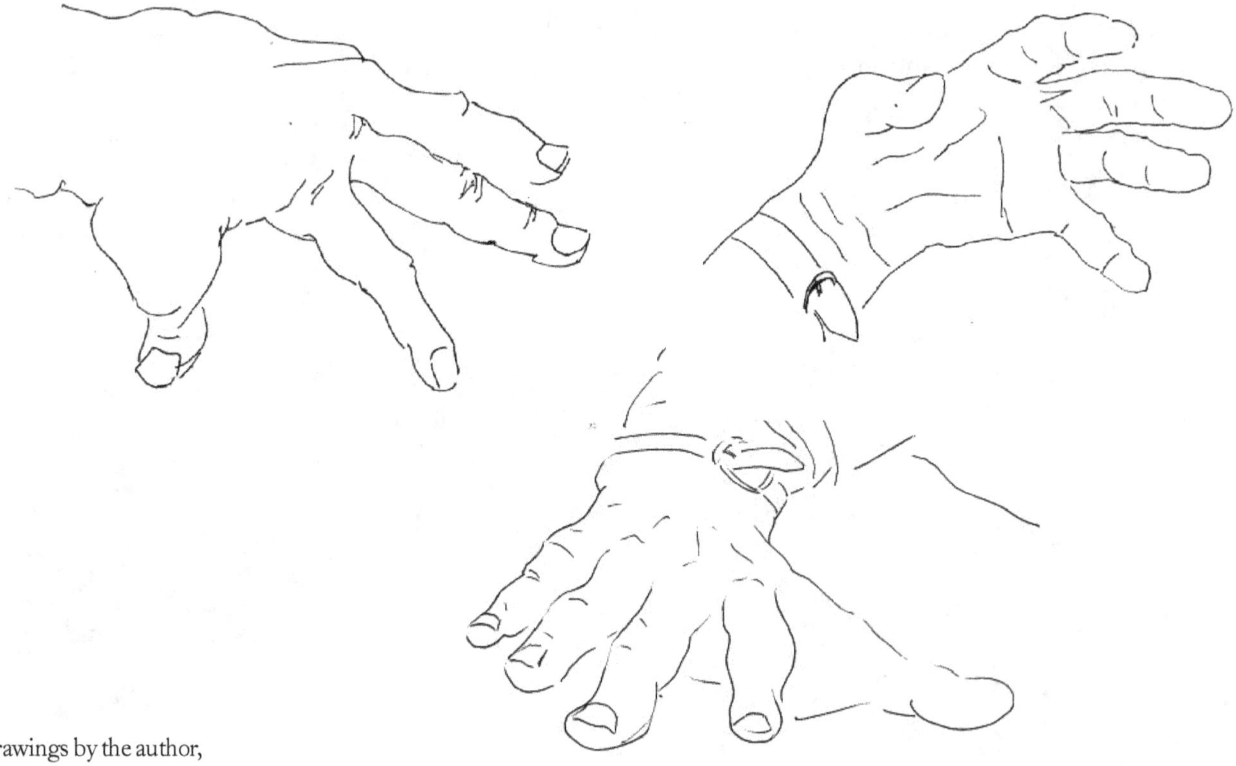

Drawings by the author,
sheet of paper 21 x 29.7 cm

movement or a precise attitude, all musculature is placed in position. It has been shown that certain regions of the brain are illuminated as much when one prepares a movement or when one executes this movement.

4. Preferably ask your model for short poses; you will get those more dynamic and interesting. Make it clear that in any case the model will move in about four minutes. This is why a pose of seven minutes is a maximum for drawing and making an outline of a vivacious painting. Long poses have another objective, which is that of working out technique; you must then carry out a series of drawings by circumambulating the model to verify the coherence of your work.

5. Keep your drawings after having dated them. Store them and get them out again in six months. After regular work you will be enthusiastic with your evolution.

Exercise 13
Objective: Create a scene with an unusual point of view

Take a chair. This is a piece of furniture whose legs and back are very often curved. Place your chair on a table, or better yet climb onto your table and leave the chair on the ground. You will have an unusual vantage point so you will not be tempted to draw your chair "by heart," that is to say to draw according to your prejudices. Get as close as possible to your chair. Its form will surprise you.

Carry out your tracing and your drawing. Notice that, in the drawing above, the chair has only three visible legs ; our brain imagines the location of the fourth leg and generally trains the inattentive artist to draw it. Do not listen to your reasonable brain that makes you believe that you see the fourth leg. The reasonable brain must keep silent when you draw; it has nothing to say about the world of perception.

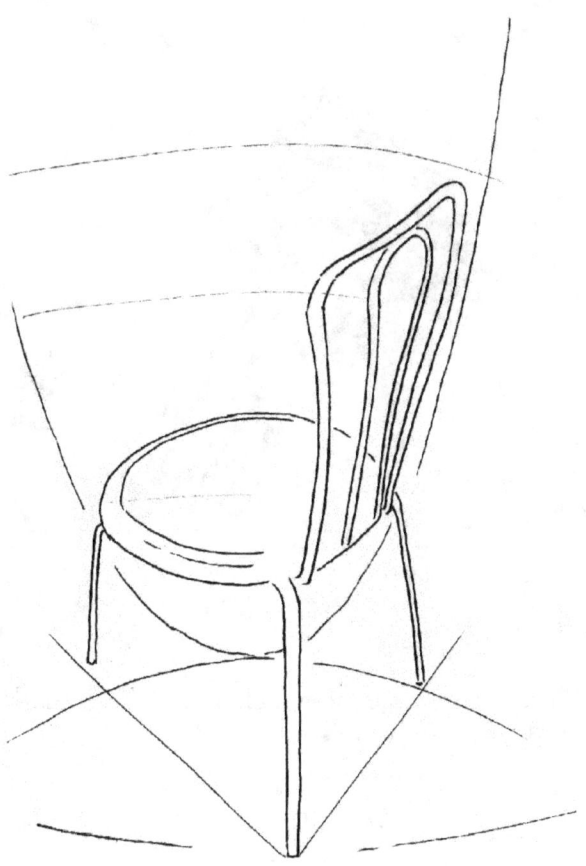

Exercise 14
Detecting a leg that is too long in Rectilinear Perspective, correction in Real Perspective

Have a model lie down in front of you slantwise. Choose your vanishing point at the navel. Trace the axis of the body. Trace the contour lines (of equal magnification) at the knees and at the heels.

At the Academy of Budapest, Jeno Barcsay, represented the contour line (of equal magnification) of the feet with a horizontal line. The left leg of the subject appears to be longer than the right leg.

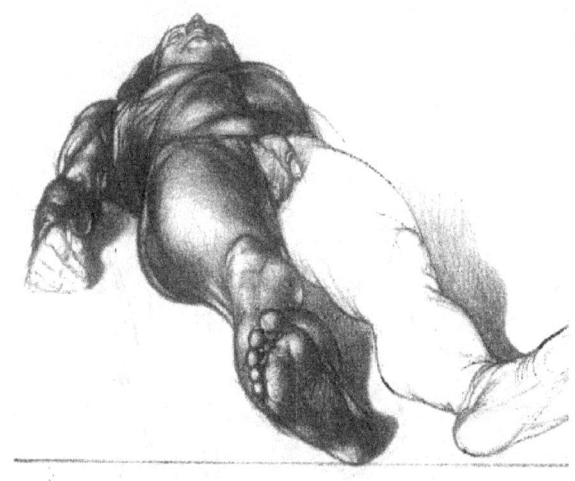

The appearance of which is not due to the different gray values.

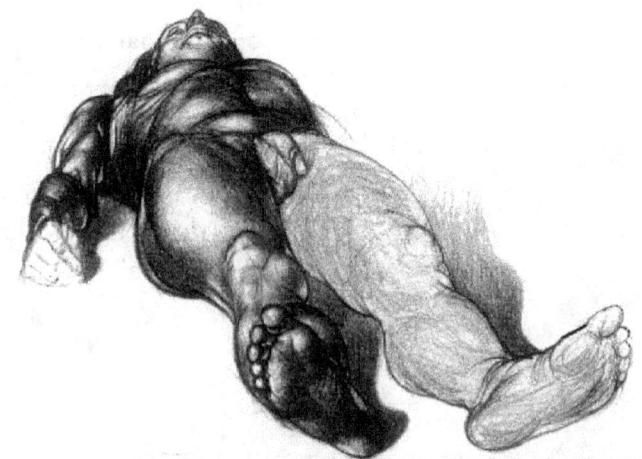

The correction of the left leg is carried out by using a contour line in the form of a quasi-ellipse perpendicular to the axis of the body.

One can make several conclusions from this drawing:

1. We have confirmed the inability of Rectilinear Perspective with regard to the treatment of space and in particular to a living model. How to imagine that one could structure space with straight lines, when nothing is straight on earth, except in the imagination of a few mathematicians.

2. It is rather Real Perspective that allows the placing of this leg at a proper level with a quasi-ellipse, which corresponds to our natural perception.

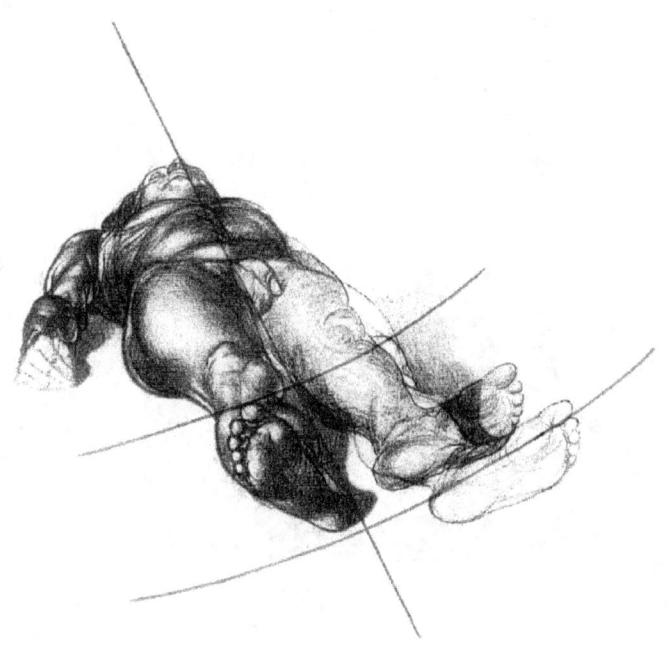

Exercise 15
Objective: Construct accurately by simplifying

You see that this drawing obtained good proportions with a minimum amount of preparatory work. It's sufficient to locate the middle and centers of each half. The middle is the navel, which is also your vanishing point and the center of the paper and the center of the picture.

Trace four contour lines *in the vertical plane,* because the bust of your model reclining on her side is in the vertical plane. Two of them pass by the extremities and the two others pass by the right breast-left knee and the right knee, in other words at mid-distance between the navel and the extremities.

Notice in this example that the two extreme curves delimit the frontier not to overlap on the drawing, and that the two other curves pass by the knees. Trace two curves in the horizontal plane, for the knees rest on the floor. The inferior curve wraps around the knees.

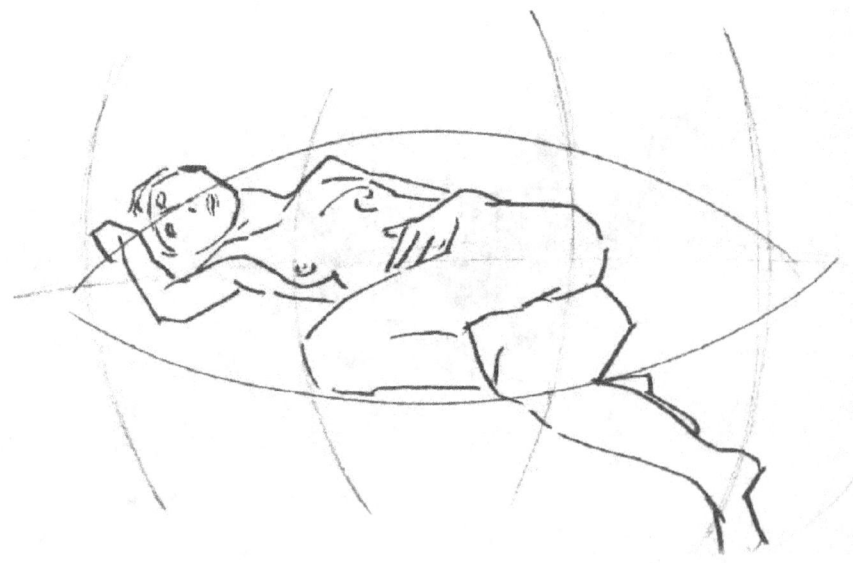

What simplicity! Make a very light outline, trace your curves, and firmly darken your outline on the grid.

Having already understood volume, vigorously begin the contour of the body segment by segment, to which you give the correct direction.

This drawing could appear difficult to set up, all in length and of three quarters. The more the artist were to take measurements with his pencil the more he would sink into cumulative doubts. Indeed, our visual system evaluates distances very poorly and has difficulty with a long form.

Moreover, the reasonable brain intervenes by saying to us that a person lying horizontally on the floor is inevitably horizontal on the sheet of paper. This is false. Fortunately, in Real Perspective, the framework becomes easy with contour lines.

Exercise 16
Objective: Construct with only a few measurements

You have found the middle of the picture that is your vanishing point, mark it with a cross; you have thus the space required for the drawing on the left, on the right, at the top and at the bottom. You have located the left foot of the person at the intersection of the contour lines. Trace the receding lines on this drawing that start from the vanishing point. Trace a horizontal line that passes by the vanishing point, and a curve in the shape of an almond whose summit is at the vanishing point and whose two branches pass by the left foot and the symmetrical point.

So not to get lost in the curves, start from a summit point at a bump or a hollow and go just to the following with a segment, locating well the direction taken. Trace a succession of small well-oriented segments; your eye appreciates the angles very much.

Notice that a regrouped pose offers several points of crosschecking and presents interesting facilities of construction. The curve that passes by the vanishing point and the left and right hollows of the waist of the woman crosschecks the left knee of the woman and the wrist of the man. The spine changes direction at the level of the vanishing point. A single curve covers the left shoulder of the woman and that of the man whose summit is between the two heads. Etc.

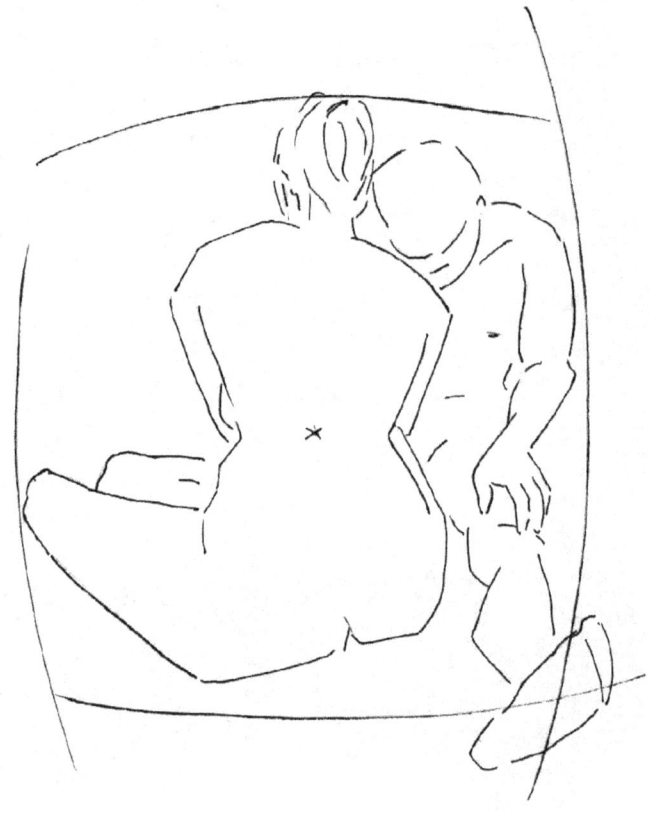

Exercise 17
Objective: understand volume by moving

Walk around your fixed model, this is a radical way of moving. With each step you will understand the volume more, even under an angle of a small gap. In one hour and a half you have the time to draw a beautiful collection.

Simplify, simplify, simplify again. Your drawing will be all the more confident and powerful.

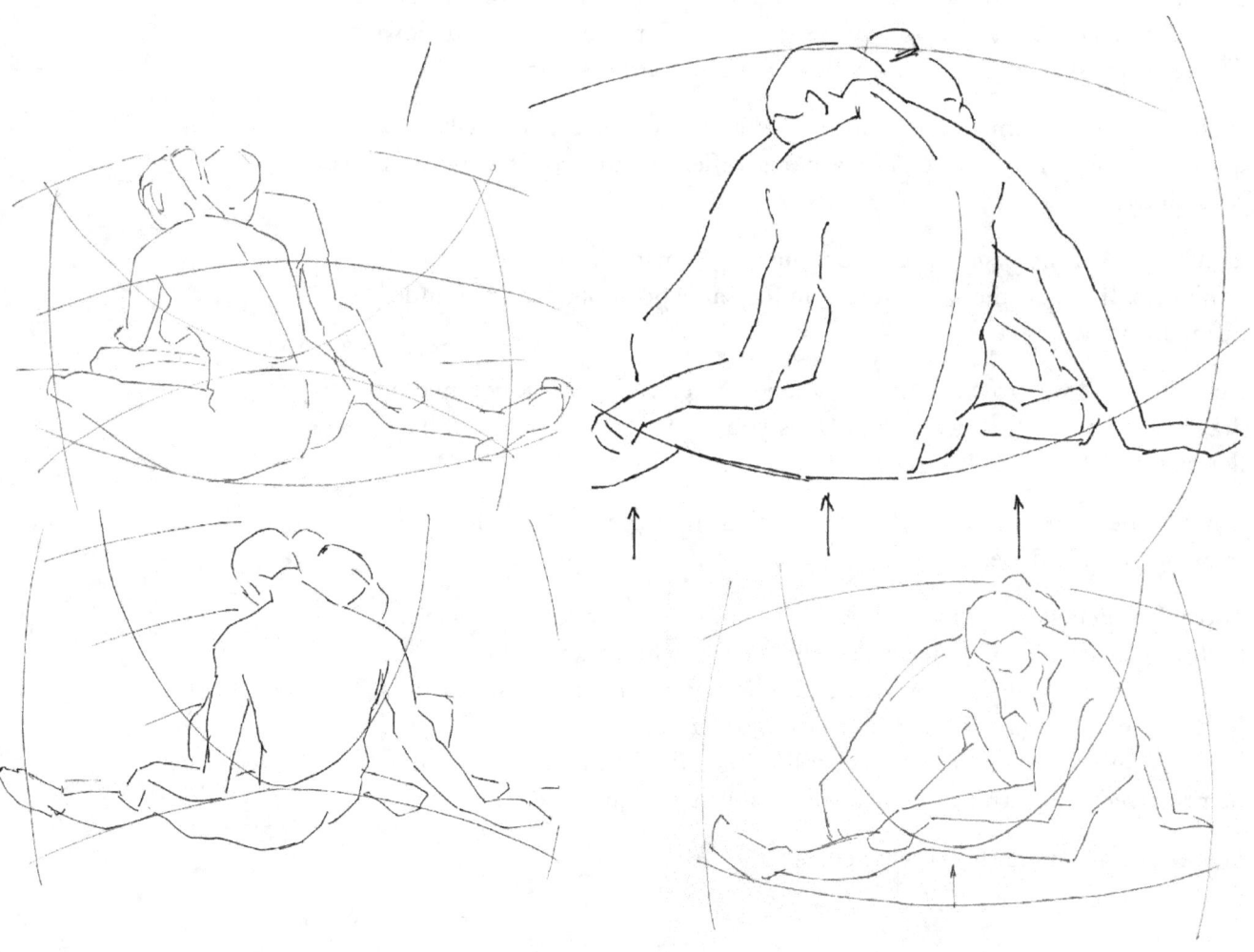

Exercise 18
Objective: analyze the space in which your model is registered

Ask your model to do a long pose, and analyze various viewpoints, not only by turning around, but by climbing onto a table, to see your model from above, or in placing yourself as close as possible to the floor, to see him from below.

The important thing now is not more understanding of the volume but the *deformation of space that accompanies the volume*. I present to you below different drawings with their analyses of the texture of space.

In the future, systematically analyze the texture of space; this will very quickly become for you an unconscious reflex of the construction of your drawings.

You will see in the pages that follow the set-up made by a raised hand in 5 minutes. It acts as the same model, in the same position, but seen under different angles.

This is a good way to work the technique and to verify the coherence of drawings between them, which enables you to be assured that you have definitely understood the volume of your model.

You will be able to note, with little training, that the construction of a drawing is immediate.

Today it is necessary to move quickly. Albrecht Dürer wrote to his silent partner Jacob Heller that he exceeded once more his estimate, because he had spent more than six months making one of the hundreds of portraits for his panel. Imagine if today an artist consecrated six months of his life to a painting, whatever it was? In a following letter Dürer concluded that he preferred to return to the more profitable technique of engraving.

Here once again are the familiar steps:

- Choose your vanishing point.

- Trace an outline.

- Imagine the grid of space as a shower of fireworks.

- Reference the points of the model, which pass the grid.

- Take one or two measurements with your pencil to reference the contour lines.

- Strengthened by the proportions brought by the curvilinear grid, trace vigorously the contours of the model. You will notice that certain drawings show several grids. This possibility could be useful for outlining the contours of a model. Take for example the axis of the model for spacing out the different parts of the body. The lines of force cross at some significant points.

You will also notice several things.

- The sketch is made in complete security, for the grid allows us to see the position and the overall dimensions of the volumes, without taking supplementary measurements other than a few key points.

- The relationship of left-hand side and right-hand side of the model are unequal due to perspective. The grid allows us to position them rapidly.

- The speed of the placement is also due to the simplification of the forms.

Consequently

- A painting brings to light the errors of a drawing. You will be pleasantly surprised when you use your drawing to make a painting.

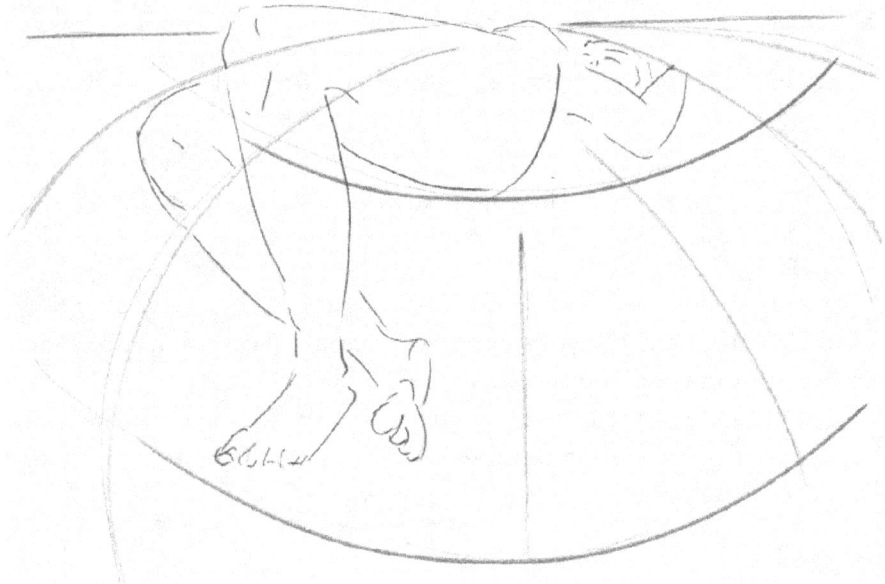

Diagram 1
Analysis of the texture of space

The initial position of the model was as follows: lying on the back, in the axis of the person drawing, the pelvis elevated. In this diagram the person drawing turned 45° counter-clockwise around the model, while remaining in the same horizontal plane of that as the model's pelvis. The vanishing point is not therefore in the axis of the model.

The legs and the pelvis occupy 90% of the volume. One is far from the manner with which Mantegna treated, in 1465, *The Dead Christ*, in which the head in the background is larger than the feet in the foreground. On the contrary we are closer to the foreshortenings of Uccello, in 1456, in his *Battle of San Romano*.

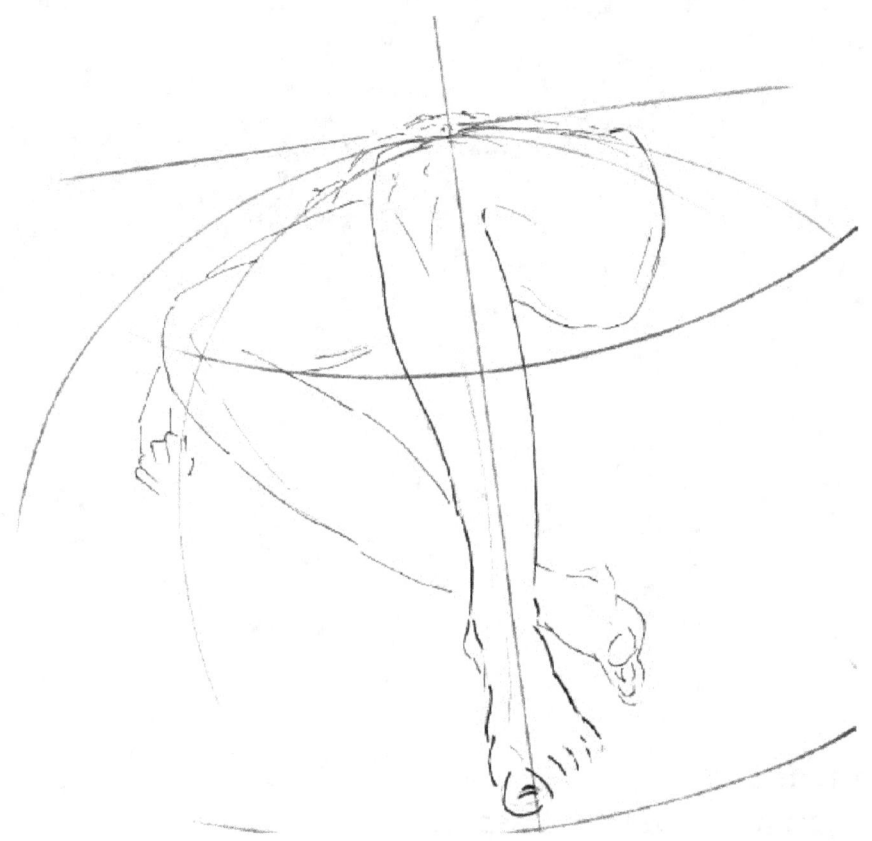

Diagram 2
Analysis of the texture of space

The artist is in the axis of the trunk of the model; in addition, he has a view from below, and the horizon line is inclined.

The head disappears almost completely, whereas the foot is very important. This situation is quite simply natural, the artist having exclusively drawn what he saw. It is not a question of hyperrealism.

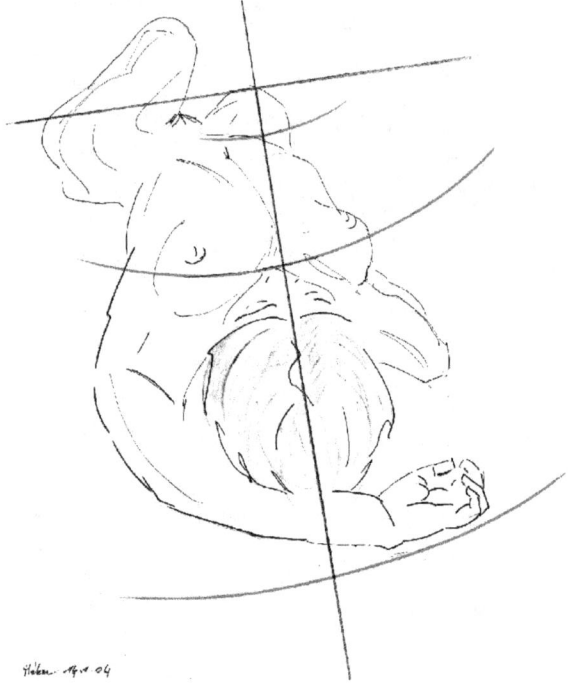

Diagram 3
Analysis of the texture of space

The artist turned a little more than 180° around the model in comparison with his movement for Diagram 2. He is this time clearly above the model. It is therefore now the head that takes a dominating importance.

Passing from Diagram 2 to Diagram 3 is very simple: the artist takes as usual the measurements *without listening to his reasonable brain,* which can only drive him to errors by telling him "you well know that the head makes an eighth of the body."

Despite this fact, the artist will have the tendency to forget his good resolutions between the moment of taking the measurement and when he presses his pencil onto the sheet of paper. It is thus that numerous perspectives are executed incorrectly.

Diagram 4
Analysis of the texture of space, looking at the axis of the body

The position in which one sees the model clearly shows the distortion in which she is found lying on different pillows; she is forced to be in an arched position. That did not however pose a problem for drawing this figure in foreshortening. The body of the model has in fact two orientations beginning from the pelvis, which is elevated.

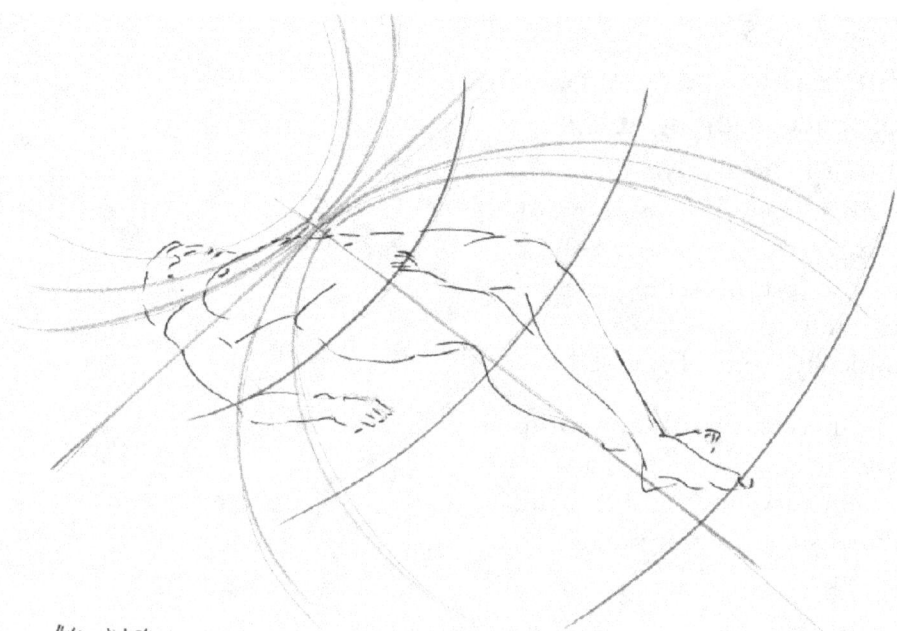

The legs were registered in the following grid, seen by an observer at the feet of the model:

- Axis of the lower part of the body,

- *Horizon line,* perpendicular in space to the axis, and consequently not horizontal on the sheet,

- *Receding lines* encircling the model, starting from the vanishing point,

- *Contour lines* passing by the reference points from which the artist has taken measurements: pubic bone, knees, and toes.

One can see that the interest of the axis of the body and receding lines is to allow the correct setting-up of the contour lines of equal magnification. attached to the model.

Diagram 5
Analysis of the texture of space, looking at the axis of the body.

By a change in the point of view of the observer we show that a foreshortening can be carried out without any difficulty from all angles.

It suffices to take some measurements and to verify with a curvilinear grid that the dimensions of the model are coherent.

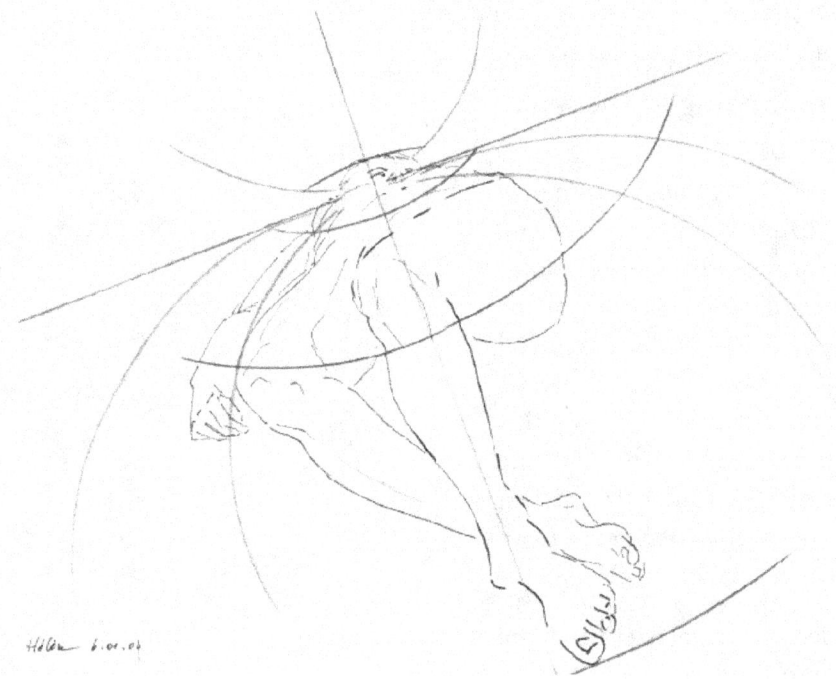

- A grid consists of: a horizon line, chosen by the artist, which passes by the shoulders of the model,

- A vanishing point chosen by the artist, situated at the corner of the right eye of the model,

- Curvilinear receding lines, issuing from a vanishing point, which encircle the model like a shower of fireworks,

- Some contour lines, perpendicular to the receding lines.

- In the present case the artist has located the reference points that allow him to spread out his drawing:
    - below the horizon line, the knees and the stomach,
    - above the horizon line, the top of the hair.

This is why one perceives above the head a concave curve inverse to those that are below the horizon line.

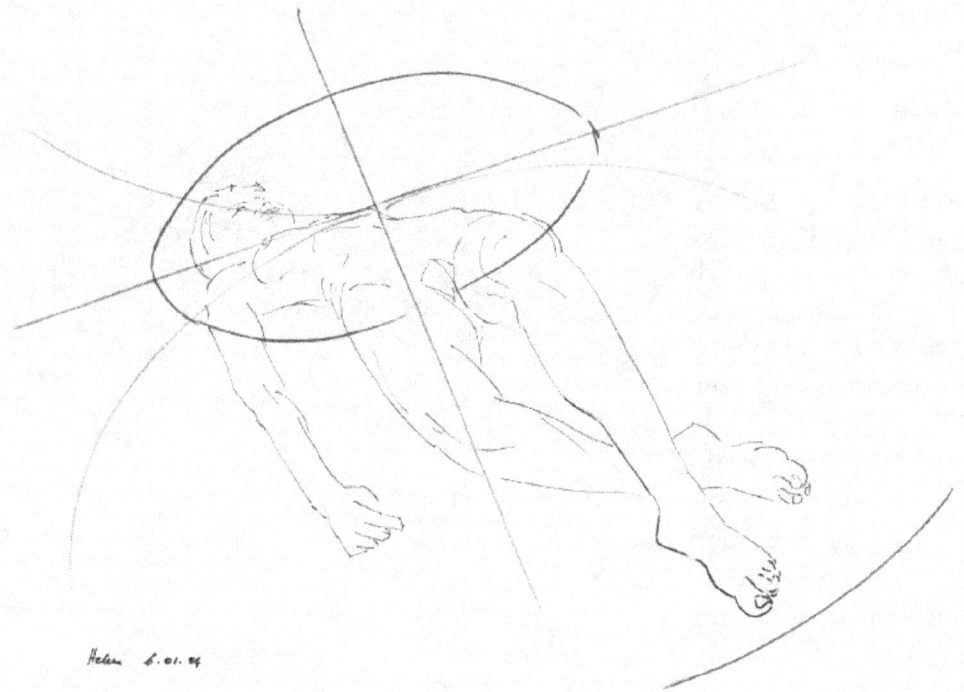

Diagram 6
Analysis of the texture of space,
looking at the axis of the body

The model having her head in the same plane as that of the body, we drew a complete ellipsoid, as calculated in Second Section Application to Architecture. In this diagram we have placed, on purely a pedagogic basis, the head of the model in the plane of her thorax.

This configuration indeed makes it possible for the artist to consider a sole plane going from the top of the hair to the knees. The artist could then trace from one part to another the horizon line, in only one quasi-ellipse, the two arcs of contour lines.

Diagram 7
Analysis of the texture of space, with two axis

Notice that the artist can choose several axes of work to graph space. At each vanishing point there is a corresponding grid. The grids will be obligatorily coherent because the contour lines of magnification pass by the reference points chosen by the artist.

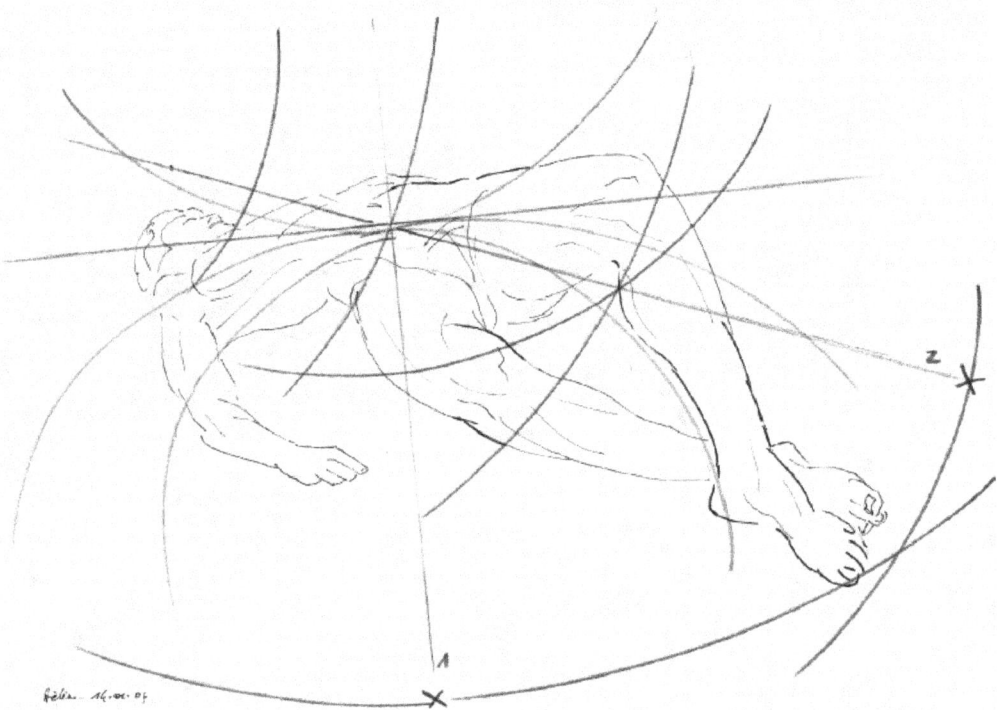

This diagram uses two axes:

- the first, an axis goes from the artist to the vanishing point that he has chosen, in this case the navel, with contour lines of equal magnification step,

- the second, the axis of the body, with receding lines and contour lines attached to the body.

The contour lines relative to these two axes give a coherent meeting point at the feet of the model.

You can now in complete security pilot your models in space. Don't be scared! To your pencils!

Exercise 19
Objective: understanding the magnifying-glass effect

We have shown the contour lines to obtain our objective, for it must translate well the fact that the left knee is about 5 feet (1.5 meters) away from the artist and the hand is approximately 10 feet (3 meters) away.

Let's not republish the mistake of Caravaggio with the *Pilgrims of Emmaus*, and do not hesitate to show the enlargement of space.

The vanishing point is to the right of the left breast. From here are issued two receding lines that allow the positioning of the contour lines of the knees and of her right toe.

The symmetrical curve of the knees passes under the chin. The top of the head remains to be positioned. In total, four measurements were taken, all the rest falling under the grid.

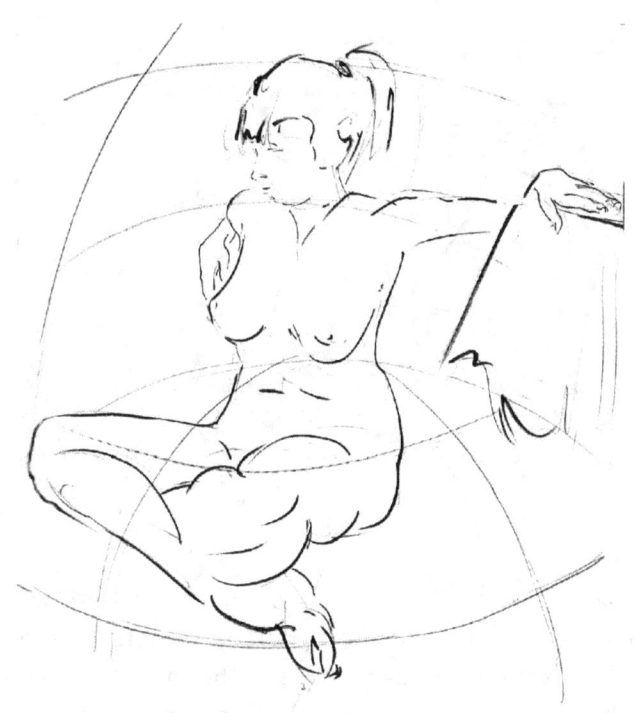

Exercise 20
Objective: do not get lost
when reference marks are lacking

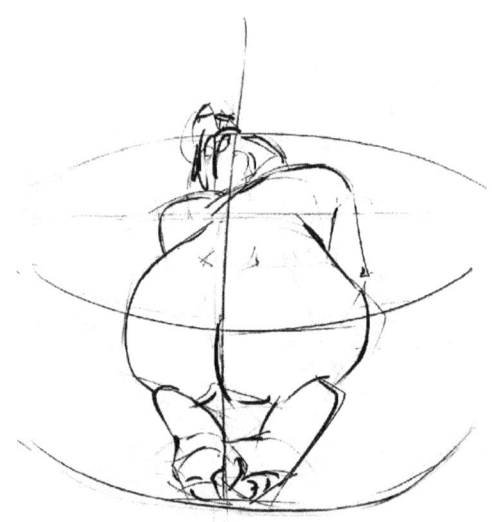

The model's back is facing you; the main thing is to know how much space and, therefore volume to grant to the shoulders and to the pelvis. No clear mark exists on this surface. We take therefore as reference marks the top of the head, the nape of the neck with the hollow of the shoulders, the line of the right armpit – left shoulder passing by the place where the hips seems to be erased, this line crosses the spinal column at the vanishing point, and finally the beginning of the buttocks and the toes.

We have four measurements to take, the grid does the rest, the proportions are good, magnifying glass effect understood. Draw what you see. Which was to be demonstrated. Do not hesitate to use the grid to construct when you feel it necessary, and then redo right away a drawing free hand.

Exercise 21
Objective: Give extreme points their just placement

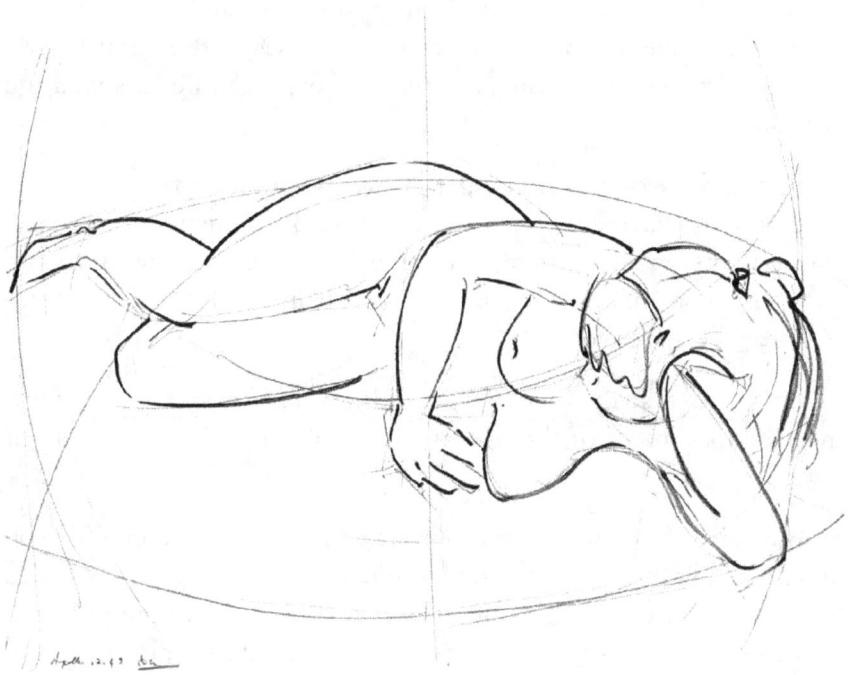

It is necessary to give to this foreshortening its appropriate position for the head, the elbow, and the right foot. The vanishing point is chosen at the navel. We seek to wrap the model's contour lines, which we place by a few measurements, and the grid gives the placement.

Compare this drawing to that of exercise 15. What are the differences and the similarities?

Exercise 22
Objective: setting-up from life

Setting up from life means drawing in the moment, catching what is front of you eyes at a given time.

You will notice that the drawing could stop in the form of a diagram or on the contrary have a supple and finished line. Only the artist knows when he has finished his drawing, in other words, when he says what he wanted to say.

With some training you will no longer even need to trace the shower of fireworks; you will have integrated it into your comprehension of space. You will be accustomed to the effects of enlargement of trigonometric space, which is your natural perception saved from errors of our culture of Rectilinear Perspective.

Ask your model to take the following attitudes and concentrate on a single objective: the placement of the model, one could also say the seating of the model.

Don't forget, as Rembrandt, to draw everyday. But it will become for you soon an exciting habit. Now I present you two drawings, examples 1 and 2, followed by six exercises, examples 3 to 8 on which we are going to play to a new game: guess for each drawing where are the vanishing point, receding lines and contour lines

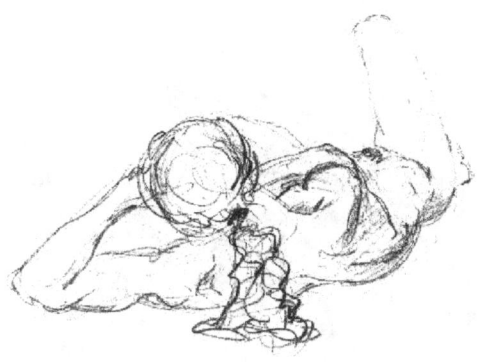

Example 1

The pose lasted three minutes because the model was in a very uncomfortable position, the right shoulder completely off the floor. The placement was easy since, once the shoulders were drawn, nothing major was left to be done. Therefore it was sufficient to:

- locate the vanishing point (under the buttocks),

- position the axis, which goes from the vanishing point from the position of the artist (this axis goes from the crotch to the right shoulder),

- position the axis of the body (which goes from the crotch to the nape of the neck),

- position the levels of the kidneys and of the nape of the neck,

- really see the axis of the shoulders.

It is necessary to become accustomed to the order of sizes in the real magnification step or face the risk of not understanding what one sees.

Do not be afraid of what you see and do not listen to your reasonable brain. Notice that the floor is not represented; the pose makes the floor's solidity an easy guess.

Drawing by the author, pencil on white paper 50 x 65cm, carried out in three minutes.

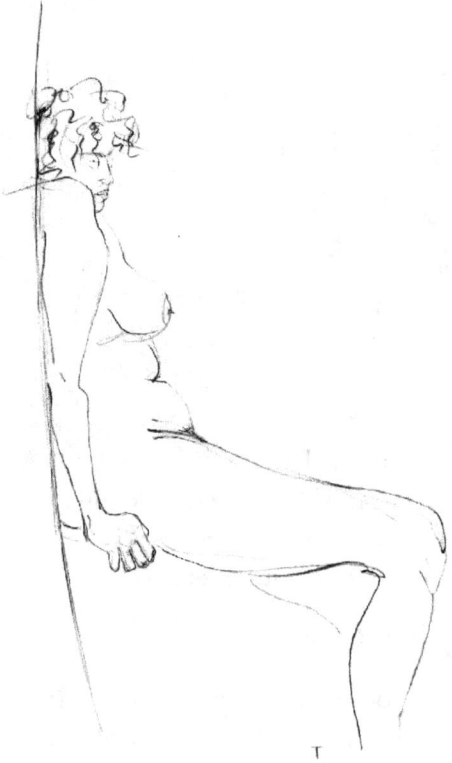

Example 2

The model is left sliding the length of a wall. You know that walls are not perceived as straight lines. This one has a concavity that wraps the axis of the model. Here the axis of the model is that of her trunk.

Recall that in *High and Low* by M.C. Escher, the walls of the house wrap around its axis.

Drawing by the author, pencil on white paper 50 x 65cm, carried out in three minutes.

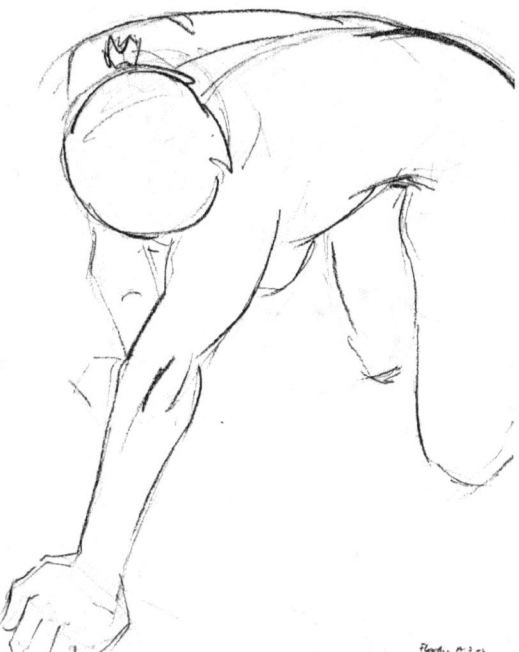

Example 3

Find

- The vanishing point,

- The receding lines,

- The contour lines of equal magnification.

Observe the force that is given by a framing brought closer to you; the approach of the model gives an augmented magnifying-glass effect.

Drawing by the author, pencil on white paper 50 x 65cm, carried out in five minutes

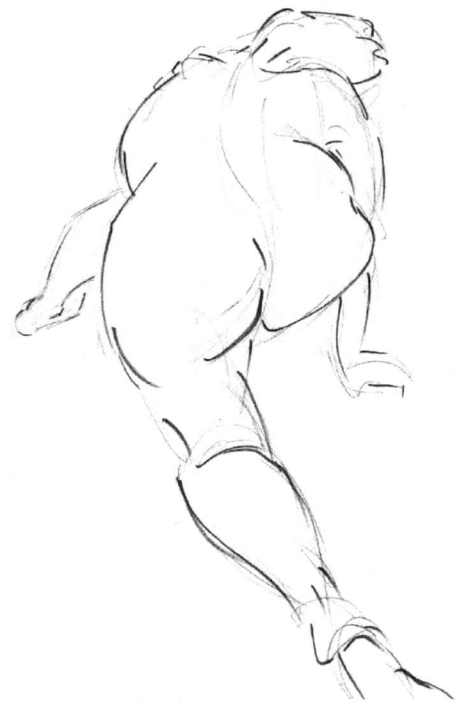

Example 4

Find

- The vanishing point,

- The receding lines,

- The contour lines of magnification.

The model has carried her right foot to the left.

Drawing by the author, pencil on kraft paper 50 x 65cm, carried out in five minutes.

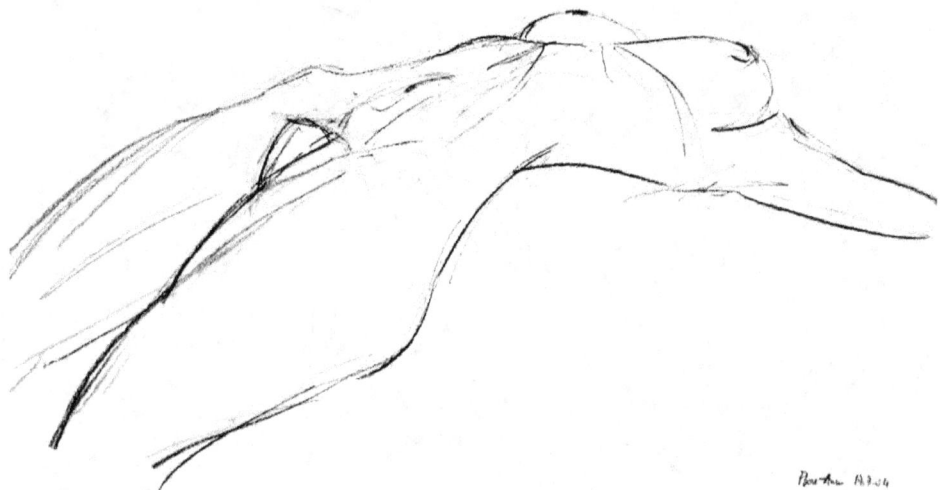

Example 5

Find

- The vanishing point,

- The receding lines,

- The contour lines of magnification.

- The model is lying on a low coffee table of small dimensions.

Drawing by the author, pencil on white paper 50 x 65 cm, carried out in four minutes.

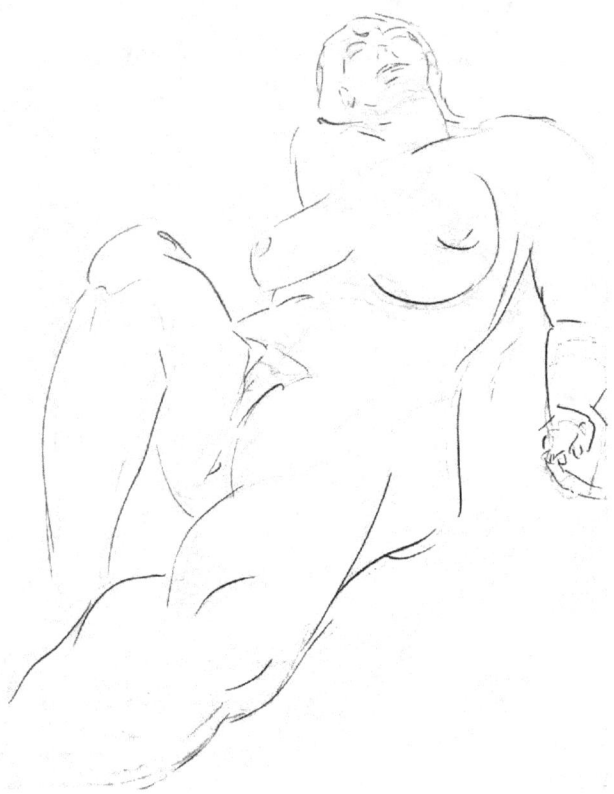

Example 6
Find

- The vanishing point,

- The receding lines,

- The contour lines of equal magnification.

The model is just in the field looking at the stars.

Drawing by the author, pencil on kraft paper 50cm x 65cm, carried out in four minutes.

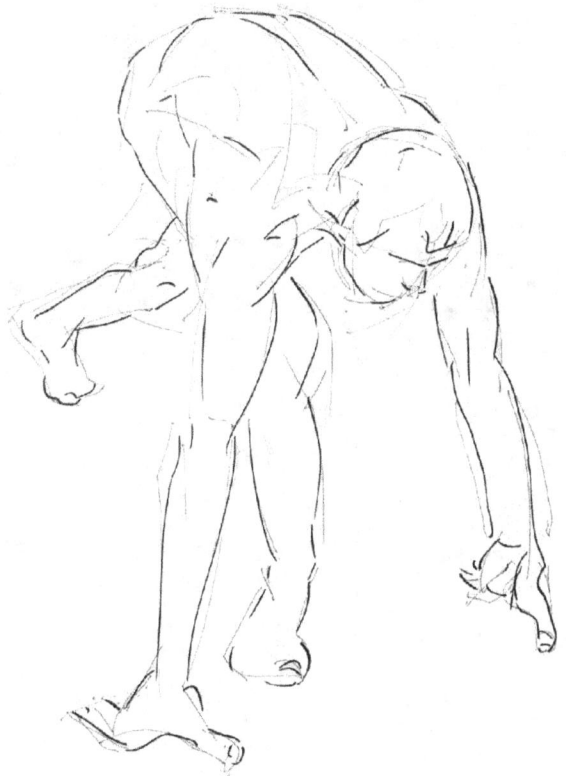

Example 7

Find

- The vanishing point,

- The receding lines,

- The contour lines of magnification.

Drawing by the author, pencil on kraft paper 100 x 80cm, carried out in five minutes.

For the model 5 minutes is very long. Begin this pose again at the next meeting.

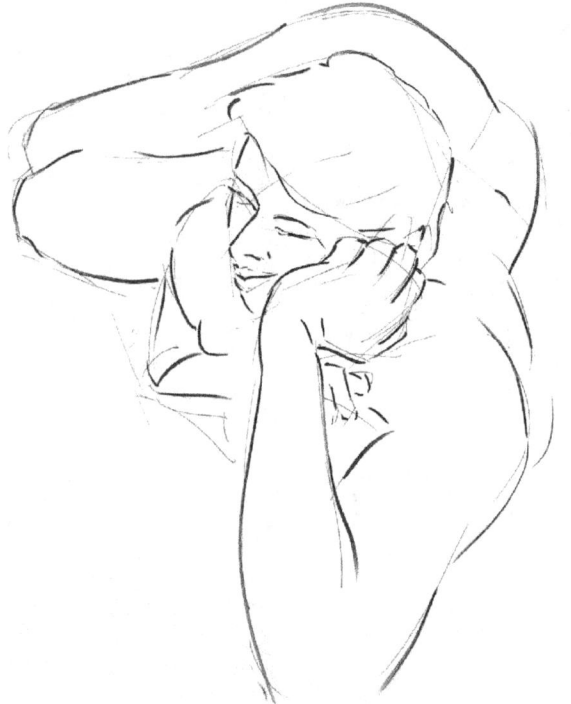

Example 8

You see that by drawing quickly you will not only draw accurately, but also with sufficient features so that this portrait is completed.

Drawing by the author, pencil on kraft paper 50 x 65cm, carried out in five minutes.

REVIEW OF THE THIRD SECTION

1. We initially gave an outline of the fascination brought by painters with the close-up. The irruption of the living made them seek the most appropriate framing. Seurat and Matisse could not search for anything else; the living was the obsession of their entire lives.

Degas constructed, Seurat searched like a photographer. Rembrandt and Matisse seized more instinctively and recommenced.

If one tried to guess a method of perspective for these works, the only thing certain is that we are not in the domain of Rectilinear Perspective, nor in that of a curvilinear spherical perspective. On the contrary the dream of Matisse seems to us very close to what we call Real Perspective.

2. Next we proposed the applications of the shower of fireworks to the treatment of volumes with curved surfaces.

We have chosen for a surface type that of a living model, which is the most demanding, because the smallest mistake on this type of volume that we know very well, in an innate manner, is immediately spotted. Control is a necessary effort for progress in the technique of drawing.

3. Finally we imagined some exercises treating perception of volume in space. We asked the reader for his contribution, for this book alone could not give it. The reader, indeed, needs to work with a model under his eyes, for he is not able to understand volume otherwise.

It was necessary to give to the reader who approaches space for the first time, not only some explanations of his natural perception of space, but also the elementary rules for executing a drawing.

We have therefore proceeded step by step, knowing that nothing is obtained without constant and reflective work.

Drawing is, above all, a work of reflection and of concentration. It leads us to questions and confrontations. It is a discipline that is not a weak-willed distraction. Drawing is a creation of culture; it also opens the door to all daring.

> "No one is forced to have recourse to my lessons, but I definitely know that whoever undertake to them will not only draw more accurately, armed with fundamental principles; by practicing every day, he will come to a deeper understanding; he will continue to search and find more than I have shown him."

> Albrecht Dürer. *Instructions for measuring*

Annex

The eye is spherical
Our ancestor the fish.

What is trigonometry?
Small illustrations for my children.

For mathematicians
Cylinder and plane.
Sphere and cylinder intersection.
Computer developments.
Cylindrical space treating curved forms.

To go farther
Documentation

Table of illustrations

The eye is spherical

Our ancestor the fish.

The evolution of species is a succession of chances. It follows that the human eye sees in degrees.

The eye is composed of a lens (the pupil) and a darkroom whose bottom is wallpapered by the retina. An object located on the horizon sends parallel rays, which converge by a dioptrically effect of the pupil, onto the center of the retina.

A foreshortened object will be seen clearly, thanks to the action of muscles that have an effect on the pupil to augment its convergence, foreshortening the focus towards the entrance of the eye and allowing the image to form on the retina.

1. In a first hypothesis, let us suppose that the eye will be fixed and that the retina will be papered on a large surface with cones. It is interesting then to compare the places where the image is formed,

- in an eye, that is to say on the retina that is spherical, and

- in a camera obscura where the background will be flat.

We see on the diagram that

- for the eye, information brought to the retina is purely angular,

- whereas for the *camera obscura* the information collected on the photo film is trigonometric, because we have the projection of the curved exterior worlds, perceived in degrees, roughly applied to a plane.

Therefore the bottom of the eye transmits, indeed, angular information to the first batteries of neurons, located in the thickness of the retina, which will digitize and transmit information to the brain.

On the contrary a camera obscura with a flat bottom, pierced by a hole (we spoke of a *stenope*), will bring trigonometric information to photographic film.

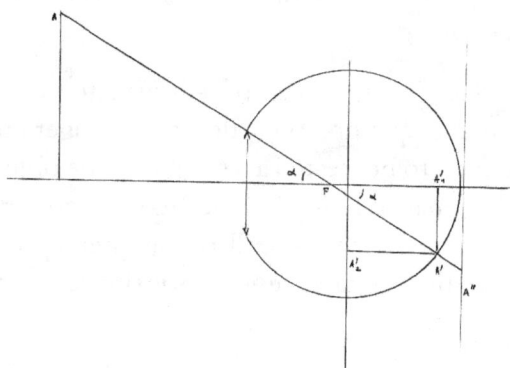

2. We know that the distribution of cones on the retina is essentially concentrated in the zone of the fovea. But the eye moves in jerks to capture the different zones of the landscape that will be reconstructed by the brain. Meanwhile the information transmitted is angular, and that the brain treats necessarily some information as angular.

To convince some, it's sufficient of note that, when we draw, we have a great skill at reproducing angles with accuracy. We can, precisely, perceive a horizon line that is not horizontal.

On the contrary we must take laboriously measurements to evaluate linear distances. For this reason to draw a shortcut it suffices to situate the middle of the drawing, the rest of the construction being instantly made by looking at the axes of the drawn figure. Taking supplementary measurements does nothing but create confusion.

3. We process the angular data read by the vestibular system of our inner ear to maintain our equilibrium.

We also process the angular data of our articulations and our muscles to direct our movements.

Angular information at the level of vision is thus consistent with the information of our other senses that need, at every moment, to be coordinated by our brain.

4. Treating angular data is a question of survival for the species. The brain is a machine of anticipation, in particular in danger and in combat. It selects the information to be treated according to the objective resulting from an established scenario. However the brain is not the only organ that contributes to this anticipation. All of our perceptive organs will transmit signals more or less intense and prioritized according to the scenario in progress.

Moreover, our muscles do not capture lengths, but accelerations: these are data depending on time, thus sources of extrapolations. The eye, already in our ancestor the fish, must be able to instantly move in the direction of a predator and give, thanks to our ocular muscles which have just worked, the necessary indications to the whole of the muscular system for an immediate strategy of fight or flight. The system of transmission must be consequently simplified to the maximum, without intermediate stages of calculations.

It is a collection of rough angular information bits that will be processed, and not a combination of trigometrical data, which would require calculations.

In conclusion

when we have a line as a physical reality in space, we know that after an angular treatment, by our eye and our brain, this line will be projected on a plane trigonometrically.

The plane is the sheet of paper of the artist or the sensitive plate at the bottom of a camera obscura. The reality of the represented world is the trigonometric figure obtained on the sensitive plate.

What happens with perceived reality? Our fictitious screen of visual perception is cylindrical because of the presence of our two eyes, and also owing to the fact that they turn more horizontally than vertically.

Perceived reality is given to us by the intersection of this cylinder with the plane defined by the straight line, in the space we are observing, and from the position of our eye.

This intersection is an ellipse. It is this ellipse, rolled out onto a sheet of paper that I represent by an arc of a sinusoid.

196 ᔑ XAVIER BOLOT

What is trigonometry?

Small illustrations for my children

The sailors of Antiquity felt lost at sea after one day of navigation. They did not have mileage odometers, speed odometers, radars, GPSs, or compasses, which are recent inventions. How to get their bearings after a day of winds variable in force and direction, in swells or tempests, when they were pushed far from the coasts of which they lost sight?

The sun shows well where the four cardinal points are, but it moves constantly and is not a fixed landmark that allows calculation of a ship's position.

There only exists a single fixed reference point in the sky, which one sees at night, which is Polaris (the North Star). The earth turns around its axis, from the South Pole and to the North Pole, directed towards this star in the sky, which thus bears its name Polaris. At night all the stars in the sky give the impression of turning around this polar star because of the rotation of the earth. This is a fixed point for sailors but also for desert caravans. Astronomers worked to benefit from this providential fixed point.

The facts of the case are as follows:

- the navigator measures his trip distance in *kilometers*;

- the star can only be located in *degrees* above the horizon, since the navigator cannot aim a string at the Polar Star just at sea level.

Astronomers thus simply established a table of correspondence between

- the angle under which they saw the star;

- and the linear course accomplished with their caravans or ship.

In the 100 years at the beginning of our era, Ptolemy in Alexandria called this table "The Table of the Arcs of a Circle". We therefore know that

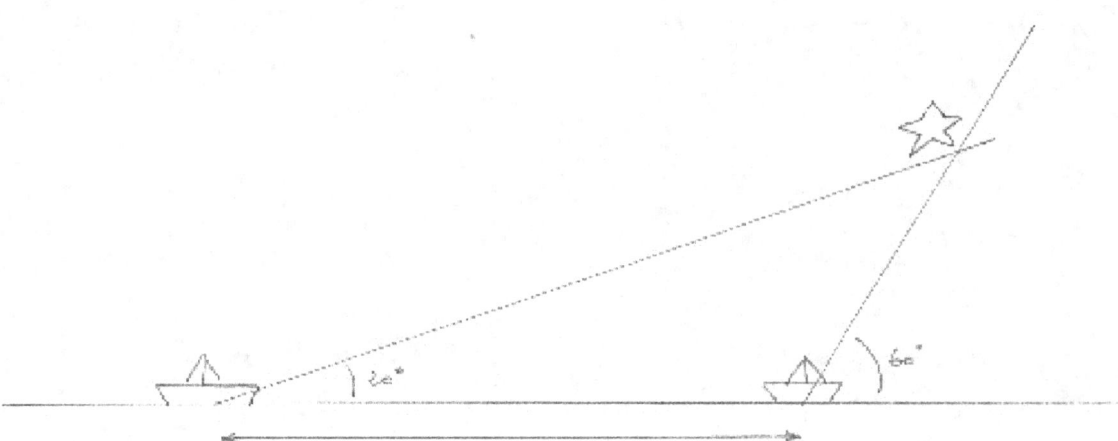

table has existed for a long time.

How was it made?

Very simply

- by tracing a circle and a radius oriented for a given angle (it's the angle under which the sailor sees the star);

- by locating on the horizontal axis of the circle (this axis symbolizes the surface of the sea) the projection of the ray and by measuring its length.

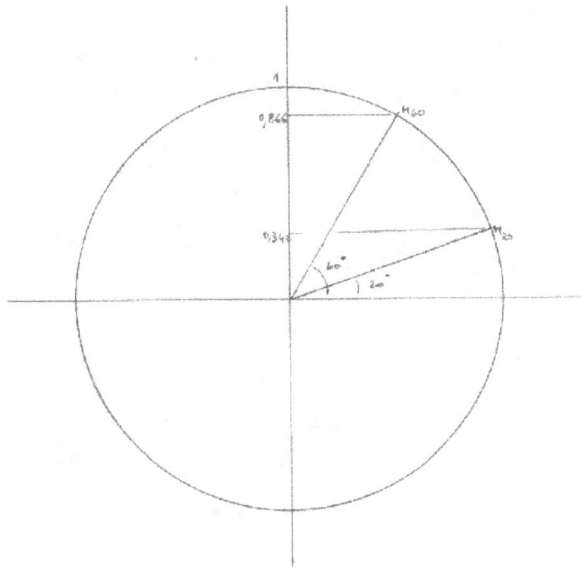

A table of arcs of a circle is made up of two columns in which are registered

1st Column   the angles of the ray

2nd Column   the corresponding lengths of the projection of the
radius on an axis of a circle.

Very well, you say, but your radius of a circle on your sheet of paper is too small and has nothing to do with the distances covered by a ship.

Yes, but the astronomer did not stop there: this time, while walking in the desert, he compared several positions of the star in relation to the kilometers covered by his caravan. He compared the kilometers covered with lengths of the projection of a ray on the horizontal axis of his circle and formed little by little his table of arcs of circles.

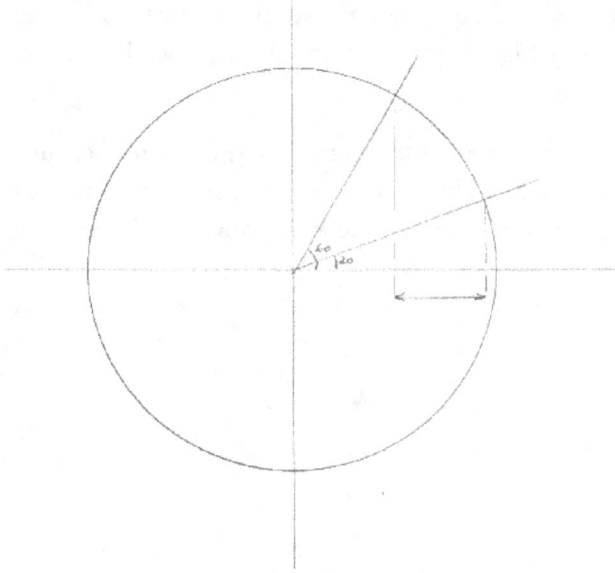

You see that a table of arcs of a circle is indispensable each time that you need to make the relation between an angle and a distance. It is however extremely simple to use.

Today the diagram of the circle and the projection of a point of a circle on its axis are used daily. Each time one deals with a circular motion, one needs this diagram.

But the misfortune came from mathematicians of the 17th century who gave the table of arcs of a circle a new name, which frightens children: "The Table of Trigonometry." They also gave to the projection of a radius on the axis of a circle an improbable name: "the sine."

We are interested in the trigonometric circle to understand several phenomena. For example, how did the architect, who built the column of Trajan in Rome inaugurated in 100CE calculate the height perceived of the frieze that decorates the column?

Indeed this frieze always seems to have the same height at the base as at the top when the column measures 27 meters. One would expect to see the decorations at the top as smaller than those at the bottom, when supposing the frieze being a big ribbon decorated and rolled over the column.

If we use the trigonometric circle we understand why the frieze measures 0.87m (2.85 feet) at its base and 1.27m (4.17 feet) at it summit, although the eye sees the base as the summit under the same angle of 1.1 degree.

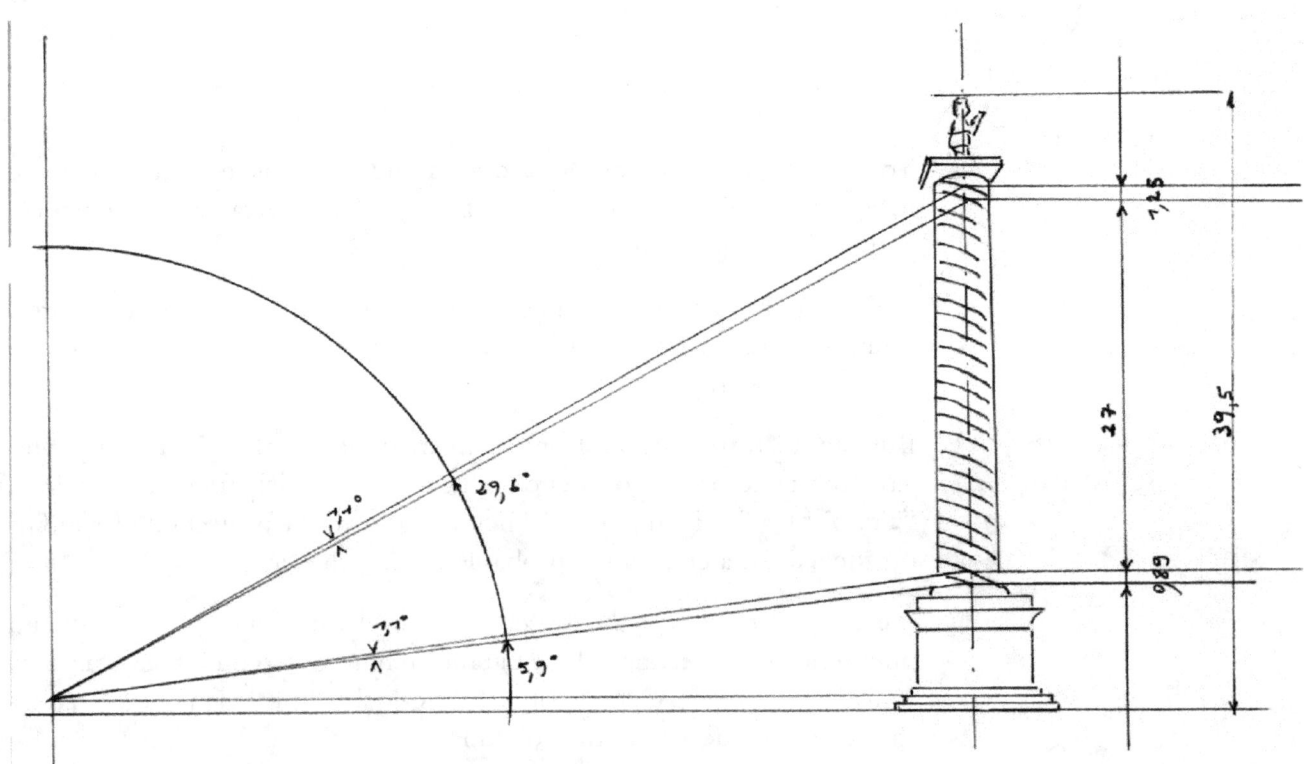

A well known beautiful curve: the sinusoid

If we take the figures of the trigonometric table and put them on two perpendicular axes Ox, Oy, we have coordinates to obtain points. Binding these points, we get a sinusoid.

This curve is neither an ellipse, nor a circle, but has a characteristic form: for the little values of angle A, it is almost straight, but it progressively curves in an accelerated manner for the important angles.

One meets this curve each time that one wants to use the value of an angle. For example when we meet a rotation, a repetitive turning movement like that of an electrical or mechanical engine, a planet in its orbit, etc.

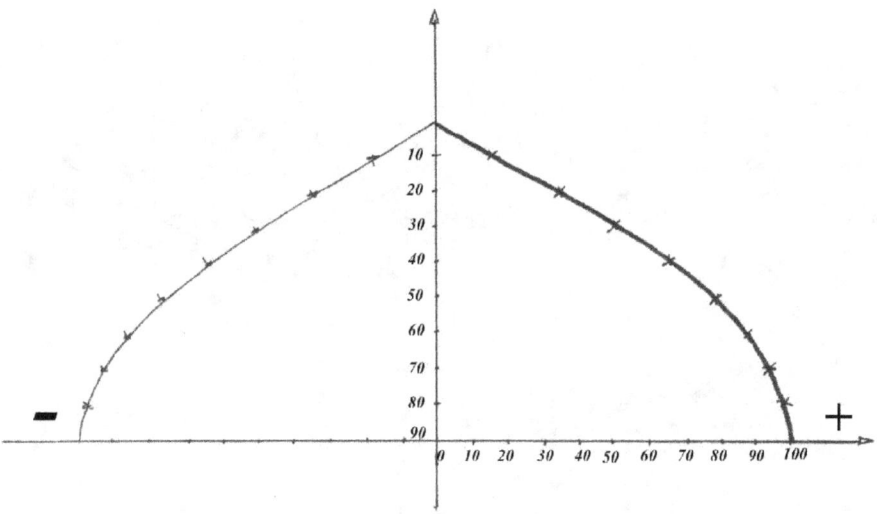

We also meet this curve when treating perspective because our eye measures in degrees, whereas the architect in meters. It is therefore natural that a straight receding line in space must be finally translated in our drawing by a sinusoid.

One sees starting from the breast of the model (vanishing point) the receding lines (that are sinusoidal arcs) like branches of a shower of fireworks. The two concave horizontal curves complete the grid.

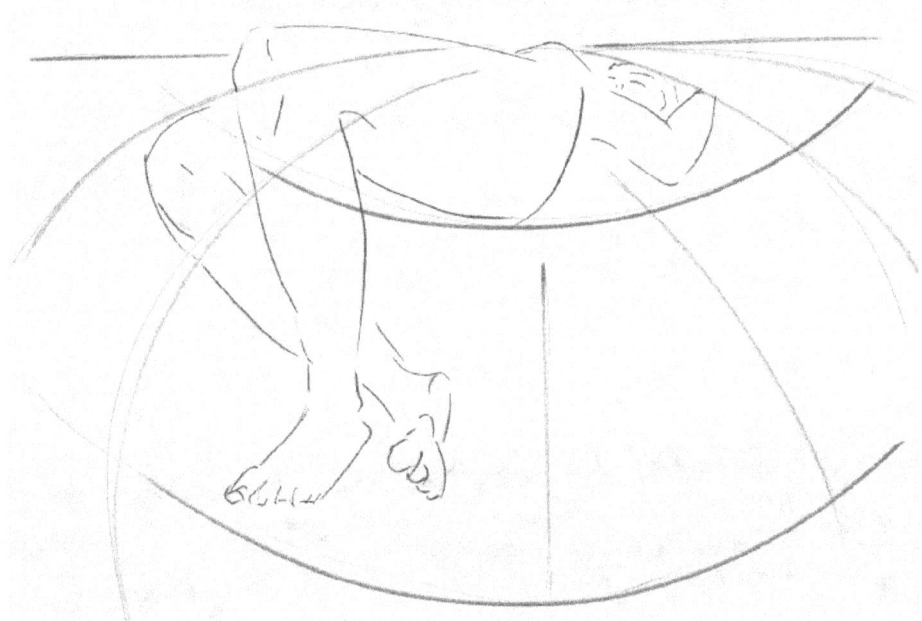

For Mathematicians

Here are some demonstrations. I reassure the artists reading this that you will find a world without any calculations when you let your body draw in a natural way. Indeed your spherical eye see with angles, your brain in its optical zone is organized to see angles, your arm, with a shoulder, an elbow and a wrist, work with angles. When this chain of angles encounter a plane, that is to say your sheet of paper, your are then in a trigonometric world, that means any straight line you see becomes a trigonometric curve on your sheet.

Never before this book have these demonstrations been written down in such a book concerning perception of space.

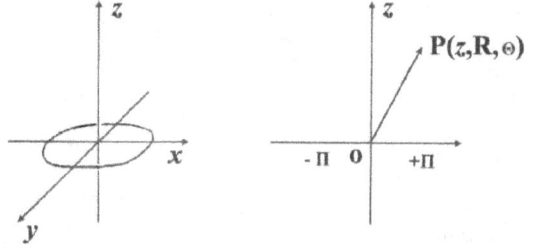

Cylinder and plane

This method of demonstration consists of retracing by equations the steps seen above.

A plane cuts a cylinder following an ellipse. Next we unroll the cylinder on a piece of paper tangent with the cylinder. So then we will note the ellipse unrolled by the cylinder is a trigonometric function.

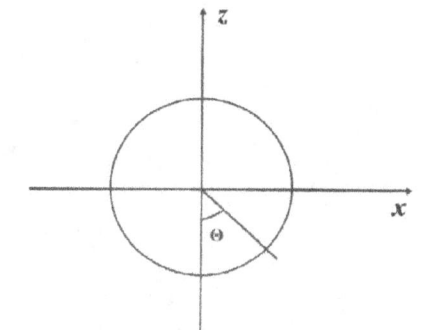

Intersection

A cylinder is represented by its equation $x^2+y^2 = R^2$ and a plane represented by its equation $x+by+cz = d$ the two equations constitute the equation of the ellipse, which is their intersection in space.

Unrolling the cylinder

Consider the polar coordinates of a point of a cylinder.

Point P unspecified is located by its coordinates R,q,z.

On the plane (x,y) we have $X = R \cos q$ and $Y = R \sin q$

which is satisfied by the equation $x^2 + y^2 = R^2$.

I introduce, in the equation of the plane, coordinates of the cylinder, which give me the coordinates of the ellipse in space:

$aR\cos q + bR\sin q + cz = d$

When we go to unroll the cylinder on a tangent plane we

create a relation:

X (linear distance unrolled) = R (ray of the cylinder),

q (angle of which one will unroll the cylinder on the plane).

$Arc(è) = X/R$ and the ellipse is unrolled on the plane of the artist's piece of paper is

$aR\cos X/R + bR\sin X/R + cz = d$

There is definitely a sinusoidal function of cartesian coordinates in this last plane, which has to be demonstrated.

It is this equation which was not established during the Renaissance, a serious lacuna leaving artists and art critics ignorant of the knowledge of our physiological perception. Therefore, they did not dare transgress the rectilinear-perspective paradigms.

Sphere and cylinder

Intersection
A cylinder is represented by its equation $x^2 + y^2 = R^2$

and a sphere represented by: $(x-x_o)^2 + (y-y_o)^2 + z^2 = r^2$

Let us develop $x^2 - 2xx_o + x_o^2 + y^2 - 2yy_o + y_o^2 + z^2 = r^2$

now $x^2 + y^2 = R^2$ and $x_o^2 + y_o^2 = R^2$

By subtracting member from member we obtain an intersection in the space of the sphere with the cylinder: $-2xx_o - 2yy_o + z^2 = r^2 - 2R^2$

Unrolling the cylinder

In polar coordinates $x = R\cos q$ $x_o = R\cos q_o$ $y = R\sin q$ $y_o = R\sin q_o$

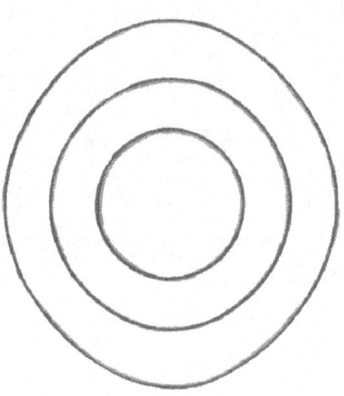

If one takes $q_o = 0$ One has $-2R^2\cos è - 2R^2\sin è + z^2 = r^2 - 2R^2$

It doesn't act therefore as an ellipse but as an ellipsoid that has the aspects of an ellipse slightly flattened.

By consequence, on our drawing paper, our contour lines (of constant magnification) are quasi-ellipses.

On the whole we have on the sheet of paper a curvilinear grid consisting of

• Receding lines in the form of sinus arcs

Contour lines (of constant magnification) in the form of quasi-ellipses.

Computer developments

Computers allows us to calculate the trigonometric magnification step to represent 3D architecture project.

Computer programs has for a longtime used parallel perspective (without the effect of perspective therefore without calculating the magnification step).

It results in the optical illusions in the figure below the two plates 1 and 2, despite appearances, have exactly the same dimension.

Notice how these optical illusions are the consequence of a cultural phenomenon. In fact our western brain, accustomed to Rectilinear Perspective, draws erroneous conclusions starting with a drawing realized in Chinese parallel perspective.

On the other hand the fact of considering the segment CD to be longer than the segments AB dates to our habits of marking as an animal of the earth. The multiple pinpoints brought by curvilinear Real Perspective helps the brain to correctly recalculate space.

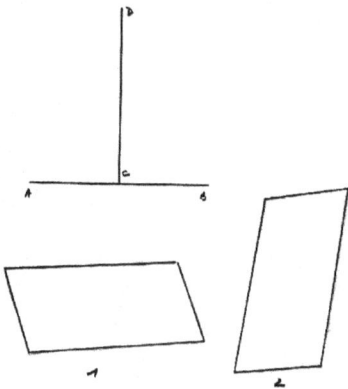

Today software fluently uses Rectilinear Perspective that declines homothetic modules with a constant magnification step known as arithmetic.

The diagram shows how the distance between two trees is progressively determined, when they are closer to the horizon.

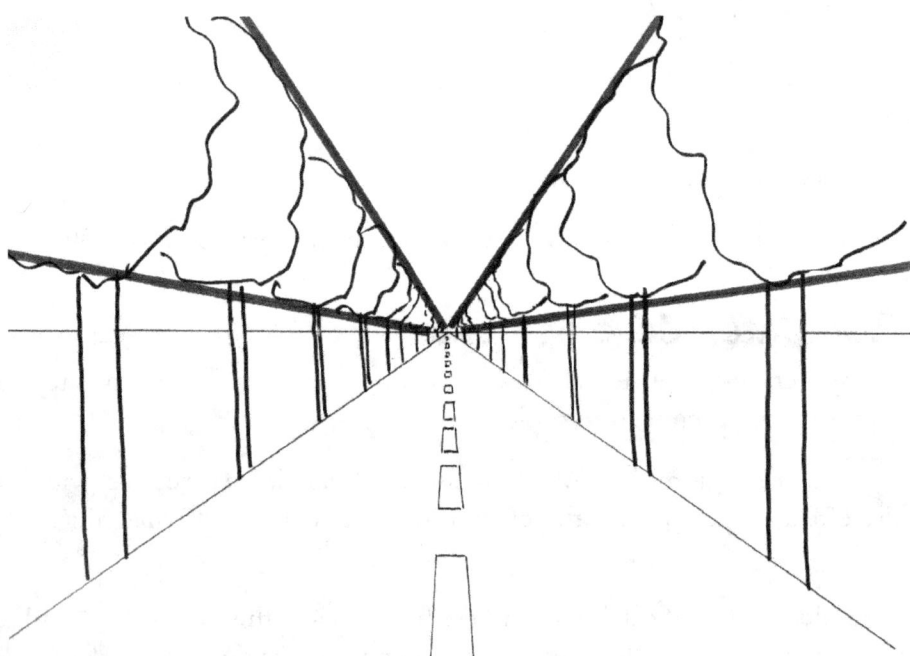

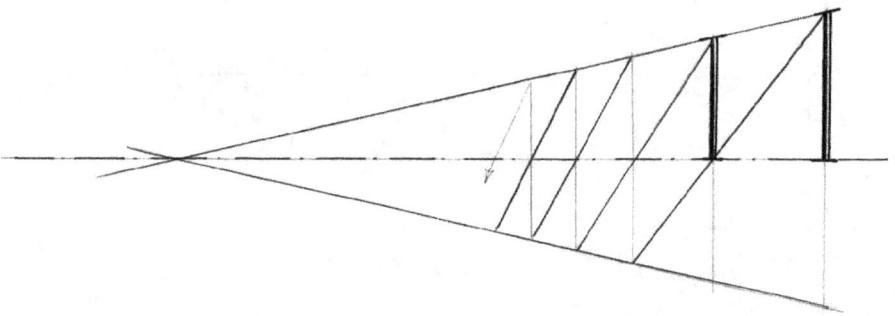

In the arithmetic progression that results from Rectilinear Perspective, the variation between two trees diminishes with each consecutive pair of trees in the same quantity. The progression of shrinkage is constant.

We will see on the following page that this is not the case in Real Perspective.

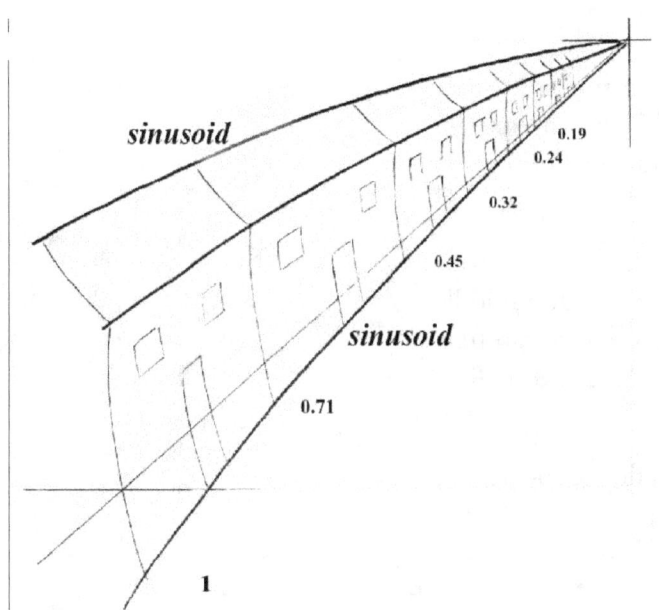

We propose to computer technicians a trigonometric magnification step to translate the effects of Real Perspective.

The contour line magnification step in the case of this figure "*Houses along a street*" is not constant but progressive as follows:

Contour line of constant magnification 5 0.19

Contour line of constant magnification 4 0.24   p4-p5 = 0.24-0.19 = 0.05

Contour line of constant magnification 3 0.32   p3-p4 = 0.32-0.24 = 0.08

Contour line of constant magnification 2 0.45   p2-p3 = 0.45-0.32 = 0.13

Contour line of constant magnification 1   0.71

p1-p2 = 0.71-0.45 = 0.26

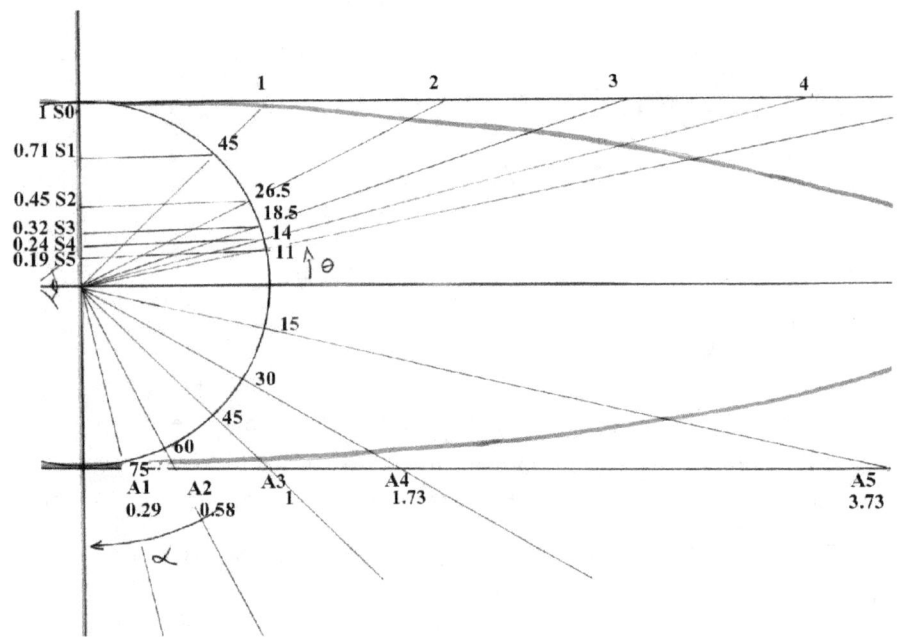

One notes the acceleration of the magnifying-glass effect from one module to another by observing the values p2-p1, etc. This confirms the observation of Wilhelm Schickardt: "The sides will gradually bend like a paunch." (First Section, Chap 2)

The enlargement of foreshortened objects is considerable. Place in front of you three apples on a table : one close to you, the other in the middle of the table and the third on the other side of the table. Measure carefully with your pencil the three apples and note the result. You are in Real Perspective.

The calculation of contour lines of constant magnification depends on the same criteria as in classical Rectilinear Perspective, namely the azimuths of

Sines and Cosines in degrees

Deg.	Sin.	d.t.	d.t.	Cos.	
0	0,000	9	0	1,000	90
0,5	0,009	8	0	1,000	89,5
1	0,017	9	0	1,000	89
1,5	0,026	9	1	1,000	88,5
2	0,035			0,999	88
		9	0		
2,5	0,044	8	0	0,999	87,5
3	0,052	9	1	0,999	87
3,5	0,061	9	0	0,998	86,5
4	0,070	8	1	0,998	86
4,5	0,078			0,997	85,5
		9	1		
5	0,087	9	1	0,996	85
5,5	0,096	9	0	0,995	84,5
6	0,105	8	1	0,995	84
6,5	0,113	9	1	0,994	83,5
7	0,122			0,993	83
		9	2		
7,5	0,131	8	1	0,991	82,5
8	0,139	9	1	0,990	82
8,5	0,148	8	1	0,989	81,5
9	0,156	9	2	0,988	81
9,5	0,165			0,986	80,5
		9	1		
10	0,174	8	2	0,985	80
10,5	0,182	9	1	0,983	79,5
11	0,191	8	2	0,982	79
11,5	0,199	9	2	0,980	78,5
12	0,208			0,978	78
		8	2		
12,5	0,216	9	2	0,976	77,5
13	0,225	8	2	0,974	77
13,5	0,233	9	2	0,972	76,5
14	0,242	8	2	0,970	76
14,5	0,250			0,968	75,5
		9	2		
15	0,259	8	2	0,966	75
15,5	0,267	9	3	0,964	74,5
16	0,276	8	2	0,961	74
16,5	0,284	8	3	0,959	73,5
17	0,292			0,956	73
		9	2		
17,5	0,301	8	3	0,954	72,5
18	0,309	8	3	0,951	72
18,5	0,317	9	2	0,948	71,5
19	0,326	8	3	0,946	71
19,5	0,334			0,943	70,5
		8	3		
20	0,342	8	3	0,940	70
20,5	0,350	8	3	0,937	69,5
21	0,358	9	4	0,934	69
21,5	0,367	8	3	0,930	68,5
22	0,375			0,927	68
		8	3		
22,5	0,383			0,924	67,5

Deg.	Sin.	d.t.	d.t.	Cos.	
22,5	0,383	8	3	0,924	67,5
23	0,391	8	4	0,921	67
23,5	0,399	8	3	0,917	66,5
24	0,407	8	4	0,914	66
24,5	0,415			0,910	65,5
		8	4		
25	0,423	8	3	0,906	65
25,5	0,431	7	4	0,903	64,5
26	0,438	8	4	0,899	64
26,5	0,446	8	4	0,895	63,5
27	0,454			0,891	63
		8	4		
27,5	0,462	7	4	0,887	62,5
28	0,469	8	4	0,883	62
28,5	0,477	8	4	0,879	61,5
29	0,485	7	5	0,875	61
29,5	0,492			0,870	60,5
		8	4		
30	0,500	8	4	0,866	60
30,5	0,508	7	5	0,862	59,5
31	0,515	8	4	0,857	59
31,5	0,523	7	5	0,853	58,5
32	0,530			0,848	58
		7	5		
32,5	0,537	8	4	0,843	57,5
33	0,545	7	5	0,839	57
33,5	0,552	7	5	0,834	56,5
34	0,559	7	5	0,829	56
34,5	0,566			0,824	55,5
		8	5		
35	0,574	7	5	0,819	55
35,5	0,581	7	5	0,814	54,5
36	0,588	7	5	0,809	54
36,5	0,595	7	5	0,804	53,5
37	0,602			0,799	53
		7	6		
37,5	0,609	7	5	0,793	52,5
38	0,616	7	5	0,788	52
38,5	0,623	6	6	0,783	51,5
39	0,629	7	5	0,777	51
39,5	0,636			0,772	50,5
		7	6		
40	0,643	6	6	0,766	50
40,5	0,649	7	5	0,760	49,5
41	0,656	7	6	0,755	49
41,5	0,663	6	6	0,749	48,5
42	0,669			0,743	48
		7	6		
42,5	0,676	6	6	0,737	47,5
43	0,682	6	6	0,731	47
43,5	0,688	7	6	0,725	46,5
44	0,695	6	6	0,719	46
44,5	0,701			0,713	45,5
		6	6		
45	0,707			0,707	45

	Cos.	d.t.	d.t.	Sin.	Deg.

Table of arcs of a circle according to Ptolemy (90-168) called since the seventeenth century "trigonometric table."

- the point of view of the observer,

- the horizon line,

- the vanishing point,

- the distance of the observer from the center of interest of the tableau,

- the principal axis of symmetry of the center of interest.

Cylindrical space treating curved forms

The magnifying-glass effect and perspective are issued from the same principles of perception in our cylindrical universe of natural vision. The description of the phenomenon is given in the Second Section "Real Perspective, Applied to Architecture". We show in this section the following things:

1. a straight line in space is perceived as an ellipse when transferred to drawing paper under the form of a sinusoidal arc with its characteristic form.

2. in practice an artist will content himself with applying these principles intuitively.

Before passing to the chapter of illustrations and exercises we give an example of the graphing of space as well as a calculation of the magnification step reserved to mathematicians. Of course the artist won't have to make such calculations. These calculations are only for perceiving an extension of the work done in the preceding chapter. The plastics artists will be satisfied to take advantage of the principles presented with the illustrations that follow.

Why be interested in a living model?

The living model is an extremely formative volume for those who search to progress in drawing, for the smallest error is immediately noticed, which is not the case for a landscape or a building.

When you know how to draw a living model and a portrait, you are capable of drawing everything. In all positions, especially with foreshortenings, Real Perspective will thus become indispensable.

You will perceive that the shortcut, which is a black beast for beginners, is the easiest thing to draw for it offers a number of reference points to you.

Is a living model difficult to draw ?

Notice that we have begun by treating a straight line in the second section, which is a simple form. But the majority of volumes are not geometric. A living model is a succession of curves.

Do these curves pose a problem? We will transform them into segments of lines to construct the placement of our volumes, and this is the essential part, the rest will be details, which you will often find useless. All that can be said is also relevant for architecture.

Graphing of space for a living model

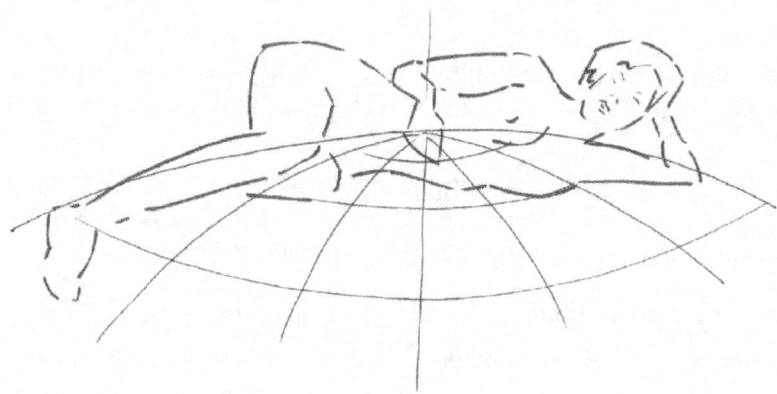

A living model that is 6.5 feet away (two meters) gives an important magnifying-glass effect.

The graph is constructed starting from a vanishing point chosen by the person drawing. The resulting receding lines are sinusoidal arcs. The contour lines (by nature of constant magnification) are quasi-ellipses.

The receding lines and the contour lines pass by remarkable points of the model chosen by the artist. The spreading out of the graph in space is then fixed by the artist with the help of a few measurements carried out with his pencil. (Where are the middle, the extreme right, the extreme left?)

These viewpoints with a large field width appears very appealing since they make it possible to include the entirety of the subject. This possibility is not given by the classics which limit their window of vision to 30° making constraints imposed by Rectilinear Perspective. It is by leaping over this constraint that David Hockney mounted his two hundred photographs of the Grand Canyon of Colorado onto a single screen.

The observer must therefore choose between several narrow, undistorted views, but to juxtapose, or a single view in wide angle reconstructed by the brain beginning with the sampling of an eye sweeping the landscape.

Calculation of a magnification step applied to a living model

Profile view

In this hypothesis the observer is:

- at a one meter (approximately three feet) distance from the model,

- one meter above the model,

- the model is in the axis of observation,

- the model is two meters tall (approximately six feet).

One sees, therefore, that the calculation must recommence each time that one of the parameters change, which would not be tiresome for a

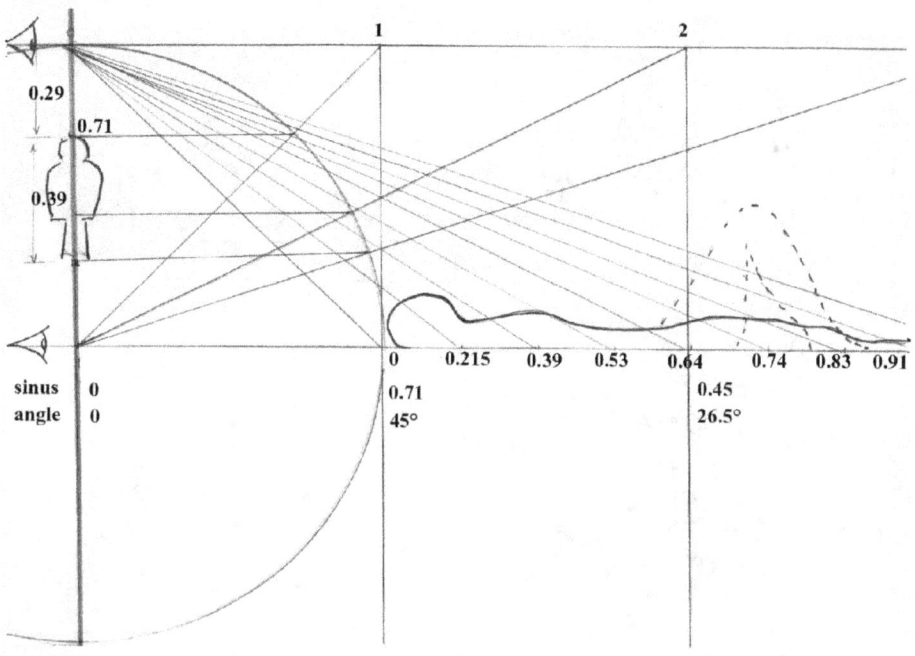

computer. The artist will be happily contented with a few measurements, if necessary.

Calculation of a magnification step applied to a living model

Profile and foreshortening
The magnification step of a profile and of a shortcut are not the same. Let's see how much.

The observer remains in the same place and the model pivots 90° around an axis placed above his head. The feet slide the length of a quasi-ellipse. One notes a global foreshortening of the model by 40%. But the impressive transformation is that of the magnifying-glass effect, which modifies all

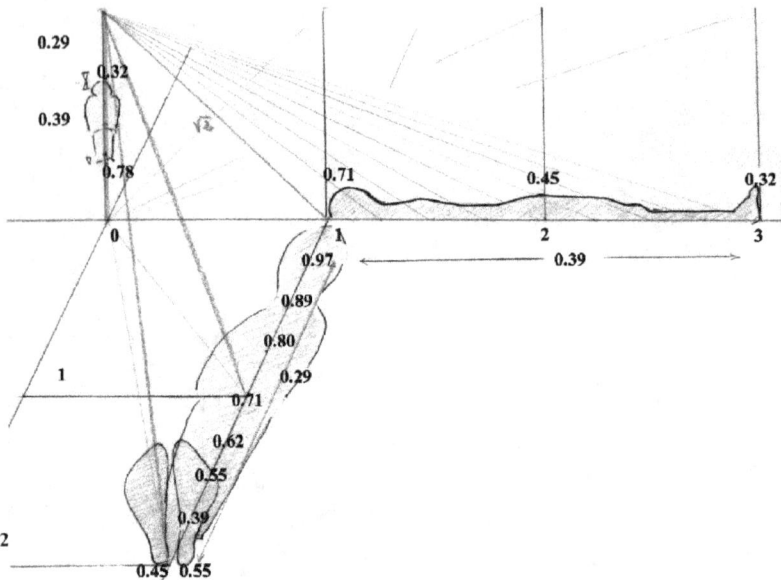

the proportions. In fact the curvilinear graph is modified and we know that the magnification step is accelerated.

The table of numbers on the two following pages accompanies the diagram, showing an example of spreading out the various parts of the body. It was made with a spreadsheet and a trigonometric table. An apprentice graduate could do it. The phenomenon of foreshortening is therefore not a view of the spirit.

The plastics artist does not need to make calculations, but must know about the existence of natural phenomena.

Calculating the magnification step of a reclining model

O in degrees		sine O	cotg O	var sine O	si cotg var sine O	From 1 to 3 %	% Cumulated
0	0,00	infini			Space	Space	
1	0,02	57,29		0,02			
2	0,04	28,64		0,02			
3	0,05	19,08		0,02			
4	0,07	14,30		0,02			
5	0,09	11,43		0,02			
6	0,11	9,51		0,02			
7	0,12	8,14		0,02			
8	0,14	7,12		0,02			
9	0,16	6,31		0,02			
10	0,17	5,67					
11	0,19	5,15		0,04			
12	0,21	4,71					
13	0,23	4,33					
14	0,24	4,01		0,05			
14,5	0,25	3,87					
15	0,26	3,73	0,0170				
15,5	0,27	3,61					
16	0,28	3,49	0,0170				
16,5	0,28	3,38					
17	0,29	3,27	0,0160				
17,5	0,30	3,17					
18	0,31	3,08					
18,5	0,32	2,99	0,0250	0,08			Plant of the foot
19	0,33	2,90					
20	0,34	2,75	0,0330		0,084615385	1	Ankle
20,5	0,35	2,68					
21	0,36	2,61					

22	0,38	2,48	0,0330		0,084615385	0,915384615	Lower knee
22,5	0,38	2,41					
23	0,39	2,36					
24	0,41	2,25	0,0320		0,082051282	0,830769231	Mid thigh
25	0,42	2,15					
26	0,44	2,05					
26,5	0,45	2,01	0,0390	0,13	0,1	0,74871794	Crotch
27	0,45	1,96					
28	0,47	1,88					
29	0,49	1,80					
29,5	0,49	1,77	0,05		0,117948718	0,648717949	Navel
30	0,50	1,73					
31	0,52	1,66					
32	0,53	1,60					
33	0,55	1,54					
33,5	0,55	1,51	0,05		0,133333333	0,530769231	Breast
34	0,56	1,48					
35	0,57	1,43					
36	0,59	1,38					
37	0,60	1,33					
38	0,62	1,28					
38,5	0,62	1,26	0,07		0,182051282	0,397435897	Chin
39	0,63	1,24					
40	0,64	1,19					
41	0,66	1,15					
42	0,67	1,11					
43	0,68	1,07					
44	0,70	1,04					
45	0,71	1,00	0,08	0,26	0,215384615	0,215384615	Top of the head
46	0,72	0,97					
47	0,73	0,93					
48	0,74	0,90					
49	0,76	0,87					

50	0,77	0,84
51	0,78	0,81
52	0,79	0,78
53	0,80	0,75
54	0,81	0,73
55	0,82	0,70
56	0,83	0,68
57	0,84	0,65
58	0,85	0,63
59	0,86	0,60
60	0,87	0,58

To go farther

"Today, despite the remarkable work of Albert Flocon, there remain too few treatises of perspective."

Pierre Descargues, *Treaties of Perspective.*

If the treatises of Rectilinear Perspective are numerous, those involving innovating perspectives are not only too few, but extremely rare, if we retain those proposed with a new vision of space supported by a scientific approach.

Luigi Vagnetti in his intervention at the Milan Congress of 1977, noted that the lack of the simultaneous use of a mathematical tool and the lack of a thorough knowledge of art history, leads to blind reactions, based on incomprehension, and to a stunting of creativity.

The Greek archives disappeared in the fire of the library of Alexandria. Vitruve was regarded as the initiator of Rectilinear Perspective. Alhazen left us a treaty of optics. Brunelleschi invented linear perspective (rectilinear), taken up and simplified by Alberti. We have shown that, in all times, numerous artists have, with their studies and experiments, contributed to the approach towards a defined Curvilinear Perspective.

Lanci, Vignola, Dürer introduced devices for drawing volumes. Leonard de Vinci drew through a window, by believing to find, in his Codex Atlanticus, a solution in spherical development. The Huyghens Codex took up these experiments of the master with spherical perspective.

Mercator developed the globe on a plane, but in a very deforming manner above the 60th parallel.

Barre and Flocon explored and determined the consequences of a spherical perspective that represented a dreamlike world.

Recently, David Hockney and M.C. Escher approached Real Perspective, that is to say physiological, in a cylindrical universe.

Bruno Ernst, the first, presented in 1947 an explanation of transformations allowing to pass from a physical world to a real and perceived world, at the moment when, according to Kim Veltman who concluded at the Milan Congress in 1977, Panofsky posed the question of a link which could exist between "vision, representation and the measurable world."

This book has modestly taken over the way of Bruno Ernst's method of calculating the structure of space in representation and derive practical consequences for drawing. Proposing "Real Perspective," in other words a physiological perspective, scientifically calculated in geometry and algebra, does not close the debate but, on the contrary, enriches it.

The other quoted authors bring us materials, sometimes very rich, preparatory to the delicate evolution that the comprehension of our space represents, but remains fundamentally in the culture of classic Rectilinear Perspective, which implicates as identical the three perceived, represented and physical worlds.

But the neurosciences teach us, if it were necessary, that our eye only informs a brain that calculates and anticipates in relation to its objectives, built on memory and emotion.

The neurosciences call into question our beliefs and how we are made to understand at which point the physical worlds, perceived and represented, are autonomous.

We present a few works allowing us to tackle this approach.

Texts in French

Alberti, *De la peinture*, Seuil, 2004.

Alberti, *De l'art d'édifier*, Seuil, 2004.

Androuet du Cerceau, Jacques, *Les plus excellents bâtiments de France*, 2 volumes, Paris, 1605.

Arasse, Daniel, *Histoires de peintures*, Denoël, 2004.

Argan, Giulio Carlo, Rudolf Wittkover, *Perspectives et histoire du Quattrocento*, La Passion, Montreuil sous bois,1990.

Aristote, *Poétique*, Poche, Edition des Belles Lettres, 1990.

Anati, Emmanuel, *L'Art rupestre Negev Sinaï*, L'Equerre, 1979.

Baccheschi, *Toute l'œuvre peinte de Giotto*, Flammarion, 1982.

Baltrusaitis Jurgis, *Aberrations, Anamorphoses, La quête d'Isis*, Flammarion, 1983-84-85.

Barthes, Roland, *La chambre claire*, Cahiers du cinéma, Gallimard, Seuil, 1980.

Berthoz, Alain, *Le Sens du mouvement*, Odile Jacob, 1997.

Bonfand, Alain, *Trois essais sur la perspective*, La Différence, 1985.

Borsi, Franco et Stephano, *Leo Battista Alberti*, Hazan, 2006-04-07

Bosse, Abraham, *Le peintre converty aux règles de son art*, Hermann Paris, 1964.

Boufard Alain, Labrot Gérard, Marion Jean-Luc, *Trois essais sur la perspective*, Editions de la différence, 1985.

Branigan, Keith - Vickers, Michael J., *La Grèce Antique*, Armand Collin, 1981.

Braudel, Fernand, *Le Modèle italien*, Arthaud,1989.

Bruce, Vicki - Green, Patrick : *La Perception visuelle*, Presses Universitaires de Grenoble, 1993.

Brucke, Ernst, Helholtz, Hermann, *Principes scientifiques des Beaux-Arts, Essais, optique et peinture*, Germer Baillère, Paris, 1881.

Chaboud, Marcel, Taton, René, *Girard Desargues, bourgeois de Lyon, mathématicien, architecte*, IREM de Lyon, Aléas, 1996.

Clottes, Jean, *Le Musée des Roches*, Seuil, 2000.

Cole, Alison, *La Perspective, profondeur et illusion*, Paris Gallimard Jeunesse, 2003.

Cousin, Jean, *L'art du dessin*, A Paris chez François Chéreau, 1750.

Cousin, Jean, *Livre de perspective*, Paris, 1560.

Comar, Philippe, *La Perspective en jeu*, Découvertes Gallimard, 1992.

Daix, Pierre, *L'ordre et l'aventure*, Arthaud, 1984.

Dante, Alighieri, *La Divine Comédie*, Les Libraires Associés, 1965.

Damish Hubert, *L'origine de la perspective*, Flammarion, 1993.

Damish, Hubert, *Un souvenir d'enfance par Pierro della Francesca*, Seuil, 1997.

Descargues, Pierre: *Traités de perspective*, Editions du Chêne, 1976.

Descartes, René, *La Dioptrique*, extraits annexés au *Discours de la Méthode*, Flammarion, 1966.

Descharmes, Robert, *Dali*, Gilles Néret, Taschen, 1991.

Deuleuze, *L'image-mouvement, L'image-temps*, Les éditions de Minuit, 1983.

Dürer, Albrecht, *Lettres , écrits théoriques, traité des proportions, instructions pour mesurer*, Hermann Paris, 1964

Dürer, Albert, *Lettres à Jacob Heller*, L'Echoppe, 1987.

Dürer Albrecht, *Géométrie*, Seuil, 1995.

Hegel, Georg Wilhelm Friedrich, *Introduction à l'esthétique et au beau*, Flammarion, 1979.

Edwards, Betty, *Dessiner grâce au cerveau droit*, Mardaga, 2002.

Ernst, Bruno, *Le Miroir magique de M.C. Escher*, Créations Taschen, 1994.

Ernst Bruno, *Le monde des illusions d'optique*, Taschen,1992.

ENSBA, *Peut-on apprendre à voir?*, L'image et l'ENSBA, Paris, 1996.

Evans, John, *La saga des sténopés*, Eyrolles, 2004.

Flocon, Albert, Taton, René, *La perspective*, Que sais-je ? PUF, 1963.

Flocon, Albert, Barre, André, *La perspective curviligne, de l'espace visuel à l'image construite*, Flammarion, 1968.

Battista Piranesi, Renouard-Laurens, 1928.

Focillon Henri, *Vie des formes, Eloge de la main*, PUF, 1943.

Francastel, Pierre, *Peinture et société*, Idées arts, Gallimard, 1965.

Get, François, *Encyclopédie des chemins de fer*, Editions de la Courtille.

Giordani, Robert et Nonce, *La Perspective dans l'image*, Editions Dujarric, 1987.

Gleizes, Albert, *La peinture et ses lois*, Imprimerie Croutzet, Paris 1924.

Gombrich, Ernst Hans, *Histoire de l'art*, Gallimard, 1998

Gombrich, Ernt Hans, *Ombres portées, leur représentation dans l'art occidental*, Gallimard, 1995.

Gromort, Georges, *Eléments d'architecture*, Vincent et Fréal, 5ème édition 1949.

Husserl, Edmund, *L'idée de la phénoménologie, cinq leçons*, PUF, 2004.

Kemp, Martin, *Léonard de Vinci*, Corbis Corporation, 1996.

Kemp, Martin, The science of art, *Optical themes in western art from Brunelleschi to Seurat*, Yale University Press, 1990. VIII- 375 29.

Klein, Robert, *La civilisation de la Renaissance en Italie*, LGF, 1986.

Jung, Carl Gustave: *Métamorphoses de l'âme et ses symboles*, 1944.

Lajoux, Jean-Dominique, *Tassili n'Ajjer*, Chêne, 1977.

Le Blanc, Marianne, *D'acide et d'encre, Abraham Bosse et son siècle en perspectives*, CNRS, 2004.

Levie S.H., Mathey, François, *Anamorphoses*, Rijkmuseum, Amsterdam, Musée des Arts Décoratifs, Paris, 1975.

Lichardus, Jan et Marion, *La Protohistoire de l'Europe*, PUF, 1985.

Ludi, Jean-Claude, La perspective « pas à pas », Dunod, 1986.

Louis, Pierre André, *Le Labyrinthe et le Mégaron*, Pierre Mardaga, 2004.

Malraux, André, *La création artistique*, Skira, 1949

Massu, Claude, *L'Architecture de l'école de Chicago*, Dunod, 1982.

Merleau-Ponty, Maurice, *Phénoménologie de la perception*, Gallimard, 1976

Ministère de la Culture, *L'art des cavernes*, Imprimerie Nationale, 1984.

Ministère des Affaires culturelles, Séminaire de formation permanente 1971-72, *Morphologie/structures*, Jean Etienne Marie, Erick Spitz, David Georges Emmerich, Jean Dewasne, René Sarger, Jean Zeitoun, Henri Laborit.

Musée d'art Moderne de la Ville de Paris, *Malévitch*, Centre Georges Pompidou, 2002.

Musée d'art Moderne de la Ville de Paris, *Robert Delaunay*, Centre Georges Pompidou, 1999.

Nietsche, Friedrich, *La naissance de la tragédie*, Gallimard, 1977.

Normand, Charles, *Parallèle des diverses méthodes du dessin de la perspective d'après les auteurs anciens et modernes*, Ch.Normand, Paris, 1837.

Olmer, Pierre, *Perspective artistique*, Plon, 1943.

Pacioli, Luca, *Divine proportion*, Librairie du compagnonnage, 1980.

Panofsky, Erwin, *La Perspective comme forme symbolique*, Editions de Minuit, 1975.

Panofsky, Erwin, *Galilée critique d'art*, Les impressions nouvelles, 1992.

Paoli, Michel, *Léon Battista Alberti*, Editions de l'imprimeur, 2004

Pèlerin, Jean, dit Viator, *De artificialis prospectiva*, Toul , 1505, fac-similé, L Laget, Paris, 1978.

Pillet, Jules, *Traité de perspective linéaire précédé du tracé des ombres usuelles et du rendu dans le dessin d'architecture et dans le dessin de machines*, Librairie du dessin et de la construction,Paris, 1901.

Platt, Colin, *Atlas de l'homme médiéval*, p. 26-30, Seuil, 1981.

Rodas-Wuilleumier, Marie-Claire, *L'idée d'image*, Presses Universitaires de Vincennes, 1995.

Saouter, Catherine, *Le langage visuel*, XYZ éditeur, Montréal, 1998.

Schneider, Pierre, *Petite histoire de l'infini en peinture*, Hazan, 2001.

Sivoukine, *Physique générale,* Moscou, 1980.

Spiess, Dominique, *Encyclopédie des impressionnistes,* EDITA, 1992.

Strieder Pieter, *Dürer,* Albin Michel, 1982.

Sutter, Jean David, *Nouvelle théorie simplifiée de la perspective,* Jules Tardieu, 1859,Archives des 4 Piliers Bourges.

Taton, René, *L'œuvre mathématiques de Desargues,* Librairie J. Vrin, Paris, 1981.

Valenciennes, Pierre-Henri, *Eléments de perspective pratique à l'usage des artistes suivis de réflexions conseils à un élève particulièrement sur le genre du paysage,* Genève, Minkoff reprint, 1973.

Vasari, Giorgio, *La vie des meilleurs peintres, sculpteurs et architectes,* collection thésaurus Beaux Arts, Editions Actes Sud, 2006

Vitruve, *Les dix livres d'architecture,* André Balland, Les Libraires Associés, 1965.

Zerri, Frederico, *Derrière l'image,* Rivages, 1998.

Nicod, Jean, *La Géométrie dans le monde sensible,* PUF, 1962.

Picard, *Traité du nivellement et un abrégé de la mesure de la Terre mis en lumière par M. de la Hire,* Etiennne Michallet, Paris, 1684.

Verdet, André, *La Vallée des merveilles,* Les Editions du Temps, 1970.

Vinci, Leonardo da, *Traité de la peinture,* Edtions Berger-Levrault, 1987.

White, Michael, *Leonardo, The First Scientist,* 1998.

White, John, *Naissance et renaissance de l'espace pictural,* traduction Catherine Fraixe, A.Biro, Paris, 1992

Texts in English

Weyl, Anne Marie - Laurence, Carl - Morocco, J., *A Byzantine Masterpiece Recovered, the Thirteenth-Century Murals of Lysi, Cyprus,* Texas Ménil, 1991.

Ching, Francis DK, *Architectural graphics,* John Wiley Sons Inc., New York, 1992.

Edwards, Betty, *The New Drawing on the Right Side of the Brain*, Penguin, 2000.

Hockney, David, *That is What I See,* Thames and Hudson, 2001.

Hockney, David, *Secret Knowledge : Rediscovering the Lost Techniques of the Old Masters,* Penguin Group, USA, 2000.

Loran, Erle, *Cezanne's Composition, Analysis of his Form with Diagrams and Photographs of his Motifs,* University of California Press, Berkeley and Los Angeles, 1944.Texts in Italian.

Alberti, Leo Battista, *Opere volgari, De pittura*, a cura di Cecil Grayson, Edotori Bari Gius Laterza Figli, 1973.

Alberti, Leo Battista, *Opusculi morali*, tradotti da Cosimo Bartoli, Venezia, 1568.

Alberti, Leo Battista, *Dieci libri di architettura*, Vicenzo Vaugris, Venezia, 1546.

Alhazeni, Arabis, *Optica thesaurus* , Basilae,1570.

Angelini, Annibale, *Trattatto teorico pratico di prospettiva*, Roma, Enrico Sininimberghi, 1861.

Angioy, Giovanni, *Della pittura in prospettiva del Rinascimento alla geometria di Monge*, Cagliari, 1973.

Barbaro, Daniele, *La pratica della perspettiva*, Venetia, Borgominieri, 1568.

Bellosi, Luciano, *La rappresentazione dello spazio*, Storia dell'arte italiana, Totino, 1980.

Bologna, Ferdinando, *Simone Martini, affreschi di Assisi*, Skira, 1968.

Boskovits, Miklos, *Cimabue e i precursori di Giotto, affreschi, mosaici e tavole*, Firenze, Scala, 1976.

Brunelleschi, Filippo, Eugenio Battisti, Milano,1989.

Calabrese, Oamar, *Piero, Teorico dell'arte*, scritti di H Damisch, D.Arasse, A. Parronchi, L.Marin, G. Arrighi, M.Apa, J.Petittot, T.Martone, G.Pittaluga, E.Battisti, Gangemi Editore, 1985.

Carli, Enzo, *Piero della Francesca, Gli affreschi in San Francisco di Arezzo*, Milano, A.Martello, 1963.

Capobianco, Michele, *Elementi di prospettiva lineare conica*, Napoli, Instituto editoriale del Mezzogiorno, 1966.

De Vecchi, Perluigi, *L'opera completa di Piero della Francesca*, Milano, Rizzoli, 1999.

Ferretti, Massimo, I maestri della prospettiva, Storia dell'arte italiana, Totino, 1982.

Fiorini, Fabrzio, *La prospettiva : limiti, tendenze, utilizzazionni e simbolismi di un sistema di raprazentazione, per una evoluzione del concetto di spazio*, Quaderni dell'Instituto di disegno, Benucci editore, Perugia, 1986.

Franchina, Lotizia, *Proposta di lettura prospettica di un giardino : il Belvedere bramentesco*. Il Giardino, Firenze, 1981.

Frederici Vescovini, Graziella, *Studi sulla prospettiva medievale*, Torino, G.Giappichelli, 1987.

Gabrielli, Margherita, *Giotto e l'origine del realismo*, Roma, G..Bardi, 1960.

Gozzoli, Maria Cristina, *L'opera completa de Simone Martini*, Milano, Rizzoli, 1970.

Guelfi, Franchini, *L'organizzazione dell'imagine nella figurazione piana : la techniche perspettiche*, La technica artistiche, Milano, 1973.

Kemp, Martin, *La sciensa dell'arte in prospettiva e percezione visiva da Brunelleschi a Seurat*, Firenze, Giunti, 2005.

Leonardo, da Vinci , *Codex atlanticus,* Milano, 1973.

Leonardo, da Vinci, *Trattato della pittura*, Rafaelle du Fresne, Paris, Langlois, 1651.

Monticolo, Roberto, Meccanislmi dell'opera d'arte, Firenze, Nardini,1987.

Orsini, Baldassare, *Della geometria e prospettiva pratica*, 3 volumi, Benedetto Franzesi, Roma, 1771-1773.

Palladio, Andrea, *I quatro libri di architetura*, Venezia, 1616.

Parrochi, Alessandro, *Studi su la dolce prospettiva*, Milano, Martello, 1964.

Piero della Francesca, *De prospettiva pigendi*, a cura du Giacomo Noccolo Fasola, Licosa reprints 1974, Firenze Eurografica, G.C. Sanzoni Editore, Firenze.

Piero della Francesca, *Scritti*, Fondazione Pi, Firenze.

Pozzo, Andrea, *Perspectiva pictorum et architectorum Andreae Putei Societate Iesu pars prima, Ptolemee, Mathematicae constructioni, cum explicatione Erasmi Rholinholt*, Parisiij, 1557.

Pozzo, Andrea, A*rchitteto*, Nino Carbinieri, Trento,1961.

Putei, Andreo, *Perspettiva pictorum et architectorum*, Roma, 1717.

Previtali, Giovanni, *Materiali e problemi*, Zerri, Frederico, *Dal Medioevo al Novecento, Storia del'arte italiano, ricerche spazale e tecnologie*, Giulio Enandi Editore, 1980.

Rosa, Agostino de, Sgrosso, Anna, Giordano Andrea, *La geometria nell'imagine: storia dei metodi dirappresentazione*, Torino, 2001.

Salvenini Francesca, *La visione e il suo doppio la prospettiva tra arte e scienza*, Roma, Larteza,1990.

Semanzato, Camillo, *Giotto di Bandone*, Editione paoline, 1966.

Serlio, Sebastiano, *I sette libri d'architettura*, Venezia,1584.

Sindona, Enio, *L'opera completa di Cimabue e il momento figurativo pregiottesco*, Milano, Rizzoli, 1975.

Sinisgalli, Rocco, *Verso una storia organica della prospettiva*, Roma, Kappa, 2001.

Tyrwhitt, Jacqueline, L'occhio mobile, la communicazione di massa, Firenze, 1969.

White John, *Nascita e renascita dello spazzio pittorico*, Traduzione di Rita e Mario Torelli, Milano, Il Sagottore, 1971.

Vasari, Giorgio, *Le vite dei piu eccelenti pittori scultori e architetti*, Jacopo Recupero, Milano, 2002.

Venanzi, Alessandro, *Le prime nozioni della perspettiva per uso del disegnatore dal vero a mano libera*, Marino Recchi Editore, 1891.

Vignola, Giacomo Barozzio, *Regole delle cinque ordini di architetura*, Lelio dalla Volpe, Bologna, 1769. Congress of Milano in 1977.

La prospettiva rinascimentale. Codificazioni et trangressioni (da Giotto a Paul Klee),

Firenze, Centro di, 1980.Atti del congresso del 11-15 ottobre 1977. A cura di Marisa Dalai Emiliani.

Apertura. Decio Gioseffi, Egle Becchi e Girglio Riva, Carlo Severi, La pratica prospettica : contributi di lettura. André Chastel, Susanne Lang, Riccardo Picciani, Enio Sindona, Renato Agenelli e Renato Zini, Daniel Arasse, Eiko Wakayama, Christianne L.Joost-Gauthier, Germano Mulazzini, Margare Daly Davis, Bruna Ciati, Eros Robbiani, Joseph Polzer, Marichia Arese, Aldo Bonomi, Claudio Cavalieri, Claudio Fraonza,Carlo Pedretti, Göttz Pochat, John Shearman, Giulio Bora, Sergio Marinelli, Claudio Zanini, Eugenio Battisti, I trattati, le questioni di teoria e di metodo. Giuseppa Saccaro Battisiti, Kim Veltman, Hubert Damish, corrado Maltese, Luigo Vagnetti, Rocco Sinisgalli, Salvatore Naitza, T.Kaori Kitao, Robert Ruurs, Paoloa Martinelli e Sabdra Pino,Lodreana Olivato, Gionanni Degl'Innocenti e Pie Luigi Andini, Kim Veltman.

Sciences and Neurosciences

Baars, B.J., *In The Theater of Consciousness*, New York, Oxford University Press, 1977.

Berthoz, Alain, *Le sens du mouvement*, Odile Jacob,1997

Brickner, R.M., *The Intellectual Functions of the Frontal Lobes*, New York, Macmillan, 1936.

Bonnet, Claude, *La perception visuelle*, Pour la Science, 1984.

Bruce Vicki et Green Patrick, *La perception visuelle, physiologie, psychologie et écologie,* Sciences et technologies de la connaissance Presses Universitaires de Grenoble 1993.

Bruyer, Raymond, *Le cerveau qui voit*, Odile Jacob, 2000.

Clark, R.E., *Classical Conditioning and Brain System: the Role of Awareness*, Science 280, 1998.

Changeux, Jean-Pierre, *L'Homme Neuronal,* Pluriel, Hachette Littératures, 1982.

Courtney SM, *An Area Specialised for Spatial Working Memory in Human Frontal Cortex*, Science 279.

Damasio, A.R., *The Feeling of What Happens, Body and Emotion in the Making of Consciousness*, New York, Hartcourt Brace, 1999.

Dennet, D., *Consciousness explained*, Boston, Little Brown, 1991.

Ernst, Bruno, *Le monde des illusions d'optique*, Benedikt Taschen, 1986.

Gregory Richard Langton, *L'oeil et le cerveau: la psychologie de la vision*, De Boeck, 2000

Griffin, D.R., Speck,G.B., *New Evidence of Animal Consciousness*, Animal cognition, press 2004.

Kaniza, G., *Organisation in Vision, Essays in Gestalt Perception*, New York, Praeger,1979.

Mandler, G., *Conciousness Recovered, Psychological Functions and Origins of Conscious Thought*, Amsterdan, Nederlands, John Benjamin, 2002.

Marr, D. *Vision*, San Francisco, CA, Freeman, 1982.

Meyer, Philippe, *L'œil et le cerveau : biophilosophie de la perception visuelle*. Odile Jacob 1997.

Ninio, Jacques, *La science des illusions*, Odile Jacob 1998.

Palmer, S., *Vision Science, Photons to Phenomenology*, Cambridge, MA, MIT Press,1999.

Perry, E Walker, M, Grace J, *Acethylcholine in mind, a neurotransmitter correlate of consciousness*, Trend Neurosciences,22, 1999.

Pérez, José Philippe, *Optique,* Dunod, 2000.

Sack, O., *The Mind's Eye, what the Blind See*, The New Yorker, July,28, 2003.

Schrödinger, Erwin, *La Nature et les Grecs*, Seuil, 1992.

Schrödinger, E., *What is Life?*, Cambridge , UK, Cambridge University Press,1944.

Seckel, A., The art of optical illusions, Carlton Books, 2002.

Squire, L.R., Kandel, E.R., *Memory: from Mind to Molecules*, New York, Scientific American Library, Freeman, 1999.

Illustrations

Drawings, scketches and photos undefined are realised by the author.

Foreword What is Real Perspective ?

P030   HG   *Ours rouge sur un fond plat*, © Jean Clottes. Californie, Mutua Flats.
             © Photo Jean Clottes.

        HD   *Le « 6.4.62 »*, Paul Roche-Ponthus. Collection privée.

P031   BD   *Sahara Tassili n'Ajjer.* Jabarun © Photo Jean Dominique Lajoux.
             Sahara (entre -3000 et -300), *Tahilahi*, civilisation de pasteurs.
             Gabriel Camps.© Photo Gabriel Camps.

P032   HG   *Fresque de l'église de Longpré*, vallée du Loir, France.
             © Photo François Lauginie.

        HD   Eiri, between 1790-1800, painting, Japan. Collection privée.

        BG   *Poterie trouvée à Tarente (-400).* Martin von Wagner
             Museum der Universität Würzburg Photo : K. Oehrlein.

        BD   *Perspective théâtrale.* Piranèse. Bibliothèque Municipale
             de Bourges.

P033   HG   *Espace sphérique* Barre et Flocon. © Edts Flammarion. 1968. *La
             perspective curviligne (de l'espace visuel à l'image construite).A.Flocon,
             Flammarion,1968.*

        HD   *Hôtel Cujas de Bourges.* Décalque sur une plaque de verre de Xavier
             Bolot. Musées de Bourges.

        BG   *Nefs latérales de la cathédrale de Bourges.* SDAP du Cher.
             Sténopé © Erick Mengual.

I. 1 The taboo

P048   *Château de Boucard*, La Nouvelle République du Centre.
             Photo Gérard Proust.

© Photo RMN / ©Jörg P.Anders. Berlin. Staaliche Museen.RMN.

P070   *Maison le Guidec*. Pietu-Bosredon Architectes. Bourges.
juillet 2004.

P071   H   *Le feu au nu*. Jean Hélion. 1983. Cliché Musée des Beaux Arts
d'Orléans, auteur François Lauginie. © ADAGP, Paris 2007.

   B   *6.4.62*. Paul Roche-Ponthus. Collection privée.

I. 3 The representation of natural perception at a standstill

P075   *Le Parthénon*. Photo de l'auteur. Avec l'aimable autorisation de
l'Ambassade de Grèce à Paris. Reproduction interdite.

P076   *Au coin d'un temple*. Temple de la Concorde. Agrigente.Sicile. Photo
de l'auteur. Sopraintendenza per i Beni Culturali e Ambianti di
Agrigento. Divieto di ulteriori riproduzioni o duplicationi con
qualsiasi mezzo.

P077   *Arnolfini and his wife* .Van Eyck. © The National Gallery, London.

P079   *Entrée de l'empereur Charles IV à la basilique Saint Denis*.
Jean Fouquet.1480. Paris. Cliché Bibliothèque Nationale de France.

P080   *Carcieri d'invenzione VI*. Piranese. Bibliothèque
Municipale de Bourges.

P081   *Scena per angolo. Architectura civile*. Ferdinando Bibiena.
Droits réservés.

P082   *Un coin d'atelier*. Eugène Delacroix. © Photo RMN/
© Michèle Bellot. Paris Musée du Louvre. DAG.

P083   *Portrait de Camille Renault*. Huile sur toile. Jacques
Villon.1944. Paris, musée national d'Art moderne – Centre Georges
Pompidou. © Photo CNAC/MNAM Dist RMN/
© Christian Bahier /Philippe Migeat © ADAGP, Paris 2007.

P084   *Espace sphérique* Barre et Flocon. © Edts Flammarion. 1968.
La perspective curviligne (de l'espace visuel à l'image construite). A.Flocon,
Flammarion,1968.

P085   *Superette*, e*space construit*. Jean Mary. Collection privée.

Intérieur, dessin à vue. Jean Mary. Collection privée.

P086   *Equirépartition spatiale cubique*. M.C.Escher.1947.

P087   *Le grand Canyon du Colorado*. David Hockney.

Grand Canyon looking north, sept. 1982 . Photograph collage ED15. 45x99 ½ © David Hockney .

II. 1 Real Perspective applied to architecture.

P097   *Perspectographes*. Dürer, exemple. Paris.

Ecole Nationale Supérieure des Beaux-Arts.

P098   *Perspectographe*. Dürer, exemple. Paris.

Ecole Nationale Supérieure des Beaux-Arts.

II. 2 Plastic art of architecture

P123   H   *Avenue Maréchal de Lattre de Tassigny*. Photo et montage.

Jean-Louis Hampe. Collection privée.

       B   *La commune de Courbevoie*. Livio Scotti. Collection privée.

P124   *Hôtel Cujas*. Bourges. Sténopé © Erick Mengual. Autorisation des Musées de Bourges.

P129   H   *Cathédrale Bourges*. Sténopé © Erick Mengual. SDAP du Cher.

       B   *Eglise St Séverin*. 1909 -1910. Robert Delaunay.

Encre de Chine sur papier Japon collé sur bristol.

© L&M Services B.V. Amsterdam 20060205.

Musée National d'Art moderne Centre Georges Pompidou. Paris © Photo CNAC/MNAM. Dist RMN./ © Philippe Migeat

P130   *Cathédrale de Bourges. Nef latérale*, SDAP du Cher.

Sténopé Erick Mengual.

P134   H   *Panthéon*. Piranèse. Bibliothèque Municipale de Bourges.

    B   *Panthéon*. Photo Aurélie Constant. Autorizzazione del Ministero per i Beni e le Attività Culturali. Roma. Divieto di ulteriori riproduzioni duplicationi con qualsiasi mezzo.

P135   G   *Colonne de Trajan*. Piranèse. Bibliothèque Municipale de Bourges.

    D   *Colonne de Trajan*. Rome. Photo Aurélie Constant.

III. I The fascination with the living

P142   H   *Sahara. Chars de Tamadjert* .© Photo Gabriel Camps.

    B   *Sahara. Tassilin'Ajjer. Iharen* © Photo Jean-Dominique Lajoux .

P143   H   *Vierge allaitant l'Enfant*. Inconnu du XVème sciècle. Musées de Bourges. inv.D.1953.4.1. et MNR 383.

    B   *Nathanël présenté au Christ par Saint Philippe*. Jean Boucher. Musées de Bourges. Cliché Musées de Bourges.

P144   H   *Saturne vaincu par l'Amour, Vénus et l'espérance*. Simon Vouet. Musées de Bourges. © C2RMF Louvre.

    B   *Les pèlerins d'Emmaüs, détail*. Caravaggio. Ville de Loches. Photo Gilles Mercier.

P145   *Le Christ Mort*. Mantegna. Pinacoteca di Brera. Su concessione del Ministero per i Beni e le Attivià Culturali. Milano Bergamo.

P146   *Fabrication d'étoffes à Leyde en 1450*. Isaac Claesz van Swanenburg. Stedelijk Museum, De Lakenhal, Leiden, The Nederlands.

P147   H   *Autoportrait aux yeux écarquillés*. Université de Liège. Collections artistiques. Galerie Wittert.

    B   *Autoportrait de jeunesse*. Rembrandt.Inv nr 11427 Eichenholz 15.6x12.7 cm Bayerische Staatgemäldesammlungen. Alte Pinacoteck München.

P148   *Le Dormeur*. Georges Seurat. © Photo RMN/ ©Michèle Bellot. Paris. Musée du Louvre.

Bathers to Asnières, study. Georges Seurat. Presented by Henz Berrggruen, 1995. © The National Gallery, London.

P149   H   *Femme à la voilette noire*. Félicien Rops. Musée Félicien Rops. Namur.

         B   *Femme dans la pénombre*. Léandre. Collection privée.

P150   B   *Chanteuse de café-concert*. Edgar Degas. © Photo RMN/ © Gérard Blot. Paris. Musée du Louvre.

P151   *Le rêve*. 1935. Henri Matisse. © Succession H. Matisse, pour les œuvres de l'artiste. Paris, Musée National d'Art Moderne – Centre Georges Pompidou. Photo CNAM/ MNAM Dist RMN /© Philippe Migeat.

III. 3 Application to Figure Drawing

P162   H   *Gisant*. Bruno Barcsay. 1930. Académie de Budapest. Droits réservés.

         B   *Gisant*. Bruno Barcsay. 1930. Académie de Budapest. Droits réservés.

P163   *Gisant*. Bruno Barcsay. 1930. Académie de Budapest. Droits réservés.

Index